Changing Minds:

In Detail

How to Change What People Think, Feel, Believe and Do

Changing Minds:
In Detail

How to Change What People
Think, Feel, Believe and Do

by

David Straker

First published in Great Britain and worldwide by:
Changing Works
Worlod yr Awel
Llanddewi Skirrid
Abergavenny
United Kingdom
www.changingworks.co.uk/books
Orders can be placed through: orders@changingworks.co.uk

ISBN: 978-0-9930416-0-0

A catalogue record for this book is available from the British Library.

Text design by David Straker
Typeset in Palatino Linotype and Verdana
Cover art by Heledd Straker
Printed and bound by Jellyfish Solutions (jellyfishsolutions.co.uk)
Changing Works is an imprint of Changing Works (Consulting and Publishing) Limited.

'Know your limits. Also know how to break them.'

— *Geraint Straker*

Contents

Preface

Why am I writing this book? And why should you trust and take note of it? You may well be wondering whether or not this book can help you. I do hope that it will.

This is something of a personal preface that tells how I came to develop a deeper understanding of how we change what others think, feel, believe and do and why I built what has become the largest website in the world dedicated to sharing information on this.

My story is one of frustration, challenge and long learning in the area of changing minds. For a number of years I was a happy geek with a first degree in engineering, quite at home in the electronics or computer lab, but all at sea when faced with a serious persuasive task. We each have our journeys and mine took a significant turn when I moved into software quality, over twenty years ago. I quickly discovered that the detail of technical quality was relatively easy, particularly when compared with the task of persuading others to go along with your changes. The engineering mindset, however, sees the world as a set of interesting problems which can mostly be solved through a combination of academic study and hands-on experience. I hence set out to learn some more.

Along the way I have worked in education, IT, marketing, sales, quality, human resources, customer support, workplace services and consultancy (internal and external). In all of this I was fortunate enough to receive much industrial-strength training and also managed to do postgraduate studies in management, education, marketing and psychology. I have always read voraciously and now have a personal library of 2000 or so books in these areas.

I write as a device partly to retain learning and partly in response to the teacher's drive to share understanding, both simplifying existing knowledge and also introducing new models and methods that I have discovered. The word I like most is 'aha', both for me and when I can help others to this enlightenment.

In 1998, after publishing five books on problem-solving, change and creativity, I started work on the website ChangingMinds.org, which has since become hugely popular with a range of different people, from psychology students to sales professionals. The popularity of the site has been a continuing spur to keep adding more information and, as of the current writing, it has over 7000 pages.

In the many kind emails that I have received have been regular requests to produce a book of the site, or at least something that condenses and restructures its huge sprawl.

And so here we are. This little tome is a long way from a copy of the website, although it of course overlaps in certain areas. It is the result of much squeezing and rethinking, and contains significant material that is not on the website. The site seeks to maximize access speeds by being largely text-based. Paper is not constrained by bandwidth and so, as a picture can add a thousand words, I have added many diagrams and tables.

You might be wondering about the purpose of the above monologue: What does it seek to achieve? Is it trying to persuade you about anything? Communications seek either to inform or persuade: Which do you think is happening here?

Perhaps this is an unfair question to ask at this point, but you might want to try this exercise when considering any communication:

1. Read between the lines, listening both to the intent of the other person and also the techniques they are using.
2. Listen to yourself in the same way. Hear your own subconscious motivations. See the methods that you are using.
3. Notice how you are responding to the other person, how you are filtering what they say and how they are affecting you and how deeply.
4. Reverse the focus again, understanding how they are processing your reactions to their words and your persuasive attempts.
5. Helicopter up and see the whole interaction within the broader context, understanding the lie of the land and how everything interacts with everything else.

If this seems a little daunting at the moment, never fear. We will be discussing this in further detail in subsequent chapters.

Introduction

How often do you have to change minds? Beyond the knotty problem of changing your own mind, most people seek to change the minds of others many times every day.

Given this basic need to persuade, how good would you say you are at it? Many would not score themselves too highly on this, yet we are all frequently successful in getting others to do things for us, from passing the salt at the dinner table to negotiating a pay rise. We naturally use such structures as social exchange and moral obligation to gain compliance to many of our requests, yet we also become frustrated when we fail in important persuasive attempts. Whether it is asking our teenage children to be home by a certain hour or getting the best price for the old car, we soon feel powerless and out of our depth just at the time when we most need to change minds.

This book is written for you, a person who is neither stupid nor incompetent, but who wants to increase knowledge and skills in changing minds. You may change minds as a core part of your job (and, as Table 1 shows, there are many such professions), you may want to improve your general persuasive abilities or you may have a specific problem in mind, from asking for a raise at work to improving a romantic relationship.

What particularly differentiates this book from many others is that it has a strong basis in psychology and seeks to teach you to fish rather than throw you wet morsels. Once you have grasped the underlying principles of how people work and the fundamentals of changing minds, you will be able to adapt these to many more situations than are described in this book.

This does not mean that this is just a psychology textbook, though many were studied in its formation. The approach taken to psychology is to lighten, condense and structure relevant parts into coherent patterns that are intended to help you understand and remember the useful systems they represent.

Table 1. Some professions and activities where changing minds is at the core of the job

Advertising	Espionage	Mediation
Acting	Financial advisors	Networking
Activism	Fund-raising	Parenting
Argument	Gambling	Philosophy
Auctioneering	Government	Poetry Police
Brand management	Human Resources	Protesting
Buying	Hypnotism	Publication
Change management	Interrogation	Public Relations
Children	Job-hunting	Romance
Communication	Journalism	Screenwriting
Confidence tricksters	Lecturing	Teaching
Conflict management	Lawyers	Terrorism
Consulting	Leadership	Therapy
Counseling	Marketing	Trade Unions
Diplomacy	Market trading	Writing

The book therefore starts at the deep end, plunging into the fundamental drivers that motivate and push us forward. It then explores the details of how we interact with the world and with each other. If you can understand these basic systems, then you are on the road to changing them – and changing things such as beliefs, preferences and mental models is one of the most powerful and difficult things to do.

There are four parts in the book. Part A goes into great detail about the components of how we think and how these may be individually influenced through persuasive methods. Part B extends this to how people interact in relationships with one another. Part C details the Core Process, a structure that is common to all methods of changing minds and gives you a basic system that can be used in any persuasive situation. Finally, Part D offers some integrative patterns of common usage in which the core pattern appears.

You may also notice that most sections fit neatly within page boundaries. This took more work but is done to make the book easier to read and especially so you can dip into it on odd occasions and nibble at the goodies within. A bit like the changingminds.org website, perhaps.

A note about ethics

Ethics in persuasion is a tricky subject. Learning to persuade can give you a powerful advantage over others whereby you can take advantage of them in ways that you know would meet with general social disapproval. Like giving a person a gun, this book can indeed be used to harm others.

On the other hand, a person who would harm others would likely do it anyway, and much persuasion happens every day that is far more damaging than necessary, when it could be done with finesse and expert ability. Take for example the punishment that parents mete out in desperation as they try to teach their children to behave (while actually teaching the opposite). Likewise friends fall out and companies lose employees over clumsy attempts at persuasion.

While the body of this book takes a relatively neutral position about the rightness and wrongness of persuasion, there are clear social implications. If you deceive and take advantage of others in a way that they perceive as unfair, then they will seek retributive justice – which may sizzle away for a long time before they get their revenge (and which may be disproportionately large). 'As you sow, so also shall you reap' is a Biblical saying that applies here. Even when people get away with things, they know this risk and may well live with a constant unease about potential retribution.

A critical attribute in changing minds is *intent*, and our evolutionary programming means that many people have basically good and socially acceptable reasons for persuasion. This book is for this social majority, seeking to help them both to be more successful and to change minds while causing less collateral damage.

The book is also for people who are the target of changing minds. If you are being persuaded, the information here can help you understand what is happening and hence make more informed and conscious decisions.

Overall, then, I believe that far more good will come from the detail given here than harm, and ask you to always consider the golden rule: 'Do unto others what you would have them do unto you'. Keep a good intent and only seek to persuade in ways that you would not mind others using on you.

Part A:
Inside The Mind

This book is based on the premise that in order to effectively change something, you must first understand it. Minds are tricky things that can be difficult to fathom, making this a doubly-difficult task. It probably makes sense to start with a tour of how we understand and interact with the world, including how we make decisions and change our minds. Although we find it convenient to talk about people changing one another's minds or how others may *influence* the process, in the end each person actually changes his or her own mind.

Psychology is a deep and endless subject and we could stay submerged for a very long time. But this would lose track of the plot as there is so much else to cover. To manage this conundrum, some simple models are used to help make sense of the dark pits of our minds.

Implications for changing minds

The truth is that none of us is a perfectly rounded individual. It is also true that good persuaders are more rounded than most. If you want to persuade then you must ditch any biases you have around psychology and get your head into the subject so you can better know what is going on in your own head. Being self-aware is the first step to self-control, which is the foundation of changing other minds.

1. The SIFT-3M Model

How do our minds work? There is no easy answer to this and the whole discipline of psychology, from personal development to neuroscience, is still only scratching at the surface. Yet if we want to be able to change minds with any reliability, we need to have some kind of model by which to discuss and understand how we think. There is any number of models available to describe the detail of individual aspects of how we think, but relatively few about how the whole thing works and none that seem suitable for our purpose in exploring how to change minds.

The overall model that has been developed for discussing our mental functioning is shown in Figure 1.1 and is described in more detail in following chapters. It is an amalgamation from a wide research and is called the *SIFT-3M Model*, taken from the initial letters of the primary actions of Sensing, Inferring, Formulating and Translating, plus the three deep systems of Motivators, Memory and Musing. It is, of course, much simpler than the very complex reality, but it is sufficient to be used for understanding and explaining much of what goes on in our heads when we make up our minds and get them changed by others.

> ### Implications for changing minds
> Understand how people make sense of the world, what drives them, how they think, how they decide and how they express themselves, and you have the basic tools for changing minds in a powerful and predictable way.

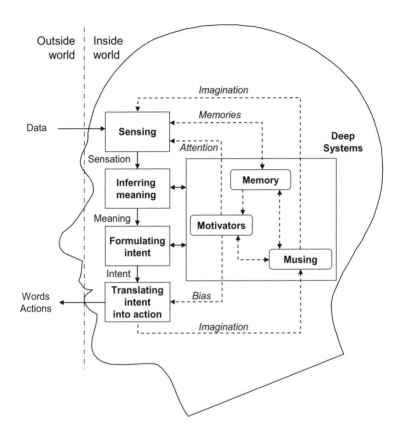

Fig. 1.1. The SIFT-3M model

George Box said 'All models are wrong, but some are useful.' The SIFT-3M Model is of course a simplification of the messy complexity of real minds but it is based on a broad reading and condensation of psychological literature. It has proven very useful in understanding people and changing minds. While not perfect, it is simple and is used as the basis for the discussions ahead.

Sensing

The first stage in creating meaning is to take input from the outside world via our five senses. This process is guided by our attention as well as being directed by goals and other drivers.

Inferring meaning

We create meaning via a complex series of filters through which we pass our sensory information, from recognizing and classifying shapes through recalling associated meaning, to forecasting the future and evaluating the results.

Formulating intent

From our needs and goals and the meaning that we infer from the outside world, we decide what to do next. This may be reactive and subconsciously-driven or may be a more thoughtful process.

Translating intent into action

It is one thing to mean something and it is another to turn this into external words and actions. 'There's many a slip twixt cup and lip' as they say, and what comes out is not always what we intend.

Memory

At the heart of our minds is our memory, which provides the basic vessel in which we hold our experiences and understanding of the world. Although simple in concept, it is tricky and elusive in nature and can feed us false information.

Motivators

There is a range of factors that motivate us and which affect both how we understand the world and the subsequent choices we make. In changing minds, if we can shape these, then we can persuade at a very fundamental level.

Musing

We also spend time reflecting and musing about the world as our imagination plays out possibilities and scenarios that help us decide what is best to do.

Inner and outer worlds

A fundamental principle of the SIFT-3M model is that there are two separate worlds in which we live. The outer world is the environment around us, while the inner world is where we try to make sense of the outer world. Like a rat in a cage, we peer out, but, by the nature of our situation, we cannot truly know what is out there. Fortunately, we are excellently equipped for handling this state of affairs and for the most part do not even notice the difference. This is both useful and a source of endless misunderstanding; we act as if our internal maps *are* the external world but, as has been pointed out, *the map is not the territory*.

Beyond our internal interactions with the outer world, an ever deeper world appears when we start using our imagination. This background thinking is capable of creating such realistic simulations of the outer world that it can be difficult for us to tell the difference between what is real and what is not. The linear nature of our conscious minds is also such that we tend either to pay attention to the outer world or to our inner thinking, where we easily become lost in daydreams and imaginings that we then project onto the outer world, causing even greater confusion and mayhem.

Implications for changing minds

Use this model to help you understand how people work, but never confuse a simplified internal map with the more complex realities of the external territory.

If you want to change the minds of others, then you have to talk to their maps or even change or create new maps for them. This is not easy, as people do not quickly change their familiar inner systems.

---

2. Motivators

One of the fundamental forces that helps us understand and decide, and which then drives us into action, is our underlying system of motivation. Much of this motivation happens subconsciously, so that we often do not know why we want things or why we do things. This is generally useful as we do not want to stop and think about every decision, but it can also lead to us making choices that are not necessarily wise.

The SIFT-3M model deliberately identifies a number of different drivers, as summarized in Table 2.1 and further in paragraphs below. These are explored, one by one in greater detail in subsequent chapters.

Table 2.1. Motivators

Driver	Quick description
Needs	Pre-programmed needs that cannot be changed
Emotions	Feelings that provide powerful motivation
Beliefs	Assumed truths we do not question
Models	Simplified models of the outer world
Preferences	Areas of choice that bias our decisions
Rules	Values and more to guide and constrain action
Goals	Things we consciously intend to achieve

Implications for changing minds

If you can understand what is driving people then you can either change these systems or work with them. If you do not understand a person's motivators then you are shooting in the dark

Needs

Needs are fundamental motivators that we all have. You cannot change or remove needs, but you can understand them and satisfy them in different ways. Needs are behind pretty much everything else that drives us.

Emotions

Emotions are powerful and primitive forces that both make us feel alive and which drive us into unthinking actions. Trying to persuade someone who is experiencing strong emotions is a tricky job. Emotions consequently need to be understood and managed carefully.

Beliefs

Beliefs are the most fundamental premises on which we base our understanding of the world. Some are derived from our own experiences, but many are received wisdoms from other people. They are often very difficult to change.

Models

From our beliefs and experiences we build complex models of the world which act as lenses through which we perceive 'reality' and decide how to understand what is going on around us.

Preferences

Each person has different preferences that form a part of their personality and affect their choices, for example in their approach to taking or avoiding risks.

Rules

In order to thrive in society, we follow various rule sets, including personal values and social norms. These tell us what is right and wrong, good and bad, important and unimportant.

Goals

Given our understanding of the world and the external pressures on us, we accept and build goals that we seek to achieve. These include personal as well as work goals.

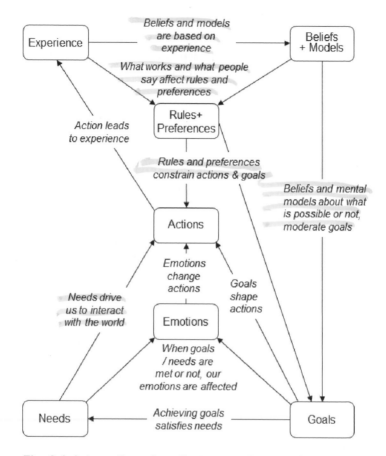

Fig. 2.1. Interaction of motivators, actions and experience

Motivators interact with one another and with the outside world in a way illustrated in Figure 2.1, each building and reinforcing one another. Together they act as a powerful force that drives us forward every day.

Implications for changing minds

If you can understand how motivators interact you can then find ways of coordinating a set of influencing actions to create powerful overall methods of persuasion and changing minds.

3. Needs

We are all programmed with deep needs that are still strongly aligned with our evolutionary past. 'Needs' here, by the way, means deep psychological needs like *belonging* rather than a need for a cup of coffee. Importantly, *we cannot deny our needs* – their grip on us is too powerful – and much, if not all, of what we do is designed to satisfy them. In this way we are like animals, driven by deep urges that we cannot challenge. Of course the human brain also has a well-developed cortex that we use for more complex thinking, yet needs still underlie even the most sophisticated musing.

As needs are at the root of pretty much everything that we do they act as fundamental motivators. They may work alone, such as when a person attacked fights for survival, but we are often driven by multiple combinations of need. For example I go to work not just so I can eat and survive. Work also provides a social environment where I can satisfy needs for interacting with others and so give me a deep sense of meaning in my life.

Managing needs in situations of change is a tricky business. Their deep nature makes them a touchy subject. In particular *needs cannot be changed*. You cannot, for example, change my need to eat or to interact with other people.

Implications for changing minds

Whenever working to change minds, always consider the impact of what you are saying or doing on the basic needs of other people. Also seek to understand what needs are prevalent and how you might satisfy or threaten them for a desired effect.

Remember also that while you cannot change human needs, you can change *how* those needs are satisfied.

Evolutionary needs

We are, at heart, primitive creatures. Yes, of course we have progressed incredibly over the past millennia, yet we still share 98% of our DNA with chimpanzees, and our basic drives are still largely attuned more to living in verdant jungles or wild plains than the complexities of our modern, interconnected world. In *the Selfish Gene*, arch-Darwinian Richard Dawkins showed us as 'gene machines' with the most fundamental driver of propagating our genes. All other needs can hence be seen as subservient to this most basic of needs.

To propagate our genes, we need to find a mate and then protect our progeny until they can feed and protect themselves. This means we must be attractive, strong and able to handle what the world throws at us. Our evolution has taught us that tribal living is good for survival and so we have developed social needs and our status within the tribe is very important to us.

Maslow's Hierarchy

One of the most famous descriptions of needs is an early entrant in all courses on motivation. This is Abraham Maslow's *Hierarchy of Needs*, in which he describes five levels of need:

- Physiological (health)
- Safety
- Belonging
- Esteem
- Self-actualization (achieving your potential)

Maslow also showed how deeper needs have a greater call on our attention and that higher needs become more significant only when lower needs are satisfied. For example when we are ill we become far more concerned about recovery than being admired by other people and achieving higher goals.

Implications for changing minds

To gain attention, stimulate basic needs, showing that these are not fully met. To address higher needs, first ensure basic needs are satisfied.

CIA Needs

If you look deeper, Maslow's five needs can be simplified further by asking what underlies the needs he describes. As shown in Figure 3.1, the lower needs are all about a need for a *sense of control*, while the higher needs are about the need for a *sense of identity*.

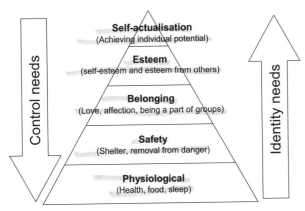

Fig. 3.1. Maslow's Hierarchy and underlying needs

These needs are closely aligned with our evolutionary drivers. Control enables us to survive and find a mate. Identity is particularly important for tribal species as it is related to your position in the pecking order, which is also (unsurprisingly) related to your ability to propagate your genes. Zoologist Desmond Morris, in *'The Naked Ape'*, confirms these two needs:

> "Animals fight amongst themselves for one of two very good reasons: either to establish their dominance in a social hierarchy or to establish their territorial rights over a particular piece of ground."

A third need that Maslow does not really cover is for *arousal*, which acts as a key force for evolution. Without being aroused, we would ignore dangers and miss opportunities for change and improvement. When other needs are satisfied, the need for arousal keeps us going.

These three needs, for a sense of Control, Identity and Arousal can be grouped together and are called the *CIA Model*. They are similar to other three-factor models, but are more accessible and useful in changing minds.

The need for a sense of control

The need for a sense of control is the most basic need and is closest to animal and evolutionary motivation. We can satisfy this need in two ways: we can either take control ourselves, making deliberate decisions about all parts of our lives, or we can cede control to others, allowing them to control some aspects of our lives. Like travel in a car, we can either sit in the driver's seat or we can be a passenger and trust that the driver maintains good control of the car.

Taking control is relatively straightforward as we make decisions for ourselves and otherwise change our actions and environment at will. Changing the minds of other people is a strong control action and can consequently be very satisfying.

A problem in life is that we cannot control everything. If everyone had to take control then society, with all its other benefits, would be impossible. We hence extend the need for control to the need for a *sense* of control. A sense of control leads to safety and confidence that we will be able to achieve wider goals.

Given that we can gain a sense of control either by taking or ceding control, we individually tend to have different preferences for these methods. Some people much prefer taking control and may end up as managers or individualists. Others prefer to give control away, perhaps seeking again the security blanket of a parental figure who will take both control and also responsibility for our well-being.

The primary condition for ceding control is *trust*. I will let you make decisions for me only as long as I trust you. Trust is also important generally in a group – I need to know that you will not take advantage of my vulnerabilities and that you will pull your weight in contributing to the success of the group.

Implications for changing minds

Find out how the other person achieves their sense of control. If they need to be in control, then let them feel they are in charge. Give them choice and show them how you can help them manage their lives. If they prefer that others provide the control, then show you are trustworthy and take control, telling them what to do.

The need for a sense of identity

Building a sense of identity is even more complex and intangible than gaining control and, long before Freud's work on the id and the ego, philosophers pondered the question 'Who am I?' Along the way since then, other important factors that relate to how we perceive our selves have been identified, such as self-image and self-esteem. 'Identity' is a complex concept but is very real for each person and the thought of losing the inner sense of who we are can be terrifying.

There are two main routes to building our sense of identity: internally and externally, both of which we use, though each of us may have quite different preferences in the balance of internal and external approaches to identity creation.

An internal construction is based very largely on an insulated set of independent musings. We decide who we want to *be* and, by focusing internally, we find that state of being. In practice, few people have a solely internal self and we also create our selves in relation to our external environment.

The externally-built sense of identity is based on such elements as our jobs, our nationality and how much money we have. Most of all, however, we define ourselves through our relationships with other people. In this way we *socially construct* our sense of identity, even creating our self-image through the perception we have of how other people see us (the so-called 'looking-glass self'). It is not surprising that significant misinterpretation in this process is a major contributor to some of our more serious neuroses.

This principle extends further when we join a group, who can have a much larger, more powerful and far-reaching collective identity than an individual. This makes the deal of ceding control to the group in return for joining of our identities generally seem like a good idea.

Implications for changing minds

Attach their identity to yours by showing how like each other you are or making your company desirable. Acknowledge their existence and worth. Praise and admire them.

Then when you ask something of them, it will be like they are asking themselves.

The need for arousal

The rich and famous have plenty of control and identity, but are they satisfied? Largely, they are no more or less happy than you or I. A reason for this is a third basic need for novelty, provocation and, most fundamentally, for *arousal* of some kind. When you have everything you need, then feelings of boredom and curiosity act as a push-pull pair to get you moving. This search for arousal is one reason why the rich (money gives control) and famous (fame strokes identity) can get lost in sex, drugs and rock-and-roll.

Arousal needs are often suppressed, either through our childhood lessons on conforming to social codes or because seeking new things can damage our more fundamental sense of control. In this vein, many of us fear novelty, and either bury it completely or constrain it to a part of our lives where we can safely play. This is one reason why seemingly-staid people can have surprisingly creative hobbies.

Everyone has arousal limits, although we each can have widely varying preferences. At one end of this spectrum people are largely numbed by normal life and may need to do extreme sports just to get a quick thrill, while at the other end, people are quickly over-stimulated (it is perhaps interesting that a part of the autism condition is that those affected cannot stem the flow of data and are easily overwhelmed).

As in Fig. 3.2, excessive arousal quickly turns into stress as our bodies and minds fight to handle changing events and potentially hazardous threats. When stressed, people will cease looking for a solution to any current problem and will seek the quickest way of reducing the stress, including cognitive or physical fight-or-flight reactions.

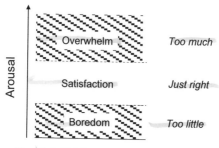

Fig. 3.2. Three levels of arousal

Cognitive arousal

Cognitive arousal is about mental stimulation. It is perhaps what you are seeking now as you read this book, as your curiosity is piqued and interest engaged. A person who is cognitively aroused asks questions, listens, watches and otherwise seeks external stimulation that helps them learn and build new mental models.

Emotional arousal

Emotional arousal is about the triggering of emotions – and strong emotions can be very powerful. It is about being human, feeling love, passion, sadness, frustration and more. Even negative emotions can be better than none as we engage in extreme and scary sports, watch horror movies and revel in the powerful feelings of anger.

Emotional arousal is more central to arousal in that cognitive and physical arousal are more likely to be accompanied by some degree of emotional arousal, while there is a less direct connection between cognitive and physical arousal.

Physical arousal

Physical arousal occurs where our bodies are in a heightened sense of arousal, typically with adrenaline coursing through our system and activating our muscles. Physical arousal includes both sexual arousal and the physical activation when we are engaged in sports and other bodily exertions.

There are deeply programmed responses to physical threats which create physical arousal and action without cognitive intervention, for example when we jump out of the way of a falling branch or block a punch thrown at us.

Implications for changing minds

Interest them. Provoke them. Get them moving. Talk about new and fascinating things. Make them curious. Stimulate their emotions. You may also find ways of giving them greater thrills, but beware of exceeding their arousal limit.

Remember that stress can be used to gain short-term compliance but does not lead to longer-term commitment. Beware of fight-or-flight reactions that are aimed at you personally.

Further needs

Beyond Control, Identity and Arousal, there are many other related needs, some of the most significant of which are shown in Figure 3.3. This indicates how needs are related and that satisfying some needs leads to the satisfaction of further needs. Likewise (and similar to Maslow's model) where lower needs are not satisfied then complete satisfaction of higher needs may be prevented.

Above the CIA needs are the more animalistic evolutionary needs for survival and procreation. There is also a host of more complex underlying needs that contribute towards achieving CIA needs and can provide additional ways of understanding and managing the motivation of both ourselves and other people.

We are not driven by all needs at all times, and at any moment one or a few needs are holding sway over our actions. This is due partially to which needs are being stimulated at that time, and also because we each have a different sensitivity to individual needs. For example some people have much stronger needs for justice and are easily outraged when they see trickery, while others simply need to dominate and have less concern about the emotional impact on their subjects.

There are additional complications, such as what external or internal conditions trigger individual needs. For example, a person with strong justice needs may have stronger concerns than others about racial or gender bias. Many such 'hot buttons' are connected directly to these deep needs.

Table 3.2 offers further detail on this longer list of needs, including implications and ideas on how stimulating or satisfying each need may be practically done.

Managing needs is, as with much of what we are discussing here, easier said than done. But needs are such fundamental aspects of how we focus and decide, they cannot be ignored. Building sensitivity and connection with others is one of the most powerful things you can do, in particular with respect to understanding their underlying needs.

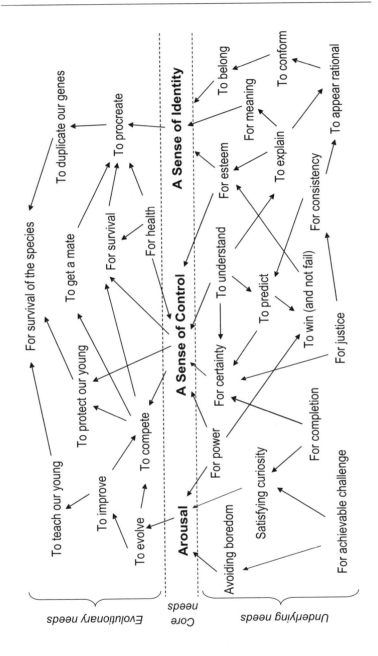

Fig. 3.3. A map of our needs

Table 3.2. Underlying needs and implications

Need	Description	Implications
Avoiding boredom	Insufficient arousal and novelty leads to boredom.	Show present as boring and the future as interesting.
Satisfying curiosity	New and unexplained things lead to curious inquiry.	Hint at intriguing possibilities.
Achieving challenge	If we are challenged in the right way, we will put effort into succeeding.	Challenge people. Set stretching goals. Show confidence in their potential.
Certainty	Certainty and confidence leads directly to a sense of control.	Show an uncertain present and confident future. Keep your promises.
Power	The ability to achieve goals through control of others.	Gain and quietly manage your power. Use it sparingly.
Completion	Things incomplete may be a threat and need attention.	Close off the past. Open the way to the desirable future.
Understanding	Understanding something helps me to take the most effective action.	Help people understand. Educate them. Beware of 'gut' decisions.
Prediction	If we know what will happen we can make appropriate choices.	Paint the path to the future. Show consequences of failure.
Winning	Losing shows us as weak and unworthy of the esteem of others.	Show yourself as a winner. Show others how they can win too.
Justice	If I am treated unfairly I can no longer be certain about social rules.	Stand up for the weak. Punish the bullies. Always be visibly fair.
Consistency	When something is consistent, I can confidently predict what will happen.	Align words and actions. Avoid mixed messages. Help them do the same.
Explanation	If I can explain I can appear expert and so be admired and get my way.	Don't just tell – explain why. Show cause and effect (both good and bad).
Rationality	Appearing rational lets others predict what I will do and so not feel threatened.	Appear reasonable. Highlight lack of reason in their arguments.
Esteem	If others look up to me my sense of identity increases.	Maintain your own self-esteem. Trade in respect.
Meaning	When I have a purpose in life I know what my life is for.	Explain why. Link things to their goals.
Belonging	If I belong to a group then I add the group identity to my own.	Clarify your brand. Make membership of your team desirable and conditional.
Conformity	If we all conform to social rules then there will be no nasty surprises.	Follow rules or break them with care. Use and change the rules.

Changing needs

As already mentioned, the first thing to remember is that you cannot change needs which are programmed into us. However, it is possible to change the actions that we take to meet our needs.

Understanding

The first action to create change is to understand what the other person does to satisfy their needs. What they say and do will tell you not only what needs are uppermost at the moment but *how* they prefer to satisfy their needs. It is also useful to identify what *causes* different needs to be triggered. Once you have this information you can find ways not only of satisfying the same needs but also offering similar routes to satisfaction that matches the other person's preferences.

It is also very important to understand yourself in terms of which needs are more important for you, how you are meeting your needs and what triggers these needs. In changing minds, it is very easy to be too busy attending to your own needs to notice and attend to the needs of others. You may also notice how they are working on you as much as you are seeking to work with their needs.

Alignment

One of the key things to remember when changing minds is that everything we do has some purpose in meeting needs. When you watch people, you should be able to link much of what they do to satisfying control, identity, arousal and other related needs. If you can connect the thread of words and actions to underlying needs, you have the key knowledge to changing what people think and do while still satisfying those needs.

Who	Talk	Subtext/comment
Them	This is annoying!	I cannot do this, which is affecting my control needs – but to admit this would affect identity needs.
You	It is. What have you tried?	Affirm needs and hence identity. Ask question that gives control and stimulates need to explain.

Trust-building

If you would take control then you must first act to build their trust in you so they will comfortably cede their decisions to you and gain their sense of control through confidence in your capability.

Talk about how you are like them in some way. Demonstrate concern for them and the things they care about. Be reliable and honest. And see Chapter 21 for much more detail.

Who	Talk	Subtext/comment
Them	He's so stupid!	It's not me that is stupid. My esteem needs are threatened.
You	It's not your fault. Maybe it's not his either.	Affirm their need first to build trust. Then suggest alternative.
Them	It's boring here. It will take ages to get home, too.	Expressing discomfort and resulting desire.
You	I'll take you back myself. Can we go via Worthing?	Demonstrate personal concern. Then ask for what you want.

Ceding

Managing needs can be something of a paradox. Changing minds may seem like an activity in which you need to take control, yet this may cause the other person to rebel, particularly if they have strong individual control needs. It may therefore be helpful to give control in order to get control.

By showing the other person that they have control, they will feel empowered to make a decision they might otherwise not make.

Who	Talk	Subtext/comment
Them	Why do we have to do it? I can't see what it would gain.	My control needs are not met. Find a rationale to hide real need.
You	Do we really have to? What would happen if we didn't do it?	Show they have control.
Them	Well, I guess we could stop if we wanted, but it would give Mike a problem.	I feel in control and am hence able to concede.

Reframing

Often when people have needs that are not met they feel bad and may project those bad feelings outwards onto contexts and people, including you. Reframing says 'look at this a different way', and allows you to channel their frustrations back into constructive action.

Who	Talk	Subtext/comment
Them	This is boring!	My arousal needs are not met. You are responsible.
You	How could we do it differently?	Stimulate with question. Reframe ownership with 'we'.

Exchange

Stroking their identity makes them feel good and more likely to support your identity needs in return. In this way, changing minds is often a system of exchange more than a one-way manipulation. We are a social species and thrive through reciprocal interaction as much as directed action.

Who	Talk	Subtext/comment
Them	It would be nice to go to see a play.	My arousal needs are not met.
You	If you pay for the tickets, I'll cancel my night out with my friends.	If you help my sense of control then I will cede on my need for identity.

Stimulation

When the other person does not seem to have any need for what you are offering, you may need to stimulate a latent need by provoking, challenging and demonstrating. Stimulation often leads to arousal.

Who	Talk	Subtext/comment
Them	I don't want a new car.	My transport needs are satisfied.
You	What do you like in a car?	Probe for needs.
Them	Well, I must say I'm a bit of a gadget freak.	I have high arousal needs
You	Let me show you something new...	Let me prod your arousal need.

Reverse psychology

When a person feels they are being manipulated, their sense of control is threatened and they may react by doing the opposite of what is suggested. Some people (and many teenagers) are rather contrary by nature and easily fall into such actions. In such cases it can be effective to 'try' to get them to do the opposite of what you want.

Who	Talk	Subtext/comment
You	You look ill. You shouldn't really go to town today.	Provoke them into going.
Them	I'm fine. I'm going to go anyway.	To assert my sense of control I will go.

4. Emotions

Emotions play a large part in our lives, but what is their purpose? There is a clue in the origins of the word: *movere* is the Latin verb 'to move'. Emotions are the fundamental system that drives us, forcing us to act, rewarding us with good feelings when we behave correctly and making us feel bad when we do the wrong things. Emotions are useful, but can also be inconvenient. Although we can influence what we feel by what we think, we still only have limited control over our emotions.

There are many emotions, although psychologists have noted that there are relatively few primary emotions and that most others can be classified as sub-categories of these. Table 4.1 lists some of these basic emotions, along with brief considerations as to how these may be managed in changing minds. Notice the common theme of managing goals and expectations – a significant cause of emotional upset is misunderstanding around our needs and goals.

The power of emotions

Emotions have varying levels of intensity and strong emotions have a greater motivational effect. As the brain chemistry changes, stronger emotions also have a greater effect in suppressing rational thinking, which can be a problem or an opportunity, depending on where you are standing.

A problem with emotions is that when we try to suppress them, they can pop up elsewhere and cause unwanted effects. Anger suppressed at work can explode in a very unwanted way back at home. Fear can appear as excessive risk aversion. Even happiness at one success can distract us from another pressing problem. Emotions may also be converted, making the origins harder to detect, for example where fear turns into anger or surprise becomes disgust.

Physicality

Emotions are also called 'feelings' perhaps because we literally feel them as physical bodily sensations, such as tensing of muscles or tingling on the skin. This is a useful clue both to help us notice our own emotions and also those of others.

When we are angry our muscles tense, our skin flushes and our teeth may even be bared. This is very different from the relaxed smiling of someone who is happy. Attention to body language hence makes many emotions fairly easy to read.

Basic emotions and triggers

While there is a wide range of emotions, many of these are variations on basic emotions. By selecting a shorter set of basic emotions, such as in Table 4.1, you can identify a useful set of emotions which may be triggered by deliberate action.

Table 4.1. Basic emotions and triggers

Emotion	Typical trigger	Implications
Happiness	Achievement of goal or satisfaction of need.	Link achieving goals to what you want them to do.
Sadness	Realization that goal will not be achieved.	Permit sadness in change. Show future happiness.
Desire	Perceived gap between goal or need and actual situation.	Build gaps to create required motivation, close gaps on others.
Fear	Threat to a basic need.	Assuage their fears. Use it sparingly for motivation.
Anticipation	Expectation of a predicted event.	Sustain anticipation of positive events. Manage anticipation of bad news.
Surprise	Unexpected occurrence of event.	Manage expectations. Create positive surprises.
Affection	Liking and caring about other people.	Be trustworthy and likeable before asking for things.
Anger	Frustration of expected achievement of goal.	Managing expectations. Direct anger constructively.
Disgust	Breaking of social rules by another person.	Avoid breaking social rules. Beware of associating with those who do.
Shame	Disgust at oneself for breaking a social rule.	Show others the risks of breaking rules. Apologize for your errors.

Emotional intelligence

Psychologist Daniel Goleman coined the term 'Emotional Intelligence' as an indication of skill in managing emotions, much as IQ is used in intelligence (hence the other common term of 'EQ'). The suppression of emotions is still remarkably common in many countries and companies, although works such as Goleman's helps lift the lid on this subject. Elements of emotional intelligence include:

- *Identifying* emotions, seeing that you and others are in an emotional state and being able to name those emotions and the effects they are having.

- *Accepting* that emotions are a natural part of the human condition and the subconscious effects they have. This does not mean making excuses for the negative effects of extreme emotion, but neither does it mean critical judging of other people.

- *Talking* about emotions, openly and lucidly and without embarrassment.

- *Controlling* your own emotions and not being driven by the emotional roller-coaster.

- *Using* your emotions in effective ways, for example considering them during decisions and putting passion into your communications.

- *Influencing* the emotions of others, creating calm or arousal as required.

Managing your emotions to create a desired impression on others is important. An over-emotional person who seems to be driven by the whim of their emotions can be seen as out of control and irrational. On the other hand, a person who shows no emotions may be seen as cold and uncaring.

Implications for changing minds

Become intensely aware of emotions, theirs and yours, understanding and accepting causes and how they affect thinking and choice. Assess their Emotional intelligence and respond accordingly. Find ways to control emotions rather than letting them control you.

Changing emotions

Given the unconscious power of emotions in driving decisions, managing the emotions of others is a constant and critical activity in changing minds. Also critical is management of our *own* emotions as emotional arousal both triggers emotions in others and seriously limits rational thinking. Emotional intelligence is therefore a core skill in changing minds.

Infection

Emotions are contagious, and others will pick up feelings that we project at them or even express in their presence. Hence, if we get angry with them, they may get angry back. If we are excited, they too may become excited.

Who	Talk	Subtext/comment
You	Wow! That's absolutely brilliant!!	Express excitement to cause excitement.
Them	Yeah! I kind of like it too.	Visible evidence of excitement invoked.

Without control, we can easily infect others with anger, depression and other negative emotions.

Bonding

When you show that you like or empathize with the other person, they will like and bond with you, considering you a friend. Then when you show emotion they will likely adjust their emotions to empathize with you. Hence when you get angry, they will be angry with you. When you are happy, they will be happy for you and hence be happy themselves.

Who	Talk	Subtext/comment
You	I really like the way you help out.	Flattery to show liking and approval of helping.
Them	Thanks, you're really kind.	I like you too.
You	Could you do this for me?	Ask for affirmed help.

Note that if the other person thinks you are flattering them just to influence them, they will likely head the other way.

Goal management

Happiness, sadness, fear, anger and other emotions are strongly linked with achievement or frustration of goals. You can use this knowledge to control emotions by the way you help or hinder others in achievement of their goals.

When you help them achieve goals, you can then ask for something in return, perhaps getting them to help you achieve your goals.

Who	Talk	Subtext/comment
You	Here, let me help you with that.	Provide assistance in achieving goal.
Them	Thank you. You're really kind.	I am happy you helped.
You	Would you like a coffee?	Ask for extended company in exchange.

Note that beyond direct goal management, you can also act to change their goals, as in Chapter 9.

Feel-felt-found

This is a specific technique that combines three steps into a persuasive narrative.

(a)   Acknowledge their feelings

(b)   Explain that others have felt the same way

(c)   Describe the successful method that those others used

This works by (a) bonding with them by acknowledgement, then (b) transferring that bond to a third party (which further legitimizes the feeling), (c) gives them action strategies by describing what those other people did.

Who	Talk	Subtext/comment
Them	This is ridiculous!	I feel angry about this.
You	I know how you feel and others have felt the same, and they found that, when they cooled down and read the details, it wasn't so bad after all.	Connect them to others, then change others and hence them.

Stimulation

Stimulating emotions can be an effective way of finding the truth as people are less able to be deceptive or cover things up when they are angered or impassioned. When they are aroused they also are less able to think rationally and are more easily influenced.

Stimulation can often be done by adopting an aroused state yourself, such as anger or excitement, effectively inviting the other person to join you in this state. While perhaps obvious, this is a primitive mechanism which few can avoid.

Who	Talk	Subtext/comment
You	That's stupid!	Carefully provoke them.
Them	Are you calling me stupid??	Aroused and angry.
You	Not unless you're thinking about doing that.	Give them a route out.

Accepting

When people express emotions, others may fear being infected by those feelings and hence back away or otherwise try to stop the person feeling that way. Yet we are emotional animals and it can be helpful to us if we are allowed to express how we feel.

Accepting and thereby legitimizing the emotions of others can hence be an effective method of building trust and bonding that leads them to be far more open to subsequent suggestion.

Who	Talk	Subtext/comment
Them	I am really upset...(cries)	I am unable to contain my emotion.
You	That's ok. There, there.	Comfort them without making any requests for now.
You (later)	Feeling better now?	Gentle suggestion that they feel better.
Them	Yes. Thank you.	I am able to speak now without feeling so upset.
You	Can you tell me more?	Getting information on which to base an intervention.
Them	Well, it all started...	I feel able to tell you confidential information.

Conditioning

In classic conditioning, a stimulus is applied to a person at the same time as a certain response appears. After a while the application of the stimulus will lead to the response appearing by itself. The famous original experiments by Ivan Pavlov were around ringing a bell when feeding a dog. After a while, the bell alone is enough to make the dog salivate. While people are more complex, this animal response may still be created. In particular, the basic nature of emotions makes them particularly susceptible to the conditioned response.

Who	Talk	Subtext/comment
Them	Can you lend me...	Unwanted action by them.
You	(loudly and suddenly) WHAT!	Make them feel uncomfortable.
	Repeat sudden loud noise when they say 'can you lend me'	Permanently link discomfort to the action.
Them (later)	Can you le...	Feels conditioned discomfort and refrains from unwanted request.

5. Beliefs

We live in a massively complex and detailed world which we have to learn to understand and handle. We cannot know it all and hence have to adopt beliefs, which are *assumed truths*. In fact, as we internally construct our own reality based on an unreachable outer world, you could say that *everything* is a belief.

A problem with beliefs is that everything else is built on top of them, including the senses of control and identity. Trying to change beliefs can hence be perceived as attacking the person, who is likely to strongly resist the pain caused by questioning their assumptions, let alone suggesting alternatives. Yet changing beliefs can be a very powerful way of changing minds, as religious missionaries know.

Table 5.1. Types of belief

Belief	Example
Existence belief	Your love for me
Associative belief	A rose is a flower
Causal belief	Treating people well makes them work harder
Comparative belief	Product A is more effective than Product B

Strength

Some beliefs are stronger as we tightly hold onto some things while are open to persuasion about others. This is a highly variable affair and some people have a greater need for belief than others.

Implications for changing minds

Understand how strongly people hold a belief and decide whether it is worth the effort (can you get the same effect another way?). Some beliefs may best be changed by weakening them over time.

Formation

Beliefs are initially formed by experience and experiment as we build our understanding of the world. A child finds that pulling a face gets attention and so tries other expressions. These experiences may then be generalized to apply in other areas, where experiment extends belief.

There are limitations to this approach, however. Even if something happens ten times, it does not prove that it happens forever (although Karl Popper helped fix this conundrum by saying that, for a thing to be true, you need to *fail* in an experiment designed to prove it false). And some things, such as many existence beliefs, cannot be proven (for example the existence of God). As a result, some beliefs are held as a matter of faith.

Faith

If we cannot prove something, then we must accept it as true. This is often done through the use of trusted *references*. For example a scientist will use accredited textbooks and the work of respected other scientists. A religious person will use holy texts and the word of the priesthood.

Not all of us trust everything we are told and many of us will actively seek to determine the trustworthiness of our reference people. The criterion for this is important: some people seek subject expertise while others use short-cuts such as job title or even appearance.

Research by Milton Rokeach showed that people who blindly accept beliefs from reference people tend to cognitively put competing beliefs far away, where they can ignore them and use generalizations such as 'they're all like that'. When beliefs are challenged, they react strongly with a 'fight or flight' response that either ignores any disconfirming evidence or attacks it. A problem with challenging a belief that has been accepted from a reference is that it calls into question all other beliefs from that source.

People who are more open about other beliefs keep these closer and have a far greater understanding and acceptance of them. They also are more able to change their own beliefs.

Implications for changing minds

Understand *how* people create and hold beliefs and hence whether and how to work with or challenge these.

Behaving and belief

As we believe, so also will we behave. Figure 5.1 shows how our beliefs about how selfish or caring people are can lead to different approaches towards other people. It also highlights the common situation that we tend to perceive ourselves in a more forgiving light than others. A known effect is that when I or my friends do well, I am likely to attribute it to skill and other personal factors, while if others do well I am more likely to attribute it to luck or other situational factors. The reverse is also true: when I fail, I will make excuses, but I am likely blame others for their mistakes. On the other hand, low self-esteem can lead me to assuming I am inferior in some way to everyone else and hence putting all others above me.

	I care more about *others*	I care more about *myself*
Others care more about *other people*	**Collaborative approach** Work *with* other people for the common good.	**Use-and-abuse approach** Take advantage of other's naivety
Others care more about *themselves*	**Nurturing approach** Take care of others, however they behave.	**Independent or competitive approach** Ignore or fight with others.

Fig. 5.1. Beliefs drive how we behave

Implications for changing minds

Work to ensure you have a strong self-esteem (but are not arrogant), so that you see others in a true light. Notice *their* beliefs about themselves and others, and work from where *they* are (not where you are).

You can also provide evidence that breaks beliefs and hence gives opportunity to change minds. If they are uncaring then show care. If they are dominant, do not conform until they are reasonable.

Limiting beliefs

We can have effective and useful beliefs that help us succeed. We can also have limiting beliefs that hold us back and prevent us from achieving our potential. For example, many people grow up believing that power and money are wrong in some way, and hence find satisfaction in being relatively poor and powerless. If they realized that it is *intent and use* that led to these beliefs, and that power and money can be used for good purposes, then they might have very different lives.

Psychologist Albert Ellis identified a number of irrational beliefs, the core of which he summarized in three common assumptions:

- I must do well, and always be liked or else I am a rotten, no-good person.
- Others must treat me in the way I want to be treated, or else they are no-good rotten people, who deserve to suffer.
- I must have everything I want quickly and easily, and nothing I do not want.

A simpler and related list was defined by clinical psychologist Taibi Kahler. His five drivers are common beliefs that affect many of us and drive us to behave in unreasonable and limiting ways.

- Be Perfect
- Be Strong
- Hurry Up
- Please Others
- Try Hard

How often have you heard a voice whispering one or more of these admonitions in you ear?

Implications for changing minds

Ensure you have no limiting beliefs that unreasonably constrain your changing of minds. Discover the other person's limiting beliefs and either work with or around these. If it helps, challenge these, but do be prepared for a battle.

Changing beliefs

Beliefs are at the root of all understanding, which makes the changing of beliefs both difficult and powerful. A challenge to beliefs can be emotionally upsetting and if I attack how you perceive the universe then I must be ready for a robust response. Yet we hold many weak beliefs which may be more open to challenge and many will appreciate the opportunity to improve their foundations of understanding.

The first stage in changing beliefs is in understanding what they are now and how strongly they are held. If you can understand the belief landscape then you can see weaknesses and ways to change what is assumed.

Evidence

One of the most powerful ways of changing beliefs is to give hard evidence to show that they are wrong. Depending on how strongly the beliefs are held, the person may remain in denial for some time, but with enough strong evidence they will eventually have to change their belief.

Who	Talk	Subtext/comment
Them	I want to work for Jo.	I believe Jo is a good manager and will be kind to me.
You	Well Jo did sack Mikey last week for coming in late. Jane has also complained about Jo.	Give evidence that Jo is not a good manager.

Challenge

The key to changing beliefs is often simply in surfacing and challenging them, showing them as inadequate for meeting need and goals. People often do not realize where understanding stops and belief begins. When we realize we hold a belief that has an irrational or uncertain basis and that better alternatives are available, then, provided the emotional impact is not too great, we may readily change.

Who	Talk	Subtext/comment
Them	That won't work.	I believe that will not work.
You	Why not? Have you tried it?	Surface detail and challenge practice.

Becoming a reference

One of the most powerful ways of changing bel
reference person. If the other person believes you at
in a particular domain, they will accept without question any
say in your area of expertise. This is the position gained by cult leaders
who dominate and dictate people's lives. It is also the position of
professors and consultants who sell their professional expertise.

Become a reference by being knowledgeable and stating your truth
clearly and assertively. In a debate do not back down unless it is
outside the area you have staked out as yours.

Who	Talk	Subtext/comment
Them	Pascal was quite a clever person, wasn't he?	I think Pascal was clever but am uncertain about this.
You	Pascal was the greatest genius of his day.	I am an expert about Pascal.

Changing the reference

If you cannot become the reference person, you may be able to change
who that person is, for example by showing your reference person as
superior to other reference people. Children try to do this when they
say 'my father is better than your father'.

To criticize a reference person is to challenge every belief based on
that person's assertions. This means that to change the reference
person, you will need strong proof of your reference's superiority, plus
a good dose of assertion as to this fact. One way of doing this is to show
that your reference is very largely the same as the other person's
reference but that your reference resolves a critical weakness in the
other reference.

Who	Talk	Subtext/comment
Them	Professor Williams has published three books in this area.	My reference person is the greatest expert.
You	But doctor Jamison has published ten books and is head of the consultative committee and he says Professor Williams is wrong in one important area.	My reference person is an even greater expert.

ilization

Where beliefs cannot be changed, then they can be used as part of the persuasion. For example a person who considers themselves expert in a topic may be flattered or co-opted onto a working group where their knowledge is occasionally required while their cooperation is gained on a range of other subjects.

Who	Talk	Subtext/comment
Them	That policy won't work unless you include conformance with the MRX standard.	I believe that the MRX standard is essential in this type of policy.
You	You know what you're talking about here, don't you? How about joining the team?	Flattery in exchange for collaboration.

Strengthening/weakening

When a person's beliefs conflict, they will choose the stronger beliefs over the weaker beliefs. Stronger beliefs are hence more dominant, more resolute and are harder to challenge. Weaker beliefs, on the other hand, may be more open to alternatives. A simple approach is to challenge only the weaker beliefs while supporting the stronger belief, at least for the moment.

You can also challenge strong beliefs not by asking the other person to give them up, but by getting them to realize that the strong beliefs are not applicable in all situation or do not cover specific detail. This approach can be incremental over time, gradually weakening the belief which may eventually be given up.

Who	Talk	Subtext/comment
Them	Jim is a great speaker. Melanie is not very good.	I believe Jim is a good speaker and Melanie is a bad speaker.
You	Jim is great with engineers, but not so hot with customers. Melanie got great reviews at the RGH product conference last week.	Weaken Jim's position and strengthen Melanie's.

Extending

Beliefs are often very limited in scope, excluding many other alternatives. This leads to simple opinions and makes decisions easy but excludes many other possibilities.

If you can leave the underlying belief intact but extend it to include other criteria, then you can change the way people decide.

Who	Talk	Subtext/comment
Them	I always use Sudso washing powder.	I believe Sudso is best (because it washes whites whiter).
You	The only powder with built-in softener is Washit.	Extend decision criteria 'best' to include softening.

Social Pressure

When people discover that others have different beliefs, then this causes them to consider possible conflict that may result, including being ostracized for the heresy of believing differently from the majority or important other people.

The implication for changing minds is to show them that people they respect have beliefs which support your objectives. If needed, you can hint at what may happen if everyone knew what the other person believes.

Who	Talk	Subtext/comment
Them	There's no point giving anything.	I believe charity is a waste.
You	Did you know that Marc and Bev volunteer with that organization?	Your friends believe strongly in charity.

6. Models

The world is a vast and intricate place and our minds, though also complex, have a limited ability to take in the terabytes of data that flow in through our senses every moment. In a remarkable feat of processing, we take these non-stop inputs from our five senses and, in real-time, we recognize shapes, sounds and smells and so are able to name and respond to the events around us.

We build detailed models called *frames of reference, mental models* or *schemas* (or *schemata*) to help us in this process, so recognizing and handling tricky situations that range from falling trees to office politics. While not as complicated as the outer reality, these models are good enough for the job at hand, recognizing things and helping us to decide what to do next. However, in doing so, they distort and filter reality as we see not which is really there but what our models present to us. In this ways, models form complex beliefs that we accept without question.

Fig. 6.1. Models as distorting lenses

Implications for changing minds

To communicate with people, speak to their mental models and do not get trapped by yours. If you change their models, you will change how they see and hence how they decide.

Model number and complexity

If an American was dropped into the middle of the Sahara desert, all he or she could see would be sand and sun, yet a Bedouin would see weather patterns, tracks of animals, past events and more. This is because Americans seldom have to survive in desert conditions and their few and limited models about deserts would be insufficient. We tend to build just enough models, each with sufficient complexity, to cope with most of what the world throws at us.

Yet in our daily lives, the models we use are often both limited and limiting and, as psychologist Abraham Maslow noted, 'A man with a hammer tends to see every problem as a nail.' On the other hand, the more models we have, the more ways we have of understanding the world. Despite the benefits of multiple models, many people are still lazy and survive with few, simple models and hence have a distorted view of the world. One reason for this is that learning and model-building are synonymous, and educated people will therefore tend to have more models of greater complexity and accuracy.

The hazards of simplification were described by biologist Ross Ashby in his 'Law of Requisite Variety' where he shows that in any ecological system, the species with the greatest flexibility are those that will prosper and survive. Children know this intuitively and will try endless new approaches until they get what they want. The more models you have, the more ways of seeing and understanding you have, the more successful you can be.

Even with greater complexity, however, mental models are still simplifications which never fully reflect reality and can contain serious defects. The key trick is to have enough models that are sufficiently accurate and complex to enable us to handle the outer world. Albert Einstein summed it up when he said 'A thing should be as simple as possible, but no simpler.'

Implications for changing minds

Learn multiple ways of seeing the world. Get educated. And never forget that models are not reality. Persuade others not only by changing their existing models but also by giving them new ones and encouraging them to see, using multiple models.

Patterns

Models may include overall patterns by which we can recognize and shape things. For example a publishing editor will have patterns for what makes a good story, including sub-patterns about how to begin and end the story, what makes a good '3D' character and so on.

Our brains are structured as pattern-matching devices and we are very good at approximate 'fuzzy-matching' of what we see to our models. We can hence make good guesses about complex situations and decide on appropriate action, as in Figure 6.2.

Fig. 6.2. Pattern-matching

Scripts

Scripts are sequences of words and actions, like the directions and words of a play, which tell us precisely how to behave in particular situations, from meeting the Pope to leaving work early.

Scripts can be shared with others to enable common rituals to be performed, as in the social acts of greeting and parting. Such rituals affirm our place in society and can be used to help detect social intruders (if you do not know how to say hello then I will exercise due caution). Scripts also allow us to perform tricky social acts such as romantic courting and challenging our superiors.

We also develop our own scripts as we find out what works and what does not work in our living contexts. Scripts thus keep us out of trouble as well as helping us achieve our goals. Scripts are also important in creating the stories that we tell ourselves and other about life.

Signals

Models may include a number of signals which trigger action and indicate points of change. They tell us when models start and stop, where things may change and when we have choices.

The dance of courtship, for example, includes many signals at which either party can break off the relationship while saving face for all concerned. A flutter of eyelashes or over-long stare can signal interest and trigger initiation, while an ignored phone call or 'let's be friends' conversation can act as a request for termination.

Implications for changing minds

When evoking a model, consider first the actions that will be triggered. When teaching a model to others, connect signals to desired actions to ensure they behave in a desirable way.

Emotions

Models often include details of what people will feel in particular situations. For example, at a funeral you may expect people to be rather upset, while at a wedding there should be more gaiety. This allows you to respond for example with sympathy or joy.

Models also *instruct* us in what we should be feeling, as in Figure 6.3, and are often so effective that we experience the appropriate emotions without knowing why. Consider how your emotions are manipulated when watching a movie. You know it is not real, but the director also knows that by projecting a model you can be made to feel happy, sad, anxious and so on.

Fig. 6.3. Models as scripts and emotional instructions

Memory

Models are also so powerful that they affect how we remember things. Memory is reconstructive in that we recall vague patterns of past events and then shape them into recognizable forms by using models to add the relevant detail.

This reconstruction includes the association of emotions with memories and we remember events that *should* be pleasant as *being* pleasant. Hence a birthday is remembered as more enjoyable than it was and we may look back on a Monday morning and assure ourselves that it was unhappy. This is particularly effective when we lump things together, remembering birthdays or Monday's events.

Implications for changing minds

Ask them to recall events that might reasonably be expected to be happy or sad, depending on the mood you want to invoke. Generalize these events to ensure that model emotions are created.

Forecasts

We build models based on the past and project these forward as we assume that both the short- and long-term future will be similar. We use models in this way to predict what may happen, from how individuals behave to how entire economies operate.

We make particular use of forecasted emotions to make decisions, as we predict the future and then see how we feel about what might happen. In this way we make significant choices about today's actions based on assumed emotions. Forecasts also lead us worry or look forward to future events, depending on how we believe we will feel.

Implications for changing minds

Talk about futures that make sense to the other people with the models that they have. If they cannot understand then build them simple models using familiar metaphors.

Ensure the models that you use have positive emotions associated with them (or other emotions you want to invoke).

Exceptions

Not all models work perfectly and we therefore have to find ways to handle the exceptions to the rules and patterns of the models we use. There are four ways that we do this: creation, revision, special case and ignoring.

Creation

When we are faced with a situation that does not fit, even moderately, with any of our models, we have to create a new model to handle the situation. For example flashing lights in the sky might make us build a mental model of alien spacecraft. This is a rare activity for many of us.

Revision

We seldom have to create entirely new models. A simpler method we use when the situation does not fit a model is to re-think the model, for example when a person starts consistently behaving 'out of character' (in other words outside our model of them) then we may change the model of them we use.

Special case

Perhaps the most common approach used when unexpected things occur that do not fit our models (other than ignoring them) is to add an exception as a 'special case', while preserving the original model for 'the norm'. For example when sales decline, a marketer may explain this as a blip caused by a competitor releasing a new product rather than any serious change in customer perception.

Special case exceptions help us handle novel situations without having to go back to the drawing board and revise our base model. This can lead to complex models with many special cases to handle daily variations. We cling tightly to our models, even when we could create far more effective ways of understanding.

Ignoring

Finally, and perhaps most commonly, we ignore things that do not fit with our models. We typically do this by closing our eyes and pretending these aberrations do not exist. If the exception recurs then we may still cling to denial, although with repeated occurrence we may eventually be forced to use one of the other methods.

Models of people

One of the main things we model is people, which is generally necessary owing to their remarkable complexity. However, as with models of more mundane things, this can cause significant problems as our simplistic models of one another lead us into assumptions that are often quite wrong and may well be socially very damaging.

A typical pattern of model use occurs when we first meet other people and quickly try reducing them to *stereotypes*. Within seconds we are pushing them into various classifications, from 'brainy nerd' to 'dumb blonde'. Once we have them neatly classified, the rest of our interaction with them is based on the model we have placed on them. If they seem to be breaking the stereotype, we will typically find some rationalization and push them back into the box. For example, if a pretty woman we have classified as 'dumb blonde' starts talking about things we do not understand, we may think things like 'She doesn't know what she's talking about' and excuse ourselves away from this confusing situation.

We also have *prototypes*, which are idealized models of particular types of people, from 'a friend' to 'a bank manager'. These are typically made up of an amalgam of the best characteristics from other people we admire, with further improvement from what we seek from such people. Hence there is the perfect parent, partner, leader, and so on. In the same way that we expect people placed in imperfect models to misbehave, if we have cast a person into a perfect model, we may well forgive them transgressions rather than accept that they are not as perfect as we hoped they would be.

Implications for changing minds

Before you meet other people, consider the model by which you want them to classify you, then get into the right frame of mind and literally act the part. When you have established yourself, you can vary how you behave for specific effect, such as breaking the stereotype to cause confusion. You also may just want to be yourself.

Also note your own stereotypes and prototypes and how you misunderstand others. The more accurate assessment you can make of others, the more effectively will you be able to change their minds.

Models and learning

A lot of education is about building and changing models. When we learn how something works, we build and change simplified internal models. Teaching is thus a process of model-building and teachers are experts at changing minds in this way.

David Kolb described a useful model for understanding how people learn and integrate models, as in Figure 6.4. First we have an actual 'concrete' experience. Then we reflect on it, seeing how it fits with our existing models. If there is a mismatch, we have to reconceptualize and change our model to fit. We then try out our changed model to assure ourselves that it is a useful update.

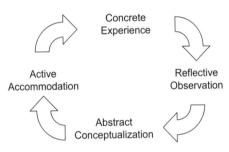

Fig. 6.4. Kolb's model of learning

Honey and Mumford built on this model in their Learning Styles Inventory where they found that we each prefer one of four different learning styles:

- *Activist*: Tries new things.
- *Reflector*: Gathers information and thinks things over.
- *Theorist*: Builds models that make sense.
- *Pragmatist*: Uses whatever seems to work.

Implications for changing minds

Use teaching methods to change models and minds. This can range from explaining, to demonstrating, to the use of experiential exercises.

Use Kolb's model and the Honey and Mumford categories to understand the detail of how people learn. Then replicate it in your changing of their models.

Changing models

Our models are effectively complex beliefs and we often receive them from reference sources, as with beliefs. As a result, models are generally difficult to change and you may decide to work with them rather than change them.

Disconfirmation

A simple way of changing models is to present *evidence* of their limitation in particular circumstances, effectively saying 'Your model is ok in other places, but it is not good enough *here.*' Extensions and revisions to the model may then be carefully offered.

Evidence may well need repeating several times and you may have to hammer home the fact that their current models are no longer good enough.

Who	Talk	Subtext/comment
Them	This bag is expensive.	I have a model of bag cost that tells me this.
You	Look at the price of these other bags.	Provide evidence that the bag in question is not that expensive.

Extension

Models often work in some contexts but lack the sophistication to handle other areas. This is typical where the other person has acquired the model from someone else and is trying to apply it blindly.

For this sort of situation the approach is not so much to challenge the existing model but to show a situation where it is not enough. This may then lead to the other person developing their model further.

Who	Talk	Subtext/comment
Them	We've got to send reinforcements to the front.	The enemy will attack at the front.
You	But what if they attack our flanks?	The enemy may also attack at the sides. How can you extend your model to cope with this?

Reframing

A related method is reframing, which changes aspects of the model (or *frame of reference*). The frame may be contained within the model or it may be in a laterally related area. Reframing says 'let's look at it a different way', which effectively says 'put that model away and let's try looking through a different lens.'

Who	Talk	Subtext/comment
Them	We need to take three weeks' rations.	There will be no other food available.
You	That would weigh too much. We must live off the land.	Reframe selves as hunter-gathers.

Challenge universality

A classic indicator that a model is being used is found where universal generalizations are applied, such as 'always', 'completely', 'every', etc. Such models are typical of simplistic black-and-white thinking that assumes there are a limited number of ways that things can be configured.

Statements may be challenged just by repeating the universal word as a question. If you can get them to break the generalization for just one instance then they will accept the possibility of there being other variations.

Who	Talk	Subtext/comment
Them	Nobody loves me.	I feel unloved and alone.
You	Nobody? Isn't there one person?	Challenge universality.
Them	Well, I suppose my mother loves me. And my brother, I guess.	I'm not that alone.

The universal thinking may also appear more subtly, for example where the assumption behind a statement is that one rule applies to all people and all situations.

Who	Talk	Subtext/comment
Them	Time for bed.	People need eight hours sleep.
You	I'm not tired.	Challenge universality: It does not apply to me.

Rejection

Sometimes models are so wrong they are not applicable in any way in the given context. When this happens you may simply refuse to accept them, rejecting suggestions out of hand.

Who	Talk	Subtext/comment
Them	Remember to bow to the Prince.	Rules of etiquette dictate bowing.
You	I don't think that's necessary these days.	Break model: Refuse and reject it.

Interruption

When they are stuck in a pattern of behaving in a certain way, people are probably following internal scripts, acting and re-enacting an obsessive performance that may be simply annoying or highly dysfunctional. Alcoholics and other abusers often fall into this category. In a similar way, people run through compulsive patterns of speech that they know are less than effective but still cannot help saying.

Patterns of behaving and talking may be broken by repeated interruption. Effectively, what is happening is that you are showing the person practically that they can stop the script at any time. There are two ways of interrupting. One is to draw attention to what the person is doing. This can help them to realize what they are doing and consciously make an effort to stop. Sometimes a more effective approach is to change the topic. This can cause confusion and acts at a more subconscious level to permanently break the pattern.

The extent to which this technique works depends on how deeply the script is embedded. A chronic pattern may need a wider range of therapeutic methods to break the compulsion.

Who	Talk	Subtext/comment
Them	It's my fault. I know it's my fault. It's always...	Stuck in pattern of blaming self.
You	(interrupting). What's that over there – is it a bird? What species do you think it is?	Interruption at random point and changing the subject. (do this repeatedly)

7. Rules

In our lives we cannot just do anything we want. There are many constraints on us that shape what is acceptable and what is not. These act as rules that we must follow when making various decisions about what we think, what we say, how we behave and what we do. Rules tell us what is more and less important, what is right and wrong, what is good and bad.

Rule sets that we follow include:

- *Personal values* that we form to guide our individual lives.
- *Group norms* that control how we behave in each group to which we belong.
- *Cultural codes* that shape attitudes and actions at group, organizational and national levels.
- *Social morals* that determine good and bad within broad populations.
- *Religious commandments* that dictate various aspects of the lives of adherents.
- *Professional ethics* that determine how specific organizations and job-related groups should behave.
- *Company policies* that must be obeyed in the places where we work.
- *National laws* that control many parts of our lives.

Implications for changing minds

Understand the rules which constrain the other person and either beware of breaking them or do so for deliberate effect. Know the rules that you follow and beware a mismatch with the rules of others.

Values

'Value' can be a confusing word as it has several meanings. Beyond the value we get when we purchase something, there are at least two alternatives when we talk about 'our values'. What are sometimes called *end-state values* are 'things we value' like happiness and prosperity. In this book, we classify these under 'goals'. When we talk of values here, we mean *instrumental values*, which are the constraints we have to follow in order to achieve our goals. Hence, for example, I may value wealth and have a goal of becoming rich, but it is against my values to achieve this by robbing banks or tricking other people out of their money.

Values are rules that tell us what is right and wrong, and what we may and may not do. They include priorities, for example that robbing a rich banker is not as bad as robbing a child. Companies often have listed 'values', but these are usually aspirational rather than descriptive and are, in effect, desired ways of behaving.

Many of us constantly evaluate (note the common derivation) other people, using our own values, of course, and judging them to be good or bad people. It is not uncommon for us to have different sets (or at least *strengths*) of values for ourselves and for other people. Those of us who are particularly self-critical have stricter self-values, but most of us are more lax with ourselves and hence judge others more harshly than we judge ourselves. We will also judge those we would put on a pedestal – including our leaders.

A good test of our values is when we are under pressure – in fact we often have two sets of values: normal values and *stress values*. Normal values may say 'be nice to people' but when you meet someone who is acting against other values you hold, it is easy to get angry and say hurtful things to them. Anger and other emotions are a common cover for stress values, where our subconscious takes over and we say things we may later regret.

Implications for changing minds

Know your own values, including stress values, and work to discover those of others. Beware when yours and theirs do not match. Get them to do things within their values. To stop them doing things, show them how these are against their values.

Social rules

A critical principle derived from our tribal past is that, in order to live in close proximity with other people without fearing them, we must agree upon some common rules about how we behave around one another. We must be able to trust others when we turn our backs on them or ask them to act for us, and so we agree to collaborate.

As a result of this social need, unwritten norms and morals develop, and it is a normal condition of group membership that these rules are followed. Complying with social rules is, *by definition*, 'good' and breaking the rules is 'bad'. New people are carefully inducted into the rule-set by various methods, from friendly members having a 'quiet word' when you get things wrong, to formal rituals and other forms of education. Transgression is often taken very seriously and the ultimate punishment for breaking these rules is expulsion from the group.

Although many social rules are unwritten, some may be enshrined in tablets of stone, quite literally in the Christian Ten Commandments. National laws also stem from the need to live together in relative harmony.

Problems can occur when personal values differ from social rules and new group members may feel permanently out of shape as they follow group rules while suppressing their own values. This can lead to tension and conflict and people may voluntarily leave to 'do their own thing'.

Rules can also lead to dysfunction, as in Irving Janis' 'Groupthink', in which groups isolate themselves from the world, acting always to preserve harmony above wider goals. Typical social rules that support the team but can be ultimately destructive include:

- Preserve harmony within the group at all costs.
- Never criticize the group or its people (especially its leaders). Always criticize people outside the group.
- Follow the leader's commands without question.
- Avoid people from outside the group as they may 'infect' you and make you bad.

Implications for changing minds

Understand the social groups to which others belong and the rules of these groups. Use the rules as levers to change minds.

Cultural rules

Rules apply within every group, from families to firms to entire nations, and the culture of one company or country can vary significantly from another.

Rules can thus be a source of conflict, and Fons Trompenaars has described a classic dilemma that highlights how these vary across cultures. If you were with a friend who hit a pedestrian in his car, does your friend have a right to expect you lie in court to save them from being fined or worse? In some cultures the answer is immediately 'yes', as relationships with friends are valued above the law. In other cultures the law comes first, and it would be considered very bad form for your friend to ask you to help in this way.

There are a number of other cultural dimensions found in national and organizational models which are condensed in Table 7.1. Note that these dimensions are variable and different groups will put a different emphasis, priority and balance point on each rule.

Table 7.1. Some cultural dimensions

Dimension	From...	To...
Equality	All people are equal	The powerful are superior
Obedience	Always conform	Consider the situation
Support	Help others first	Help yourself first
Time focus	The past is important	The future is important
Time sense	Things organized in time	Things out of time
Risk	Be safe and conservative	Take risks; be flexible
Work	Collaborate with others	Get the job done

Across many cultural dimensions is a general theme of 'we vs. me', which tells people how important it is to consider their duty towards others as opposed to looking after themselves. Also found in cultural models is a 'we vs. they' focus that gives clear instruction on how to interact with people outside your cultural boundaries.

Implications for changing minds

Understand national and organizational cultures and factor these into your interactions. Beware of transgressing these rules. Use them as levers of change.

Changing rules

The more widely shared and the stricter rules are, the harder they are to change. A good approach is to determine the strength of the rule before challenging it, as changing or breaking rules can have serious implications for the other person and they may consequently strongly resist any advances. Transgressing social rules can lead to serious punishment, while changing personal rules is, in effect, changing *who the person is*. Rules also are often deeply held and may be self-sustaining, for example through the clever inclusion of a rule that 'it is wrong to change these rules'.

Contradiction

Given the many rules that control our lives, it is not unsurprising that they often contradict one another. This principle can be used to interrupt the rule the person is following by invoking another, contradictory rule. This at least causes confusion and, if the new rule is of higher priority, will cause them to quickly change.

Who	Talk	Subtext/comment
Them	It's wrong to betray a confidence.	I have a rule I must obey.
You	It's more wrong to protect someone who has hurt your friends.	My rule is more important than your rule.

Rule-maker challenge

Where social rules are defined by social leaders, you may be able to challenge the authority of the person making the rules. Some people like being in charge and will grab the baton of authority, while other will cede authority to whoever is most assertive, even if they do not really agree. Their latent rebellion may be provoked by making a challenge of the rule-maker.

Who	Talk	Subtext/comment
Them	Mike says I have to do it.	Mike makes the rules.
You	Who says Mike is in charge? Can you decide for yourself?	Mike does not have authority over you.

Rule-maker change

Where social rules are accepted from social leaders, you may have to find and work on these leaders or perhaps become one yourself. If you can change the rules, you can change many people at once. You may even go up a level and change the rules about changing the rules!

Who	Talk	Subtext/comment
Them	Mike says I have to do it.	Mike makes the rules.
You	Well I say you do not. And you'll find that Jan and Griff agree with me.	Mike does not make the rules. I do.

Challenge

Rules often act at subconscious levels and may be challenged by surfacing and questioning them, showing how they conflict with the context and with one another. For example a group rule may be shown to conflict with a personal value and the person may successfully be encouraged to 'be themselves'. In the reverse situation, they may be reminded of the consequences of breaking social rules.

Who	Talk	Subtext/comment
Them	I'll just get you a cup of coffee.	I am inferior to you and must demonstrate this by serving you.
You	Let's make one together.	We are equal. There is no need to serve me.

Enacting

Perhaps the most powerful way of spreading your values, and particularly if you are or seek to be a leader, is to consistently use these rules in how you act and behave. Thus, for example, if you want people to be curious and open, then you might ask more questions and listen actively to others.

Who	Talk	Subtext/comment
You	Enough of this late working. I'm off now. Go home soon yourself.	Enacting model of work-life balance.
Them	Ok. I'll just finish this.	Wow. Now the boss has gone, I can go too.

Invoking their rules

Companies have policies, guarantees and other rules that they say that they follow, although this is not always true. If you invoke these, you are simply asking them to follow their own rules, which they can hardly fail to do.

Who	Talk	Subtext/comment
You	Do you have a company policy for product returns?	I know you have one.
Them	Yes...	Uh oh.
You	What does it say about how long your lifetime guarantee lasts.	I know how long it is.
Them	Er. It doesn't. It just says lifetime.	I don't have a leg to stand on here.
You	Ok. So I guess when your CEO signed off on these he understood that a lifetime includes the duration for which it is being used.	I'll take it up to the CEO if I need to.
Them	Tell you what – how about if I give you one of our latest models as a replacement?	I have to follow the policy. We can't fix the old model. Well at least I won't get into trouble for it.

8. Preferences

One of the things that add to the diversity of the human condition is the different ways in which each of us chooses and makes daily decisions. In practice these choices are not random and we do not toss a coin for every decision we make. Neither do we make perfectly logical or rational choice, selecting what truly is best for us. Instead, we have personal preferences that bias our decisions, leading us to choose that which fits best with what we have come to know and love and avoiding those things that cause us undue discomfort.

Table 8.1 highlights some of the major dimensions of preference that we use when making choices. By these decisions, we not only are different or similar to other people – we also *become* who we are.

Table 8.1. Differing human preferences

Preferring this...	...or this?
Attraction towards interests.	*Avoidance* of discomfort.
Extraversion; being with others.	*Introversion*; being with self.
Conformance to rules.	*Contrarian,* breaking of rules.
Judging and blaming others.	*Understanding* why things happen.
Detail focus; delve into data.	*Overview* focus; seeing big picture.
Notice *similarity* between things.	Notice *difference* between things.
Logical decision-making.	*Emotional* decision-making.
Organizing predictable outcome.	*Open* to, and ready for, change.
Thinking about things. Plan focus.	*Doing* things. Action focus.
Avoiding emotional overload.	*Seeking* emotional arousal.
Pessimistic view; being fearful.	*Optimistic* view; being hopeful.
Avoiding risks and failure.	*Taking risks*, handling failure.
Fighting for your rights.	*Fleeing* to live another day.
Persistence and determination.	*Trying* then giving up.
Visual thinking.	*Verbal* thinking.

Pain and gain

One of the patterns of choice we make, as noted by Aristotle and then Sigmund Freud, is based on the fundamental principles of experienced pain and gain, discomfort and comfort, hurt and happiness.

Imagine that you are a young child again and that you ask your mother for something. Whether she patiently listens and explains why you cannot have it, snaps tiredly at you or gives in to your wheedling, you have learned something that works and what it costs you. You hence will develop preferred ways of going about interacting with others, based on the equation of pain and gain in childhood learning.

Our experiences in comfort and discomfort therefore transmute into preferences that often become attraction or avoidance, actively seeking some things and carefully avoiding others, from the company of other people to the excitement (or not) of extreme sports. This again translates into effective motivational systems of reward and punishment, also known as carrot and stick or push and pull. This is expanded on in Chapter 25 (Pain and Pleasure).

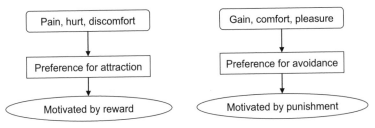

Fig. 8.1. Pain, gain and motivation

Preferences around pain and gain aggregate up and some people are more motivated by things which are attractive while others are distrusting and are more motivated by avoidance, as in Figure 8.1.

Implications for changing minds

By observing and understanding this basic difference, you can form strategies on the balance of pain and gain method. Do be careful with the balance of this: the best approach is often initial pain to get them going followed by regular gain that gets positive motivation towards where you want them to be.

Types

One of the most commonly used models in assessment of personality measures preferences is based on four double-ended spectra, as Table 8.2. It This originates from Jungian archetypes and the most common system is the Myers-Briggs Type Inventory (MBTI) although other variants exist, for example the Keirsey Temperament Sorter.

Table 8.2. Jungian preferences

Factor	One type	Other type
Energy source	*Extraversion*: Gets energy from being with people.	*Introversion*: Recharges batteries in peace and quiet.
Data gathering	*Sensing*: Focus on data, detail and bottom-up.	*Intuition*: Focus on ideas, big picture and top-down.
Decision-making	*Thinking*: Choice through logic and reason.	*Feeling*: Choice through what seems or feels right.
Living	*Judging*: Structuring and organizing for best way.	*Perceiving*: Keeping options open for maximum choice.

This leads to sixteen different 'types' as briefly caricatured in table 8.3, which also shows an approximate distribution in the population. Note how 24% are STJ, which is the controlling, conforming style approved by many schools, organizations and governments.

Table 8.3. Jungian type caricatures

ISTJ (12%) Doing what should be done	ISFJ (8%) A high sense of duty	INFJ (4%) An inspiration to others	INTJ (6%) Always room for improvement
ISTP (4%) Ready to try anything once	ISFP (4%) Sees much but shares little	INFP (4%) Noble service to help society	INTP (4%) A love of problem-solving
ESTP (3%) The ultimate realists	ESFP (5%) You only live once	ENFP (8%) Giving life an extra squeeze	ENTP (5%) Non-stop exciting challenges
ESTJ (12%) Life's administrators	ESFJ (8%) Genial hosts to the world	ENFJ (5%) Smooth-talking persuaders	ENTJ (6%) Life's natural leaders

Traits

While preferences are generally developed choices based on experience, we also make choices based on inherited factors. Rather scarily, research in behavioral genetics and the study of separated twins has also shown that much that we had once assumed was learned is actually inherited.

Freud saw personality as being a battleground between three components: the primitive life and death drives of the Id, the conscious and reasoning ego, and the ethical super-ego that managed values and conscience. Each of these parts may be seen as having preferences.

Since Freud, various personality models have been developed, that seek to identify and assess key traits. Table 8.5. shows a comprehensive set of traits identified in the 1920s by Raymond Cattell.

A simpler model is known as the 'Big Five' (Table. 8.4) and usefully can be fitted into the OCEAN acronym. This is widely used, although some people prefer the longer 16PF (Table 8.5).

Table 8.4. 'Big Five' traits

Factor	Description
Openness	Curiosity and seeking of new ideas
Conscientiousness	Working dutifully and seeking order
Extraversion	Enjoying company and seeking excitement
Agreeableness	Collaborating and avoiding disagreement
Neuroticism	Tending to anxiety and impulsiveness

Implications for changing minds

Appeal to the super-ego for morals or the baser mores of the id as appropriate. Talk rationally to the ego. Observe and understand the subconscious traits that people have, then play to them or deliberately prod them to stimulate reaction.

Table 8.5. '16PF' traits

Factor	Low	High
Warmth	Reserved, impersonal, distant, cool, detached, formal, aloof	Warm, outgoing, attentive to others, kindly, easygoing, participating, likes people
Reasoning	Concrete-thinking, lower general mental capacity, less intelligent, unable to handle abstract problems	Abstract-thinking, more intelligent, bright, higher general mental capacity, fast learner
Emotional Stability	Reactive, emotionally changeable, affected by feelings, emotionally less stable, easily upset	Emotionally stable, adaptive, mature, faces reality, calm
Dominance	Deferential, cooperative, avoids conflict, submissive, humble, obedient, easily led, docile, accommodating	Dominant, forceful, assertive, aggressive, competitive, stubborn, bossy
Liveliness	Serious, restrained, prudent, taciturn, introspective, silent	Lively, animated, spontaneous, enthusiastic, happy-go-lucky, cheerful, expressive, impulsive
Rule-Consciousness	Expedient, nonconforming, disregards rules, self-indulgent	Rule-conscious, dutiful, conscientious, conforming, moralistic, staid, rule-bound
Social Boldness	Shy, threat-sensitive, timid, hesitant, intimidated	Socially bold, venturesome, thick-skinned, uninhibited, can take stress
Sensitivity	Utilitarian, objective, unsentimental, tough-minded, self-reliant, no-nonsense, rough	Sensitive, aesthetic, sentimental, tender-minded, intuitive, refined
Vigilance	Trusting, unsuspecting, accepting, unconditional, easy	Vigilant, suspicious, skeptical, wary, distrustful, oppositional
Abstractedness	Grounded, practical, prosaic, solution-oriented, steady, conventional	Abstracted, imaginative, absent-minded, impractical, absorbed in ideas
Privateness	Forthright, genuine, artless, open, guileless, naive, unpretentious, involved	Private, discreet, non-disclosing, shrewd, polished, worldly, astute, diplomatic
Apprehension	Self-assured, unworried, complacent, secure, free of guilt, confident, self-satisfied	Apprehensive, self-doubting, worried, guilt-prone, insecure, worrying, self-blaming
Openness to Change	Traditional, attached to familiar, conservative, respecting traditional ideas	Open to change, experimenting, liberal, analytical, critical, free-thinking, flexible

CIA Preferences

The level of need for control, identity and arousal (as in Chapter 3) varies between individuals. Control and Identity needs can combine for four different styles as shown in Figure 8.2.

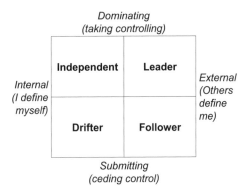

Fig. 8.2. Control-Identity grid

Leaders like others to look up to them and to be in charge. At parties they are the 'life and soul' and are typically surrounded by others as they hold court. They may be social leaders, work managers or both.

Followers need recognition from others, but do so by ceding control and trusting leaders to help them succeed. In parties, they circulate and chat, enjoying the company of others. At work, they are good team players and often contribute well to overall business success.

Independents are fiercely their own people, going their own way and do their own thing. At parties, they may listen or argue, not really caring whether people agree with them. At work, they succeed on their own terms. In teams they can be argumentative or work separately.

Drifters withdraw from the world where they can, living in their own internal world. At parties, they sit in the corner and leave as soon as possible. At work, they keep their heads down and do their jobs but do not really participate in team activities.

Arousal preferences layer on top of these, for example a leader with high arousal needs will work on high risk projects, while those with lower overwhelm threshold are more likely to stay within the confines of the current business.

Bias

Preferences and traits also show up in the bias that we put into our decisions. Again this may well start in early programming as we develop stereotypes and pick up bias for and against other social groups from our parents and friends.

Many people have bias towards themselves, forgiving their own foibles while easily blaming others for small transgressions (although people with low self-esteem may put others before them). The same effect continues with our friends and we will easily choose them over others, almost by definition.

Bias is often subconscious and we easily become unwitting racists, ageists or sexists. Careful self-monitoring can help reduce this, but we can seldom eradicate all bias.

Implications for changing minds

Watch the choices that people make for signs of bias. Then either align with that bias in your interactions with them or otherwise challenge or make use of it.

Context

The context within which any preference is expressed can have a significant effect on the choices made. Thus a person may be dominating and dour at work while they are friendly and cheerful at a social club and quietly submissive at home.

This is one place where the differences between traits and preferences may be seen, as genetic traits are much more likely to be visible across all contexts, although conscious suppression and contrary preferences may mean that they are not always apparent.

Implications for changing minds

Just because a person displays a preference in one situation does not mean they will choose the same everywhere. Test their preferred approach in each context.

Changing preferences

One of the most important things to remember in changing minds is that, while we have many similarities, we are all individual and what works with one person may not work with another. The first trick in working with preferences is therefore to identify them. For example, if a person is cautious in decisions, you may note that they are risk-averse, while if they talk with enthusiasm about a skiing holiday, you might conclude that they are risk-seekers. As with any assessment, the more evidence that you gather, the more certain you can be about your conclusions.

Alignment

The basic principle in playing to traits and preferences is to align your arguments with them. If a person is risk averse, then to avoid and downplay their risks where you want them to go and increase their risks where you do not want them to go. If they think visually, then draw pictures and use visual language, and so on.

Who	Talk	Subtext/comment
Them	I see the acquisition as hazardous.	'I see' is visual language. 'hazardous' indicates risk aversion.
You	Look, buying has its dangers but it would be worse if our competitors made the acquisition.	Use visual language. Make alternative risks greater than risk they are avoiding.

Denial

The reverse principle to alignment is to deliberately take an opposing action of some kind, acting in a contrary way to deny them their preferences. If a person is risk averse, then create risk. If they seek control, take it away. This will act as a form of torture and they will flee the reversal and chase after the comfort of a preferred alternative, which of course you can provide.

Who	Talk	Subtext/comment
Them	We must be careful.	I seek low risk and control.
You	We have already passed the point of no return.	Highlight unavoidable risk.

Name and shame

Another approach that can be used, particularly with socially undesirable preferences such as the use of stereotyping or politically-incorrect actions, is to name them. If a person feels accused even of harmless bias then they will consciously work to prove that they are in control of their thought processes rather than risk the social exclusion that is the classic punishment for social transgression.

Who	Talk	Subtext/comment
Them	He's just a stupid wop.	I do not like Japanese people.
You	You just insulted our Japanese guest!	Point out the social gaffe.

Bad for you

Preferences are susceptible to conscious consideration. If you can show that the habitual choices that the other person is making are against their real interests then, depending on how deeply ingrained the preference is, they may change their decision criteria.

Who	Talk	Subtext/comment
Them	I think I'll wear the purple top and orange skirt tonight.	I have a preference for bright and loud clothing.
You	Have you noticed that when you wear 'dayglo' clothes that nobody wants to talk with you?	Point out the social price of indulging in personal preferences that others dislike.

9. Goals

As we have discussed, we are driven to achieve our needs, but are constrained in the way we can do this. We therefore need to make conscious choices in setting ourselves goals that we consider worthwhile and which we have some realistic chance of achieving.

Goals are what we *decide* to do and seek to achieve. We often set goals for ourselves, such as 'lose weight', and, although we do not always achieve them, the presence of the goal motivates us to take some kind of positive action.

A note: there are many definitions of the tasks that we set ourselves and in this model we use the word 'goals' to include all forms of intended action and achievement, including:

- Objectives
- Tasks
- Actions
- To-dos
- Commitments
- Mission
- Plans
- Key Performance Indicators
- Targets
- *(and so on)*

Implications for changing minds

To get people to do things, set them goals! It also helps to show how these goals will satisfy their needs and align with their beliefs, values and preferences.

Purpose

One of the most fundamental questions we can ask ourselves is 'What is it all for?' Some of us wander aimlessly through life, but those who know why they are doing what they are doing are motivated far more strongly.

The most basic purpose is 'survival'. Sometimes we do what we do just so we can eat and be safe. Yet you can also have higher goals of growth and achievement beyond yourself and your immediate circumstances.

Extrinsic and intrinsic goals

Author Dan Pink divides people into those with extrinsic aspirations (type X) and those who are more intrinsically motivated (type I) . Ask a type X person what they want and they will likely talk about fame and fortune, or similar 'profit goals'. Ask a type I person and they will describe deeper 'purpose goals', such as helping their children grow up into successful adults, devising new technologies or changing the world in some way.

Studies by psychologists Edward Deci, Richard Ryan and Christopher Niemiec found that people with intrinsic goals led more satisfying lives. Those driven by extrinsic goals (such as position and wealth) often suffered from increased anxiety and depression, even while achieving their goals. One reason for this is that focusing on 'things' and 'me' rather than relationships and higher ideals tends to focus people inwards where they can lose perspective and start to fear loss more than looking forward to achievement.

Implications for changing minds

Ask people 'Why' and 'What for' to find their purpose, and maybe provoke them into developing greater meaning in their lives. Then link greater purpose to intrinsic goals.

If they are more extrinsically motivated or have strong short-term goals, you may need to help them achieve these first before they are ready for the more challenging questions.

Forming goals

While the formation of goals can be a relatively straightforward conscious activity ('I am too heavy: I must lose weight'), a number of different factors influence our decision-making process, as indicated in Figure 9.1.

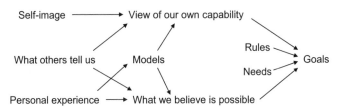

Fig. 9.1. Formation of goals

We first decide what is possible from a combination of experience and collected perceptions which range from accurate scientific information to distorted and limited opinions. We then put ourselves into this equation and decide whether we are at all capable of achieving this and whether it is worth the effort. We also, of course, temper these decisions through our values and other rules.

From these deep musings, we also spread our goals over time. These can range from simple, short-term goals such as making a cup of coffee, to intermediate goals such as completing a project, to life goals such as increasing the sum of knowledge in a chosen field. Our goals should align and support one another, but this is not always the case. In particular, life and work goals can conflict, and when we are driven by short-term urgent problems, we can easily lose sight of the shore.

External goals

While we set personal goals that range from getting to work on time to world domination, we also accept goals from external sources which we accept as authorities who can command or advise us. Hence in the transaction of work, we take on goals from our employers in return for what we hope is fair pay and working conditions.

The commitment we place on external goals that are agreed in a form of contracted transaction may vary greatly depending on the trust and loyalty we feel towards the other person or organization.

Interests

As well as more specific goals, we also have general interests, such as when a person has an interest in motor sport. Interests can certainly lead to goals, such as attending motoring exhibitions or winning races, but without a clear definition of success they tend more to be general motivators that guide evaluations and decisions.

Interests can be confusing and annoying when they are difficult to pin down and when people have not developed individual goals from them. People may not even consciously know what their interests are.

Interests are also important when we are inferring meaning (Chapter 13) as we compare everything we experience against interests in order to spot opportunities on which we can capitalize.

Positions

In negotiations, people often take positions, much like in warfare where an army takes a position on a hill and then defends it with all their might while the enemy tries to dislodge them from this position. When two people take positions, then the result is either stalemate or bitter defeat for one party or the other.

When people are stuck in interests, it helps to chunk down to what they specifically want. When they are stuck in positions, the reverse is true and the first step is to chunk up to find their interests. In the negotiation classic 'Getting to Yes', Fisher and Ury suggest that you 'focus on interests, not positions'.

Implications for changing minds

If the other person does not seem to know what they want, start by looking for interests by asking what is important to them and how they spend their time (or would like to). Then help them develop goals that align both with their interests and also what you want from them.

When people take fixed positions about things and then just blindly defend these, first ask 'why' to find the interest behind the position and hence gain agreement at this higher level. Then introduce alternatives to let them achieve their interests in ways other than their initial position.

SMART

A common acronym that is often used to determine whether goals are useful and are more likely to result in them being achieved is SMART:

- *Specific*: It is clear what 'success' is and is not.
- *Measurable*: It is possible to determine progress towards achieving the goals and whether the goals have been fully achieved.
- *Achievable*: It is reasonable that the goals may be achieved within the given timescale, with the given resource.
- *Relevant*: The goal aligns with the higher purpose, such as company strategy.
- *Timely*: There is a sensible date or time set by which the goal should be achieved.

Achievable challenge

Having clear goals can not only be very motivating, it can also make you cheerful. Mihaly Csikszentmihalyi has shown how the happiest people are those who constantly take on challenges and consequently get lost in the 'flow' of work. He calls these people 'autotelic', from the Greek auto (=self) and telos (=goal).

The trick with motivating challenge is to place the goal somewhere between the easy and the unattainable. Ideally, it is towards the further end of this spectrum, although it must be seen as feasible by the people involved. When people achieve things they have not achieved before, they feel a great sense of exhilaration.

Curiously, Csikszentmihalyi found that there is a work-play paradox, whereby when we are at work we dream of holidays, yet when we lie on the beach we are bored. We are in fact happiest at work when we are working on what we consider to be worthwhile goals.

Implications for changing minds

When motivating others, particularly in business, use SMART goals.

Also find the right point where the other person feels excited by the possibility of the achievement. Test for this when setting goals.

Dissatisfaction, satisfaction and delight

There are three levels of satisfaction, based on three levels of goals. We hardly notice when our basic requirements, such as for clean bathrooms, are satisfied. If they are not satisfied, however, then we quickly become dissatisfied. This is a no-win, easy lose situation and you should always deliver the basics in a reliable and sound way.

The second level includes the conscious goals that people are seeking. Satisfaction of these is very variable and the more you deliver, the happier they are.

The third level is where people have needs that they have not recognized and turned into conscious goals. If you can satisfy some of these, it often leads to delight. However, if delights are offered without satisfactory delivery of more basic needs, then the result can be frustration and annoyance.

Commitment

It is easy to under- or over-commit to a goal. Weak commitment is given to goals that never seemed achievable or where we do not fully trust the person for whom we are working. Goals that are contrary to our values also never gain full commitment as we constantly feel uneasy about 'bad' consequences.

When we fully commit to a goal it becomes bound to our sense of identity such that if we fail, we will feel shame, anger and other powerful emotions.

Chapter 24 discusses commitment in further detail, in particular around sustaining it within an agreed course of action.

Implications for changing minds

When serving people, ensure you reliably and efficiently satisfy their basic requirements. Listen to their conscious goals and deliver well on these. Then add the icing to the cake, delivering one or two extra delights.

When you have helped people get the right goals, next work on building commitment so they will continue to work with a will towards achieving the goals.

Conflicting goals

Most people have many things they want achieve in all areas of their lives, and a great deal of energy is spent juggling these balls, trying to sustain progress in them all and meeting the delivery dates at least for the most important ones.

Especially when other people set goals for us, which may happen at home, work and our social lives, it is easy for these to conflict with one another, at the very least in the requirements for our time. A very common 'work-life' conflict is between time spent at work and time spent at home.

Goals have priorities and, when they conflict, we have to make difficult choices. For example a person who has personal goals of becoming rich and to help other people may be faced with a dilemma if they are asked to donate significantly to a charity.

Revising goals

Once we have formed goals and particularly if they are important to us or we have a strong preference for closure on our commitments, we tend to stick to them unless something happens to convince us otherwise. Some goals, such as protecting the family, are closely related to fundamental needs are unlikely to change (although the methods by which they are achieved may change). Others, for example finding a coat on a shopping trip, are more easily abandoned or changed.

Typically it takes repeated failure for people to change their goals. Even given a simple task such as finding a named card in a deck of cards, if the card cannot be found then the person will typically repeat the search by multiple methods before concluding that the card is missing and the goal is unachievable. In this case the goal might change to avoiding embarrassment.

Implications for changing minds

Understand the multiple pressures on people to deliver in different arenas. If you want to add more things for them to achieve, try either to reduce their other goals or increase the priority of the goals you are adding for them.

Changing goals

Goals are much easier to change than most of the other human drivers. As they are generally consciously derived, a rational discussion can often be sufficient to get the person to change direction. If you are in a position of authority, changing goals may be as easy as telling the other person to do something.

Identifying goals can be done by asking *probing questions* (see Chapter 20) that discover what the other person is seeking and the reasons why they have chosen these goals.

Chunking

Chunking is a simple method that moves thinking between lower-level detail and higher-level abstraction. *Chunking down* asks *how*, seeking the practical methods, and can be used to show how goals are difficult to achieve. *Chunking up* asks *why*, seeking the higher purpose for doing something. You can thus chunk up to a higher goal and then down to a different way of achieving it.

Who	Talk	Subtext/comment
Them	I want to go to Paris.	My goal is to visit Paris.
You	What for? Why Paris?	Chunk up: seek real purpose.
Them	Because Jane is there.	My goal is to visit Jane.
You	How long do you need with her? Could you phone her instead?	Chunk down: seek detail. Seek alternative way to satisfy goals.

Repurposing

Repurposing is a word that is used to describe goal change by changing the underlying purpose. This can be done by asking and thinking about questions such as 'What are we trying to achieve? Why do we come to work each day?

Who	Talk	Subtext/comment
Them	We need to cut costs.	Cutting costs will save the business.
You	How will that save the business? If we are to survive, we must rebuild our entire market.	Cutting costs is narrow and insufficient. We must think big.

Visioning

Visioning starts from the higher goal, selling an exciting view of the future and so building desire for that future. The ultimate goal then becomes to achieve the vision, while other intermediate goals can be derived in rational planning activities.

To sustain motivation, vision should be memorable. This can be helped with visual images and brief description. It can also be made more immediate by framing it in the present tense.

Who	Talk	Subtext/comment
Them	How can we get there quicker?	I don't like to travel.
You	Imagine you could walk out of this door and into your destination.	Stimulate curiosity.
Them	How could you do that??	Puzzled but intrigued.
You	Imagine a door-to-door luxury service. Chauffeured to and from a home-from-home sleeper train.	Paint the picture.

Plan-busting

Chapter 11 discusses how musing about what might happen in the future leads us to setting and changing our goals. As Figure 11.2 shows, forecasts lead to plans which we then follow until they no longer work. However, before we change goals we may well try changing our plans.

Changing another person's goals may hence be done by *plan-busting*, showing them that there is no way their current goals can be easily achieved with *any* plan of action, and the only recourse is to go back and re-examine the goals that are driving the plans.

Who	Talk	Subtext/comment
Them	I will try asking Jane.	My goal is ask Jane.
You	Jane is out.	Your plan to achieve your goal will not work.
Them	Ok, how about Tim.	Minor change, same basic plan.
You	Nobody here knows about it.	Your plan to ask a person will not work. You need to think again.

Probing

If you keep questioning the other person they will be forced to think hard about what they really want. Use the standard set of questions about what/when/why/how/where/who to probe into their rationale.

Who	Talk	Subtext/comment
Them	I want to go shopping	I have a goal that will be satisfied by shopping.
You	What are you looking for?	What is the underlying reason for shopping?
Them	I want a new coat.	I have a goal that will be satisfied by a new coat.
You	When do you need the coat?	Tell me more about your goal.
Them	I am going to the book launch next month.	I want to look good at the book launch.
You	Why do you need a new coat?	You have several nice coats already
Them	I need a coat to go with my blue suit.	My suit and coat must match.
You	Your grey coat looks really smart. How about getting a new suit to match that?	A new suit is cheaper than a new coat.

10. Memory

Human memory is an irritating and strange thing. You can be introduced to someone and forget their name in seconds flat, and then spend a conversation desperately hoping someone else will say their name. You can try to remember something only for it to sit at the tip of your tongue, annoyingly just out of reach. Even when you do remember something, it can be strangely lacking in detail or even be completely incorrect. And yet you can easily recall some things that happened years ago.

Types of memory

We have two parts or maybe more (depending on who you talk to) to our memory. *Short-term memory* has about seven 'slots' for chunks of information on which we are working. This constrains what we can think about at once, and if we do not remember what we see and hear quickly then we effectively forget it.

Long-term memory is just that, where we store and recall long-term information. We have different types of long-term memory, depending on what is being remembered:

- *Procedural memory* lets us remember how to do things.
- *Declarative memory* contains facts and events.
- *Semantic memory* includes knowledge of concepts and meaning.
- *Episodic memory* contains high-detail memory of a short period of time (usually something significant).

There also seems to be an intermediate *working memory* somewhere between short- and long-term memory, where we juggle things of current interest.

Recall and recognition

An important aspect about long term memory is how we store and recall information. Most memories are effectively lost when we are unable to bring them back to conscious thought. Most annoying is what is called the 'tip of the tongue phenomenon', whereby you know there is something there, but cannot quite recall it.

Even when we do remember, we seldom recall every detail, yet we are still surprisingly good at recognition. Few can recall every detail of a familiar friend's face, yet will recognize them from only a partial view of their face, even if it is pulling all kinds of expressions.

The extent to which something can be remembered is generally correlated with the method of storage, and specific techniques can be learned to enable far greater recall, particularly of concrete facts.

Implications for changing minds

A good memory is very useful for remembering facts about the other person. Learn how to encode memories so that they are easily recalled.

Memory and reality

We believe our memories, usually without question. Memory and perceived truth are hence synonymous, yet studies of police interrogations have shown what Freud discovered years before: memories can be wholly constructed or significantly modified. When questioned intensively about whether a past event happened, we repeatedly imagine the event happening until we cannot distinguish it from a real memory.

It is notable that we do not remember exact images but patterns from which we *reconstruct* memories. This can make remembering detail a shaky affair.

Implications for changing minds

Just because a person remembers it, it does not mean it is true. To change the truth of a past event, question the memory. To create a memory, repeatedly ask if it happened.

Association

Any one memory or idea is linked to a surprising number of other memories. As Figure 10.1 shows, thinking about an elephant can lead on to a wide range of subsequent thoughts.

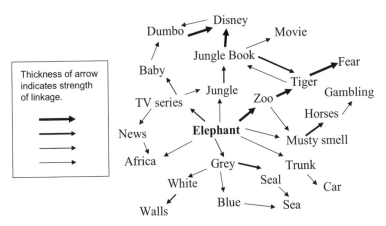

Fig. 10.1. Associated thoughts and memories

Association between items often happens when they occur at the same time. A common way of remembering where you put things is to think about what you were doing at the time. Association also happens through shape: hence we link cigars and pencils (this is a root of Freud's concern about 'phallic symbols'). Association also happens through other relationships, such as opposites (e.g. black and white).

Memories that are associated with strong emotions are particularly easy to recall, giving us another method of memorizing, although this can also be a problem in the case of traumatic events that you would rather not remember. Much therapy is concerned with fixing this problem, for example by 'turning down the volume' on the emotions or by deliberately breaking the association between event and feelings with repeatedly interrupting the process.

Implications for changing minds

Explore their associations and create new ones, strengthening links by triggering emotions and weakening links by distraction.

Primacy and Recency

When given a list of things to remember, we recall the first things on the list (the *primacy effect*) and the last things on the list (the *recency effect*). So which is most effective? Psychologist Solomon Asch asked some people about a person described as envious, stubborn, critical, impulsive, industrious and intelligent. He then asked other people about a person described as intelligent, industrious, impulsive, critical, stubborn and envious. The second group rated the person more highly than the first group, showing primacy as more significant. He also found the second and third items on the list had some primacy effects.

In other studies that separated experience and recall in time, it was found that the recency effect is more effective for recent memories, while the primacy effect is best when the message and recall are separated in time, such as between adverts and purchase.

Another recency effect, called the *availability heuristic*, is a principle by which we believe something is more likely because we have heard about it recently. Hence people who hear about city attacks become more fearful, even though the actual crime rate may not have changed.

Implications for changing minds

If you want people to remember something within a conversation, put it at the beginning. If you want them to remember it later, add a summary or reminder at the end. If you want them to think something is likely, tell them it has happened recently.

Context

Have you ever gone upstairs and had to go back downstairs to remember what you went up for? Memories are often linked to the context in which they were created and to recall the memory we may need to change where we are, the mood we are in and even the time of day and how we are dressed.

Implications for changing minds

To get somebody to recall something, get them into the right context (at least mentally). To get them to forget, move them, both physically and mentally.

Contrast

Try to remember this list: Cat, dog, brush, door, spade, duck-billed platypus, orange, leaf, house, handle, book, chair, picture.

You might well remember cat and dog (primacy effect) and chair and picture (recency effect). You are also very likely to remember the duck-billed platypus, which stands out as something unusual as well as being a rather long descriptor. If you are given a list of similar items to remember with one different word in the middle, you are more likely to remember the word that stands out. This is the *Von Restorff effect*.

We recall things that are unusual, primarily because our basic system of perception uses contrast to distinguish between separate things.

Implications for changing minds

If you want people to remember anything, make it stand out from its surrounding context.

The power of today

What we thought and felt in the past is powerfully affected by what we think and feel today. For example a study of the effects of speeches on students found that those who were persuaded found it difficult to imagine that they had ever thought differently. In the same way, a depressed person finds it difficult to remember feeling happy and a person about to happily drink their tenth pint of beer does not think about the hangover from last week when they declared they would never drink again.

In effect, as we recall the past we layer how we think and feel now on top of the memory, effectively changing our memories to suit our current mood.

Implications for changing minds

Get people to recall memories useful for persuasion when they are in the right mood to affect the memory. As necessary, help them into the right frame of mind first.

Changing memories

While it may seem odd to think of changing memories, in practice many memories are already distorted and can be very harmful, for example where traumatic childhood memories trigger anxiety in adults.

Suggestion

Changing memories is surprisingly easy, as the police and lawyers know – all you have to do is question the detail and suggest alternatives, and people will eventually replace real memories with false memories. Therapists also know this, and use various methods to soothe and change harmful memories.

Who	Talk	Subtext/comment
You	Who was there?	Seek information.
Them	Jane and John.	Give memory.
You	Could Sam have been there?	Probe for detail you want.
Them	Um, well, he could have been.	Try to imaging Sam there.
You	Don't you think he was there?	Suggest Sam is there.
Them	Yes. Yes, I remember him now.	Construct memory of Sam there.

Encoding

Important in changing minds is ensuring that people remember those things that you want them to remember (and perhaps forget other things). You can hence help them use methods of encoding into memory those things you want to re-trigger at a future date.

You can, for example, make things more memorable by using the primacy, recency and Von Restorff effects. You can also use repetition, emphasis, visualization or associative linking together of memories.

Who	Talk	Subtext/comment
You	Look at the ivy on the walls. You know our friend Ivy? Imagine her climbing the wall. Ivy on the walls.	Create unusual visual image of woman called Ivy climbing the walls. Repeating Ivy and walls.
Them	Mmm.	Memory being encoded and mused about.

Recoding

Therapists may use deliberate methods of getting their clients to change or downplay traumatic memories, for example by replacing the memory with one which is defocused, distant and incoherent. The same principle can be used in reverse to create vibrant and pleasant memories, making the memories bigger, brighter and sharper.

Who	Talk	Subtext/comment
You	Take that bad memory and turn it black and white. Is it black and white now?	Black and white images are often less emotive. Check they can do it.
Them	Yes – it is less uncomfortable now.	Confirmation they have changed the memory.
You	Now make it foggy and the sounds indistinct. Can you see it's all fuzzy now? Are the sounds hard to understand?	Further changing of memory so it is less troublesome. Include visual and aural memory.
Them	Mmm. Yes. It's not so clear now.	Further confirmation of change.
You	Now push the picture into the distance, making it small. Notice how the sounds are getting quieter too.	Change memory again to be less distinct.
Them	Ok. That's better too.	Continued confirmation.
You	What's the time? What are you doing tonight?	Break them away from the memory.
Them	Eh? It's four o'clock and I'll be going to the club with Harry.	Evidence they have stopped thinking about the memory.
You	Now try think about that time again. What's there?	Move them back to the memory.
Them	Er, it 's really small and, well, no bother now, really.	Confirmation that the memory has been changed.

Naming people

In conversation, help people remember your name by repeating it, for example by quoting what someone else said to you. In a new group, you can ease the conversation and help group bonding by using people's names both to stroke their identity and to help others fix this important information in their memories.

11. Musing

When we have a moment to spare we indulge in the very human practice of thinking and general musing. We think about what has happened in the past, constantly dredging up memories of past events to relive happy days or wonder about those things that we find harder to explain. We think also about what might be, wondering what the future might hold as we project forward from the past and present.

This is also the place where we reconsider our motivational systems and rebuild models, values, goals and so on. Such changes are not done lightly and we often need to take time to think about what it all means.

Background thinking also happens in the subconscious. While we are doing other things, our subconscious keeps on chewing the cud of our latest issues, although it does tend to pop suggestions into our conscious minds at the most inconvenient of times.

What we are not good at doing in our musing space is keeping up with the non-stop real-time flow of data that constantly assails us, but that is not what it is for (the front line SIFT system takes care of this). A key purpose of musing is as a system *builder*, creating and improving the processes and mechanisms by which we handle the world. If something we believe does not happen as expected then we will examine the beliefs and models involved and see if we can change them to be able to explain the latest unexpected events.

Implications for changing minds

If you can change how people muse and think deeply, you can change the motivators and systems by which they decide.

Double-loop living

We have two loops by which we can make sense of the world, As in Figure 11.1. The outer experience provides us with 'real' data with which we have to contend and gives us the information with which we can build our internal models.

We can also 'play' internally, running possible future scenarios and musing about what might happen. This is so realistic the actual parts of the brain used for sensing and emoting are stimulated as if things were really happening. Dreaming acts in the same way and can fool us into believing that our dreams are real.

You can usually tell when people are musing as their eyes glaze over and they pay little attention to the outer world. The may stare into an imagined reality and their lips move as they talk to themselves. If you talk with them, they may well respond with non-language noises, such 'Mmm', Uh-huh' and so on.

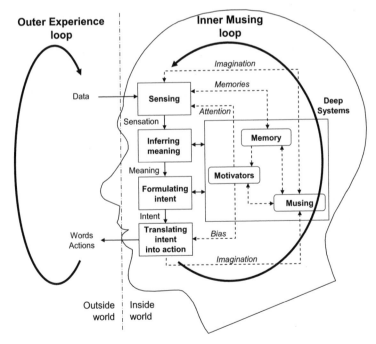

Fig 11.1. Experience and Musing loops

Forecasting

One of the things we do a lot of when we are musing is trying to predict what will happen in the future. This is a critical skill because if we know what will happen we can ensure we are ready for it. We can also think about the actions we might take to achieve our goals and see how effective they might be. Forecasting is therefore important in such as setting and managing goals (Chapter 9), inferring meaning (Chapter 13) and formulating intent (Chapter 14).

What we effectively do in forecasting is imagine a scenario where we do something in the outer world and consequent events occur. In doing this we plug directly into the SIFT system and actually experience the imagined future, as in Figure 11.1. From this musing, we see what might happen and how we would feel about it, and hence determine whether the potential actions are worth taking.

One of the problems with forecasting is that our pictures of the future are heavily tainted by our current models and views. For example 1950s futurist scenarios show high-tech hover cars, yet gender roles still portray the unspoken norm of the day, with domesticated housewives and patronizing husbands.

This happens in the short-term too. Thinking about a possible happy future is very difficult when you are not happy now. Reality necessarily takes priority over imagination, for example thinking about flying while walking downstairs could cause a hazardous tumble. This is one reason why closing your eyes is very effective when imagining as it shuts out any real-world interference or priority interrupts.

Implications for changing minds

First catch them in the right mood to make the decision you want or work specifically to get them thinking positively, perhaps by moving them in small, easy steps.

Then facilitate the process of imagining futures. Say 'Imagine...' or 'What if...' and guide their musings into the future you want to happen. Show them that the future you can create for them is good and that the changes you propose will essentially lead to that future.

When forecasts fail

As we seek to achieve the goals we have set ourselves we live in a constant state of checking that we are on track. But what happens when our forecasts fail? Figure 11.2 shows this effect.

In Loop 1, experiences are used to check that our forecast is still on track to achieve our goals. Most of the time this is just fine and we carry on using our predetermined plans.

In Loop 2, our forecast shows us that our current plan is not working as expected, so we go into a quick loop of revising our plans and projecting them into the future to determine whether the new plans are likely to work. Assuming we find a suitable plan, we then return to the everyday loop 1.

But what happens if we cannot find a plan that will work? We are then sent back to loop 3 in which we have to revise our goals. This is not easy and requires significant musing. This double-step before we change goals means we will sometimes bang our heads against a brick wall of impossibility before accepting the necessity of change.

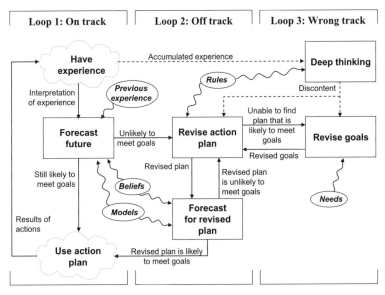

Fig. 11.2. Forecasting, plans and goals

Subconscious processing

One of the problems with musing is that it is a slow process and sometimes you need to just leave your subconscious alone to think by itself.

Incubation, where you put an idea into the back of your mind to let your subconscious work on it is very powerful in creativity and otherwise thinking about problems and issues. Graham Wallas described this in 1926 as a critical part of the creative problem-solving process. This is initiated by *preparation,* which involves first thinking hard about the problem to give data to the subconscious and let it know that resolution is important. Incubation involves not thinking consciously about it at all, which usually requires some distracting activity like sport or reading. *Illumination* is the 'aha' moment when the solution is realized and *verification* is the reality testing of the result.

Intuition also acts in a similar way, as the subconscious offers up suggestions unbidden to conscious desires for solution. Just because you do not know how you know something, it does not mean it has no value.

Psychologist Guy Claxton has shown that slow thinking often asks better questions and gives better solutions than everyday thinking. It is curious and leads to learning and wisdom. Slow thinking also suits the development of tacit skills, as opposed to the rapid acquisition of explicit knowledge. As a carpentry apprentice practices planing a wooden surface time and again, they develop a *feeling* for how to hold and use the plane.

The subconscious nature of slow thinking, as with incubation and intuition, acts without the constraints of language and is hence free to act with indescribable concepts. We can in this way develop a deep understanding of the world around us with what we sometimes call *instinct.* To use this style of thinking requires that we are confident enough to trust our instincts and thoughts that we cannot explain.

Implications for changing minds

Do not expect minds to change immediately. However, if you can plant seeds and tend the seedlings, then you may receive a bumper crop of commitment.

Changing musing

As the processes of musing are largely subconscious, changing these is not particularly straightforward. The one advantage of this, however, is that the conscious mind does not interrupt the process!

Disconfirmation

A person's beliefs, models, rules and other systems will continue to be sustained for as long as their experience confirms that they still work. When they experience disconfirming evidence, they will often at first ignore it. You will likely need to provide continuing and very obvious evidence until they realize that their inner world no long matches the outer experience and that a change is necessary.

Who	Talk	Subtext/comment
You	Mike was arrested last week.	Disconfirming evidence about Mike.
Them	But he is such a nice person!	Refusal to consider Mike bad.
You	He was in a fight outside a club.	More evidence about Mike.
Them	Maybe he was picked on. Surely?	Seeking to excuse. Grasping at straws.
You	He had a knife and attacked an innocent person.	Even worse evidence.
Them	But...he was always so nice to me.	Starting to change model of Mike as always nice to everyone.

Challenge

If you challenge their models, rules or other motivators, they may well be forced to reflect upon what you have said, testing their models to see if they work and perhaps thinking of an appropriate answer (and checking that this is valid before explaining it).

Who	Talk	Subtext/comment
Them	We must wait here.	I believe there is a rule that prevents us progressing.
You	Why? Who says?	Challenge belief.
Them	Ummm.	Muse about source and hence validity of belief.

Isolation

The problem with much deep change is that a person's friends and cultural associates will oppose any change in their thinking and try to persuade them back to the old ways. Isolating the person while they are rethinking their life is a method used by many institutions, from monasteries to universities.

Projecting

Get them to think about the future by talking about the future. Take what is happening now and extend it into a new future. Show how other influences may change what might normally be expected. Talk about a time when they have not planned and expose the future vacuum. Then when they show uncertainty, give them a pleasant future to choose.

Who	Talk	Subtext/comment
You	I think I'm going to go to town next week. What about you?	Talk about the future.
Them	Mmm. I'm not sure yet.	Projecting an empty future.
You	Would you like to come with me.	Provide them with a pleasant future.

Seeding

Seeding uses a very appropriate agricultural metaphor for planting ideas that people may later think of as being their own. New ideas require patience, care and a safe climate in which to blossom and grow. Sound like you are musing yourself, saying things like 'What if...' and 'I wonder...' and then back off as you see them musing about the possibility you have spoken.

Who	Talk	Subtext/comment
You	I wonder what it's like in New York now?	Ask an open question, then stop.
Them	(later). Let's go to New York.	Idea has filtered through. Person thinks they thought of it.

12. Sensing

We have five senses with which to take input from our surroundings. Each sense gives us very different data which allows us to detect many of the vibrations and arrangements of molecules around us, as in Table 12.1. From this storm of data, our minds work at the speed of sensation in a system of dynamic perception and meaning-making that allows us to survive and prosper in the sometimes rather inhospitable world.

Table 12.1. What can we sense

Organ	Sense	Can detect...
Eyes	Sight	Electromagnetic radiation (red to violet) Brightness, contrast, hue, luminance Distance, dimension, location Objects, focus, distinctiveness Movement, locus, speed, acceleration
Ears	Sound	Physical vibration (pitch, 20Hz to 20kHz), volume Waveform (different sounds), quality Music: notes, scale, chords, harmony Words, speech
Skin	Touch	Pressure, temperature, pain Sharpness, roughness, texture, vibration Shape, location
Nose	Smell	Strong/weak smells Pleasant/unpleasant smells
Tongue	Taste	Sweet, salt, sour, bitter, savory, spiciness Also in eating, we use temperature and texture (via mouth touch), plus appearance (we 'eat with our eyes').

Sensory preferences

Imagine as a child that, in your relatively random learning, you find that sounds give you significant pleasure. Perhaps it is the sound of a toy or perhaps your mother's cooing voice. Perhaps you found your visual sense most fascinating, with bright toys and stimulating surroundings. The result of pleasure is that we pay more attention to its source, reveling in it and seeking further pleasure, Thus we develop preferences for one form of sensing over another, much as Chapter 8 describes how we develop preferences for the company of others, levels of risk and so on.

Our sensory preferences change how we communicate and hence can often be detected. People with a preference for visual sensation often have a strong internal visual system, literally thinking in pictures. This can lead them to talking quickly as they try to explain the flashing internal show before it passes. Their rapid speech limits their breathing, which is snatched in shallow breaths between words and leads to hunched shoulders and a higher-pitched voice. Those who prefer sounds slow down more as they take pleasure in the varying sound of the words they speak.

Our sensory preferences can also come out in the words we speak, and those with a visual preference will say things like 'That looks good' even about abstract concepts, as they make internal images about the idea. Likewise those with a sonic preference may say 'That sounds good' (because for them, it actually does). Likewise a tactile person may say 'That feels good' and one who is sensitive to smells may say 'That smells good'.

Much trust is built on similarity, and people will trust those who seem to have similar sensory preferences, even though they may not consciously notice the similarity.

Implications for changing minds

Pay attention to what people say and how they say it to discover their sensory preferences. Then show you are like them by replying in the same way, with similar sense-based words, spoken with similar speed and pitch and with matching body movement.

Attention

We guide our senses via our attention, which we shine like a torch towards areas of interest. Table 12.2 shows some of the ways that our attention may be grabbed by different stimuli.

Table 12.2. Grabbing attention

Attention-grabbing method	Examples
Stimulating sensitivity	Flashing lights Piercing notes Acrid smells
Overload	Blinding lights Loud sounds Extreme heat or cold
Contrast	Red on yellow Sudden silence Sweet and sour sauce
Threat	Person with a knife Branch falling from a tree
Opportunity	Free! Easy! Sale! A chance to meet goals

When we are paying attention to something we are *not* paying attention to other things, which makes this important for changing minds, as all marketers know well. In our modern 'attention economy' there is an increasing number of companies clamoring for a share in the fixed limit of attention that we have. This can lead to an exhausting overload of stimuli as each marketer tries to out-do the last.

Implications for changing minds

Without attention you have little opportunity to change minds. If you want them to listen, first find ways to attract their attention, although beware of creating sensory overload that triggers a fight-or-flight reaction.

Distraction can also be very useful. Moving attention *away* from one thing can be as useful as moving it towards something else.

Attention zones

We have two main zones of attention that can vary in size, as in Figure 12.1. Our *zone of focus* is relatively small and is where we are paying most attention. Our visual zone of focus is literally about an inch in diameter.

We also have a wider *zone of awareness* where we are not focusing, but where changes can still catch our attention. Sometimes we shut down that outer zone – for example where a teenager playing a video game can see and hear *only* the game.

A third state is like a martial artist, where the zone of focus is expanded to take in a large part of the available world. It is an almost trance-like state, where their heightened sensitivity lets them react instantly to events around them.

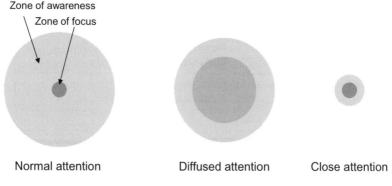

Fig. 12.1. Zones of attention

Implications for changing minds

Understand the sizes of their attention zones by noticing the way in which the other person is paying attention to things. Place stimuli in the zone of attention to get consciously noticed. Use the zone of awareness to subtly snag attention.

Distraction

Note that while conscious attention is often desirable, it can block subtle messages intended for the subconscious. Attention can hence sometimes be used in the way of a stage magician, to distract your conscious mind while the real business is going on elsewhere.

A point worth noting is that conscious persuasion that engages the person's full attention is generally more powerful for long-term change than subconscious persuasion, although this usually takes more time and effort. Using a peripheral route that avoids serious conscious consideration by the target person may get short-term compliance but does not lead to longer-term commitment.

Implications for changing minds

Rather than just attracting attention, *manage* it. Use different stimuli to direct it in a way that gives you the best chance of changing minds. Use central, conscious persuasion for long-term change. Use distraction and peripheral persuasion for quick and simple persuasion where longer-term buy-in is not so important.

Personal spaces

We each have a certain amount of 'body space' around us which we treat as private territory, probably because there is potential for first-strike attack if others get that close to us. If anybody invades this space then we may either back off or push the other person away.

Edward Hall identified four concentric zones:

- *Intimate*: touching to 10 inches. For close friends and family.
- *Casual-personal*: 18 inches to 4 feet: Informal conversation with friends.
- *Social-consultative*: 4 to 12 feet: Formal transactions.
- *Public*: Over 12 feet. Addressing groups of people.

When touching the body, some places are more permissible than others. Briefly touching arms, shoulders and back is often accepted. Touching the face and sexual areas is rarely permitted. Invasion and touching are often used as deliberate acts of domination.

The strange question of time

If you ask scientists what there is out there in the universe that we can sense, they will probably tell you of four things: space, time, energy and matter. This leads to an interesting paradox, because we can only sense space, energy and matter with our five senses. So how do we sense time? The alarming answer is that it is an internal construction. We 'make up' time, which perhaps is one reason why time flies or drags, depending on how much fun we are having.

We construct time in a number of very different ways. Some people see past, present and future as closely overlapped while others separate them out. There is also a differing focus on the past, present and future, for example with some considering the past to be more significant while for others the present or future has greater importance. Figure 12.2 illustrates this with circles.

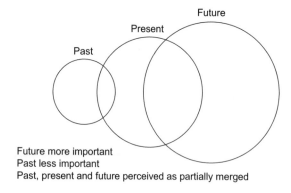

Future more important
Past less important
Past, present and future perceived as partially merged

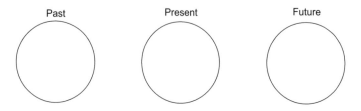

Past, present and future equally important
and cognitively kept very separate

Fig. 12.2 Perceptions of past, present and future

Representing time

We live in three-dimensional space and often use this to represent intangible concepts, including time. There are two interesting points about this, as indicated in Figure 12.3. Firstly, time typically gets imagined as a line or road which may be straight, curved, left-to-right, back-to-front, U-shaped and so on. A second perceptual effect is that some people perceive themselves in the 'railroad tracks' of time, with the future coming straight at them, while others place themselves outside time, looking down at it.

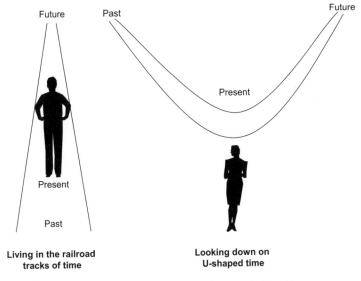

Living in the railroad
tracks of time

Looking down on
U-shaped time

Fig. 12.3. Different ways of perceiving time

Another effect is that when we think about the past or future, we do so through the lens of today's thoughts and feelings. Thus a smoker, satisfied by the nicotine, forgets the craving of a minute ago and is sure they can give up any time. Or a teenager, told they will think and feel differently when they are older, considers the notion preposterous.

Implications for changing minds

Identify how people perceive time and either tune what you say to align with this or deliberately change their perceptual method.

Changing minds and sensing

An implication of the limited focus that we use when sensing the torrent of data from the world around us is that to change minds you must first stand in the spotlight of attention. If the other person is sensing elsewhere, then you might as well not bother trying to communicate with them.

Contrast

Using contrast is an effective principle for gaining attention. A loud sound will make people look if it is quiet, but not if the noise level is already high. A bright foreground will stand out against a darker background. A cold breeze will be noticed in a hot environment. A sudden movement will be noticed when things are still.

Who	Talk	Subtext/comment
You	AHH!	Faked accident to allow sudden movement and loud noise.
Them	What?	Give attention.
You	Sorry, I stubbed my toe. Just look at this!	Attention gained, move to sustain it.

Stimulation

Stimulate their senses in other ways. Touch can be very powerful, for example a light touch on a person's arm (or other safe area) sends a strong signal. Smells are quite primitive and can be very significant, from the smell of coffee and good food to the deliberate smell of a seductive perfume.

Who	Talk	Subtext/comment
You	(touching their arm) Look at that painting.	Physical arousal and directing attention to reds and yellows.
Them	Woh! That's bright.	I am over-stimulated.
You	It is. What do you think about this one?	Redirect them to the one you want to sell.
Them	That's much nicer.	I am pleasantly stimulated.

Overload

The human sensory system can only take so much. A bright light, loud sound, heavy touch or noxious smell will make them move away from the stimulation. You can also cause overload gradually, using the way stress works in an accumulative manner, with each little stressor adding up.

Under-stimulation

In a perhaps non-intuitive and opposite approach to overload, a faintly detected stimulation will make the other person crane forwards as they seek to find out more about what it is. Having made the commitment to find out more, they are then hooked into sustaining that attention.

Who	Talk	Subtext/comment
You	(whisper incoherently)	Getting them to listen harder
Them	What?	I do not understand. I want to understand.
You	Do you think you could spend more time here with me?	Ask for commitment.

Alignment

Identify their preferences for sensory attention, for example by listening to the language they use, and use these in your communications.

Who	Talk	Subtext/comment
Them	That looks like a good idea.	'looks like' is visual language, showing tendency to use
You	Let me show you something.	Reply in visual language and play to the visual sense, showing them something they can look at.

In a similar way, you can align time orientation to the way they mentally perceive and structure time.

Who	Talk	Subtext/comment
Them	Things aren't what they were…	Focus on past.
You	So for next year now, let's make today the 'good old days'.	Turn the present into the future past.

Invasion

Invade their body space, moving closer to them than they feel comfortable. This can be done under the guise of whispering a confidence or moving closer to hear them.

Touch them in safe zones such as on the arm. Touch their back to guide them physically in a desired direction.

Be very careful when invading their body space – it can easily be interpreted as a threat and invoke a fight-or-flight response.

Retreat

The opposite of invasion is retreat. Moving backwards away from them, even slightly, invites them to follow. If they are interested in what you have to say (or just in you) then if you step away they will step towards you.

Movement

There are many forms of movement you can use to gain attention, for example:

- Something moving towards a person will trigger a subconscious defensive reaction.
- Rocking lightly back and forward can destabilize them, making them more ready to move.
- If you get them engaged on a topic and then turn to go still talking, they may well follow you.

Describing what you are saying by sculpting the air with your body and arms also sustains attention. Use mobile eyebrows and a generally expressive face. Keep mobile to keep attention.

Distraction

Sometimes you *do not* want the other person to notice something. A simple way of doing this is to create 'inattentional blindness' where, by forcing a close attention on one thing, you can cause them to miss even very 'obvious' other events.

13. Inferring Meaning

When we first receive information from our senses, it is just a set of electromagnetic and physical vibrations. From this raw data we must first recognize what is there and then work out what it all means. This is the process of *inference* – there is no inherent meaning in the world around us – so we infer our own meaning. This has a very significant importance for communications as it means that, for any given set of information, everyone will infer an individual and, at very best, slightly different meaning.

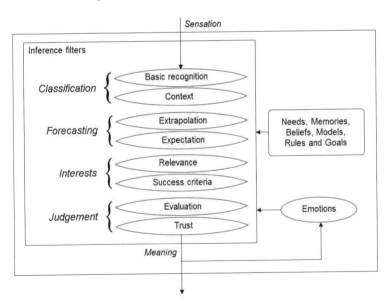

Fig. 13.1. Inferring meaning

Classification

An early step in finding meaning is *basic recognition* of what we see. We do this through a system of pattern-matching and classification, using our memories and models. This is very useful for fitting new experiences into existing models, but it can lead to us missing what it actually something different. It is also one reason why business people often miss changes in the marketplace until it is too late.

The surrounding *context* is also important for making sense. A gun in a museum is different from a gun in the hands of a man in a bank – and even then what he is wearing can change the meaning. When examining problems in business, it is common to see only immediate causes, missing the implications of the broader context. Taking a wider perspective is a very useful approach for leaders where they can bring greater understanding to business problems.

Implications for changing minds

Whatever you describe something, make sure the other person can recognize it, unambiguously. Look for confusion and do not pass it by unless you deliberately want to create it.

Forecasting

We are constantly concerned about the future, seeking to predict what will happen so we can control our actions and environment. We hence *extrapolate* from our experiences to forecast what might happen next.

An early process in finding meaning is assessing what we sense for threats. Our subconscious can take over our bodies when there is a physical threat, making us react before our slower conscious thinking gets going. We also constantly scan for other threats, for example in the words of other people.

As well as looking forward, we also check out our *expectations* from our previous forecasts. If things do not happen as expected, we are surprised and have to decide whether or not to change our forecasting model. This is something we do not do easily.

Interests

When what we see has relevance for our goals and other interests, we notice and pay particular attention. We notice other cars which are the same make and model as ours. We notice business news about our customers and competitors. This is the connection of our goals to our attention.

We also pay attention to our goals and the criteria we have set up to tell us if we are on track to achieving them or have just succeeded. When we are successful our brains reward us with a little squirt of the brain's natural opiates, making us feel good about our achievement.

Implications for changing minds

Align what you say and do with whatever means 'desirable' and 'success' to them, either showing how you help them succeed or how their interests are being threatened in some way.

Judging

Another layer of meaning we add to our experiences is based on using our various rule-sets to *evaluate* whether what we see is good or bad, right or wrong. We judge both one another and also ourselves – often using different rules for each.

An important form of judging is where we assess situations and people to determine whether we can *trust* them. This is related to forecasting, as the actions of someone who is trustworthy can be predicted with confidence. Trust is critical for persuasion and is explored in detail in Chapter 21.

Implications for changing minds

Make sure they judge you as good and right by following their rules, at least initially. Always act to gain and sustain their trust. If needed, show chosen others to be untrustworthy.

The effects of emotion

Emotions are closely connected with all stages of inferring meaning, both in the meaning we create and the way that meaning affects our emotions. Emotions and meaning hence act in a circular fashion. When I infer meaning, I invoke emotions as a result of what I have understood. And while I am inferring meaning, this process is contaminated by current emotions, as created by previous inferences. Thus the emotional impact of each experience infects and shapes the emotional impact of subsequent experiences.

Table 13.1. Emotion and inference

Inferring	Emotion	Why
Classification	Confusion Contentment	Cannot recognize something All is as expected
Interests	Anger Delight Sadness	Frustration of goal-achievement Goals met Goals not met
Forecasting	Surprise Fear Anticipation	Experience not as forecast Extrapolation indicates threat Extrapolation indicates success
Judging	Disgust Shame Fear	Others do not follow rules I did not follow rules Person cannot be trusted

If we are upset or angry with someone, then we will interpret their actions very differently to when we are feeling affectionate towards them. When we perceive threats to our needs, we will fear. When our goals are frustrated and our forecasts proven wrong, we are likely to get angry. Meeting goals, on the other hand, leads to happiness.

There is also a view that we deduce meaning from our emotions. Hence if I feel aroused when in the company of a member of the opposite sex, I might conclude that I love her. This is not an empty theory and has been proven by several cunning experiments.

Implications for changing minds

Recognize and manage the other person's emotions and its impact on how they create meaning. Get the other person in the right mood before persuading them.

When there is no meaning

Most of the time we find reasonable meaning in what we experience and so happily go around the 'normal loop' in Figure 13.2. But what happens when we cannot find valid meaning? This is a surprising, confusing and uncomfortable experience, and there is a very strong temptation to deny the invalid meaning.

If we choose not to seek further understanding we then will typically take one of three routes to return to, or stay in, the comfort of the normal loop.

The easiest action is simply to ignore what has happened and hope that it does not happen again, staying in the 'normal loop'. This is typically what happens when somebody says something that we do not understand. Rather than questioning them, we nod and hope that they will explain further or simply not return to the subject.

The next choice is to follow the 'denial loop', assigning a cause to what happened, explaining it away by such methods as blaming others or creating pseudo-scientific theories. We may even change our memories. This seems radical but it happens surprisingly often. It is typically done at the subconscious level, making it a particularly pernicious way of making us ignore a potentially significant new reality.

When we accept that we cannot find a satisfactory meaning then we are forced to face the situation of not-knowing and seek a way of increasing our understanding in the 'learning and change' loop. For many people this is a very uncomfortable place and they will only accept it when they realize there is no other course of action open to them. Even then, they may grasp at straws, seeking any answer that will relieve their distress.

The true learning state is one of acceptance of the lack of meaning, perhaps even with a sense of excitement at the possibility of new learning. When you are ready to learn, you seek explanation but do not grasp blindly at it. Possible new meanings are handled with interest, turned over and examined with curiosity and care.

Implications for changing minds

Prevent denial and persist until they reach a learning state. Then they will be very open to changing their minds.

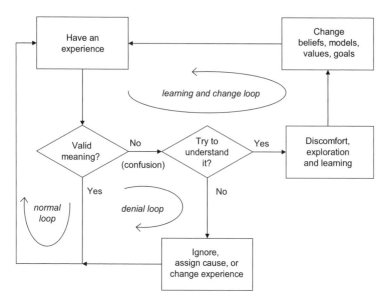

Fig. 13.2. When there is no meaning

Meaning and musing

The learning and change loop of Figure 13.2 uses the processes and systems of musing, as in Chapter 11, and may involve the full imagination loop of Figure 11.1. Musing hence tests new beliefs and models to see what meaning they would make and how they integrate with other motivators.

Meaning and memory

The sense we make of experiences now is based on what we remember of previous experiences, faulty and limited as these are. Meaning is thus affected by what has happened recently and what more distant events can be most easily called to mind.

Implications for changing minds

Make events that will be useful for future meaning easy to recall. When persuading, first help them bring relevant memories to mind.

Changing meaning

Meaning-making is a complex mechanism, which makes it surprisingly easy to change the meaning that others infer. The real trick is in doing this accurately and reliably. One way is to work on the deeper systems of beliefs, values, models, etc. that are used within the meaning-making process. The alternative is to work directly on the process, explicitly guiding the inferences that are made, for example by directly or subtly suggesting the conclusions that should be drawn.

Confusion

Deliberately make any sensible inference difficult to draw. This has the effect of forcing the other person either to think hard about the real meaning or accept without question any subsequent meaning you offer.

Who	Talk	Subtext/comment
You	If you warma bella works canna dwit now.	Confusing mumble.
Them	Eh???	Does not make sense. Move to confused state.
You	If you want to believe this works, you can do it now.	Add real persuasive line.

Reframing

Reframing says 'look at this another way', inviting the other person to use different models or rules, thus changing their perceptual lens.

One of the easiest ways of reframing is to extend the current frame, for example by adding new information. As current motivators are not challenged, you are unlikely to get much resistant. Changing the frame completely can also be effective and simple if, rather than denouncing their frame, another frame is offered as an alternative choice.

Who	Talk	Subtext/comment
Them	The HR manager won't approve.	HR manager framed as judge.
You	What if his opinion didn't matter?	HR manager reframed as irrelevant.

Emotion-then-meaning

Use a two-stage process of getting the other person to a desired understanding and inference of particular meaning. First work to create the appropriate emotion and intensity, for example by invoking a happy memory, and then deliver the message that invokes the desired meaning and with which they will associate the emotion.

Who	Talk	Subtext/comment
You	Didn't we have a wonderful time last week!!	Invoke happiness by recall of happy time.
Them	Yeah! It was really great.	Emotion moved to happiness
You	What do you think about this great new system?	Make request.
Them	It's wonderful!	Positive emotion shapes evaluation.

Suggestion

Suggest possible interpretations of a situation, effectively telling the other person what meaning they should infer from it. This is very often done with a bold and confident assertion. If you seem sure then many will accept what you say as true (this is the basic method of much religious preaching).

Who	Talk	Subtext/comment
You	I think he looks rather stupid, don't you?	Offer meaning of a another person's appearance.
Them	Yes, he does rather.	Accept interpretation of person's appearance.

Suggestion can also be subtle and sly, as may be used in hypnosis, slipping messages to the subconscious while distracting the conscious mind with irrelevant other matters.

Who	Talk	Subtext/comment
You	Look _by_ there, next to _the dress._	Emphasis says 'buy the dress'.
Them	I'd rather look at the dress.	Accepted subconscious suggestion.

14. Formulating Intent

We cannot ponder forever, and either directly after inferring meaning or as a result of some deeper musing, we have to decide what we will do. There are two routes through this activity, as identified by psychologists Richard Petty and John Cacioppo and illustrated in Figure 14.1. We can take time to consciously think and decide what to do or we can use short-cut decisions, for which we have many strategies. This makes sense, as we simply do not have the time to think through every action we take. The problem, however, is that the short-cuts can easily result in poor decisions and damaging actions.

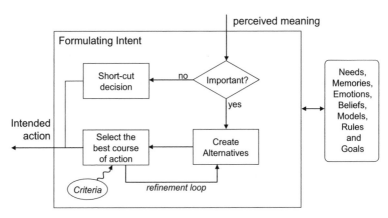

Fig. 14.1. Formulating intent

Implications for changing minds

Understand how people decide and the impact of motivators on this process. Then act and talk to guide them to the decision you want.

Short-cut decisions

In the non-stop flow of actions we take, we have very little time to think about what we will do. As a result, many of our decisions use simplified short-cut decision methods like those in Table 14.1. Most of the time, this serves us well, enabling us to focus our time on the more important decisions.

Short-cut decisions can also be a deadly trap when the tried-and-true no longer gives us an effective result. This is typical in times of change, where methods and criteria for deciding can go from being assets to liabilities.

Table 14.1. Short-cut decision mechanisms

Method	Trigger	Action
Fight-or-flight	Sudden unexpected event	Massive bodily change in preparation for battle or fleeing.
Habit	Familiar event	Repeat a well-established pattern of behaving rather than think more deeply about the situation.
Rules-of-thumb (heuristics)	Familiar decision point	Use quick and simple rules to decide. For example, 'Don't ask the boss to sign anything on a Monday.'
Models	Decision	Use pre-existing mental models to simplify the situation and hence ease decision-making.
Intuition	Vaguely familiar event	Make irrational decision, assuming the subconscious will ensure this is correct.
Pleasure-Pain	Something desirable (or undesirable)	Decide based on satisfaction of short-term need rather than rational decision.
Social rules	Other person says or does something	Blindly follow rule, e.g. agree with other person because 'It is rude to disagree', 'I might look silly', etc.

Implications for changing minds

To get quick compliance, slip things past the conscious guard through one of the short-cut decision mechanisms. Be aware, however, that such methods do not produce lasting change – for this you need to stimulate conscious choice.

Creating alternatives

When making considered decisions, the ideal full process is to start with a divergent exploration to find a wide range of possible alternatives. Both detailed analysis and creative discovery method may be used for this purpose.

The structured method of finding alternatives is to do a top-down decomposition, breaking choices down into successive layers of detail in a 'decision tree', as Figure 14.2. In extreme logic we can assign probabilities and utility to each of these, although we typically make such assessments less consciously.

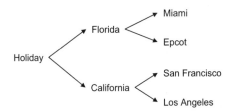

Fig. 14.2 Decision tree

A very common creative way of building alternatives is to brainstorm or otherwise collect a wide set of possibilities and then winnow it down to the best alternative. In practice, people have different preferences for for the extent to which they use judgment and action over slower musing of possibility.

It can be a very useful action to slow down this process, holding up the decision-making until an adequate range of possibilities is sufficiently explored. How much time should be spent here of course depends on a combination of the real (not imagined) pressures and the potential benefits being sought.

Implications for changing minds

Facilitate the process of creating alternatives. Avoid or distract them from things that they might choose but you do not want. Include choices that they are unlikely to choose in order to hide the real choice that you want them to make.

Selecting ideas

From the range of possible alternatives, the next stage is a convergent process of evaluation by which the best solution is decided. The classic approach to this is to identify and prioritize decision criteria and then apply them logically to each possible alternative, as in Figure 14.3.

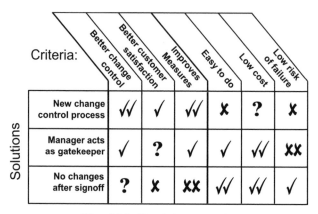

Criteria: Solutions	Better change control	Better customer satisfaction	Improves Measures	Easy to do	Low cost	Low risk of failure
New change control process	√√	√	√√	✗	?	✗
Manager acts as gatekeeper	√	?	√	√	√√	✗✗
No changes after signoff	?	✗	✗✗	√√	√√	√

Fig. 14.3. Decision matrix

In practice, while a structured and logical method may be helpful for important decisions, a number of other approaches are often used, especially under stress or where collaborative agreement is required:

- *Socialization and emergence,* where ideas are discussed and the most equitable solution emerges from the dialogue.

- *Politicization and power-play,* where individuals advocate their own preferences and use political tactics, which may be negative, to get their choices adopted.

- *Incubation,* where the solution is ignored until an idea and rationale 'pops into the head'.

- *Satisficing,* where high stress levels leads to selection of any solution that will reduce this, no matter how suboptimal.

Implications for changing minds

Manage the decision criteria and the process of choice that they use. If you want real commitment then facilitate a rational process, otherwise compliance can be gained subtly.

External choices

We do not always make choices from internally generated ideas and much of our decision-making is from alternatives presented to us by other people or by the circumstances in which we find ourselves. In such situations we choose in roughly similar ways, although the influence of other people can be significant when we are deciding within a group context, as discussed in Chapter 18.

Two-stage deciding

When we make decisions we are sometimes faced with a wide range of alternatives, for example when we are looking for a house we may end up with a big stack of details. Rather than examining each in detail, we typically use a two-stage process, first reducing the pile to a shortlist which we then consider more carefully before we decide which to visit.

The shortlisting stage is usually a *negative* selection process where items are *rejected* for *not* meeting basic criteria (too expensive, wrong area, etc.). The second stage is then one of *positive* selection, where the process aims to choose one or more, based on key criteria (big kitchen, four bedrooms, etc.). Choice may not stop here and further two-stage decisions may be added, for example by doing a drive-by of selected houses before choosing those to visit.

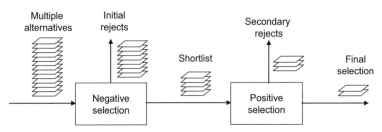

Fig. 14.4. Two-stage selection

Implications for changing minds

When they have many alternatives, give them simple selection criteria for the first stage so you get onto their shortlist. Then give them more details that meet their positive selection criteria.

Decision preferences and biases

We all have a number of areas in which we have preferences for decisions and actions in one direction rather than another, such as those shown in Figure 14.5. Preferences are often learned early in life and stay with us as unconscious biases that affect our decisions in many subtle ways, as discussed in Chapter 8.

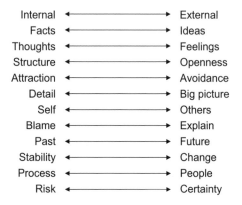

Internal ⟷ External
Facts ⟷ Ideas
Thoughts ⟷ Feelings
Structure ⟷ Openness
Attraction ⟷ Avoidance
Detail ⟷ Big picture
Self ⟷ Others
Blame ⟷ Explain
Past ⟷ Future
Stability ⟷ Change
Process ⟷ People
Risk ⟷ Certainty

Fig. 14.5. Some of our preference spectra

Each preference is effectively a spectrum and we each prefer some position between either extreme. Where we are on each spectrum at any one time is influenced by several factors, such as our emotional state and whether we are at work or at play. We nevertheless tend to have a preferred 'home position' where we are most comfortable, plus a 'range of comfort' across which we can happily move. This leads to bias as we tend more towards one end of the spectrum than others.

We often have biases about people, typically based on whether they are like us and our friends (the in-group) or are different to us in some way. Out-group people often get stereotyped in highly simplified and unjust ways. Chapter 18 discusses further the impact of groups on decisions.

Implications for changing minds

Understand the natural biases and preferences that the other person has and either use these or find ways of counteracting them.

Decision traps

We may think that we are good at making decisions but beyond preference and bias there are many more psychological traps that the unwary decision-maker can fall into when making decisions, some of which are described in Table 14.2.

Table 14.2. Decision traps

Trap	Description	Example
Ambiguity effect	We prefer a known probability to an unknown one.	Rather than 'risk' changing jobs I stay where I am, even though I am unhappy here.
Anchoring	We base decisions on recent events and decisions.	Employee satisfaction is 60% at one of our factories. I assume other factories are around the same figure.
Availability Heuristic	We presume that what comes most easily to mind is statistically most likely to happen.	High press coverage of corporate scandals leading me to suspect my managers and colleagues.
Bias for action	We need to appear decisive or assume a quick decision is better than taking time to decide.	I seem to spend all of my time fire-fighting and I feel like a hero when I succeed.
Bounded rationality	We are naturally limited in what we can understand.	A company executive makes a massive investment based on few, simple criteria.
Confirmation bias	When we make a decision, we pay more attention to data that proves us right.	I implement a new motivation system and then commission a study that 'proves' that it works.
Conjunction fallacy	Assuming that the overlap of two separate events is more likely than just one of the events.	It seems more likely to have a powerful competitor who slashes prices *and* attacks your product than have a powerful competitor who only slashes prices.
Cover-ups	We deliberately lie to avoid expected discomfort.	I have to report bad figures to the board next week, so I hold back some numbers until next month.
Endowment effect	We over-value the things we own.	I try to sell my rusting old car for a high price.
Gambler's fallacy	We think we can forecast random events.	I think I am on a winning streak, so take higher risks.

Table 14.2. (continued)

Trap	Description	Example
Hot-hand fallacy	We assume success breeds success.	Because I have won three times in a row, I think I will win again.
Loss avoidance	We avoid certain types of loss.	I refuse a bet where there is a 90% chance of doubling my money (vs. 10% chance of losing everything).
Misunderstanding of statistics	We make 'statistical' guesses that are wildly wrong.	I assume that I can easily grab 10% of the market (so do many competitors).
Overconfidence	After we make a risky decision, we believe it is more likely to succeed.	I invest in a new computer system and hence assume that it will work first time without any problems occurring.
Perfectionism	We desperately want to make the right decision.	If there is not enough data on a new product I will not allow it to be launched.
Procrastination	Rather than risk a wrong decision, we make no decision.	I put off meeting with a difficult employee.
Representativeness heuristic	Assuming that similarity in one area means similarity in another.	Because a customer was aggressive, I assume others from the same company will also be aggressive.
Satisficing	When we are feeling stressed, we seek any solution to relieve the stress rather than the best solution for the company.	An employee is threatening to sue for racial bias. Even though I know they are wrong, I pay them off to keep things quiet.
Single-frame thinking	We make decisions based on a single viewpoint.	I make an autonomous decision to buy the furniture and am very surprised when people are unhappy about this.
Sunk-cost effect	Once we have made an investment we are loathe to pull out.	A gambler tries to get back winnings by increasing the stakes.

Implications for changing minds

Understand the traps that can snare you and avoid falling into them. You can, of course, steer other people towards them or otherwise use them in various persuasive actions.

Changing formulation

Getting people to change their formulation of intent is largely about influencing *how* they make decisions. As with other areas, this may be done by changing the deeper systems that act to support and guide decisions, such as the constraints imposed by values.

Rational methods

Rational methods of persuasion appeal to the conscious mind, asking it to think about what we say and hence agree with us. These methods are more effective at creating long-term change than quick methods that get short-term compliance but no long-term commitment.

Logical argument

This method is preferred by intellectuals and people with preferences for logic and rational judging. Aristotle and the early Greeks defined rhetorical rules that survive to this day.

Who	Talk	Subtext/comment
Them	I want to go to the beach.	Original proposal.
You	But the forecast is for rain.	Logical refutation.
Them	It doesn't matter if we are swimming.	Counter-argument.
You	But our things will get wet.	Logical refutation of counter-argument.

Giving facts

A simple method of changing minds is to appear not to persuade but simply to give the other person the facts by which they can work out the right answer for themselves in their own time.

Who	Talk	Subtext/comment
You	BJR are having a sale next week.	Providing information.
Them	Uh huh.	Absorbing the information.
You	What are you doing next Friday?	Provoke/test decision.
Them	Hmm. Well we could go to that sale, I suppose.	Thinks and makes decision.

Changing motivators

`If you can change the other person's goals or models (which they use to plan how to achieve their goals), then you can change how they decide.

Who	Talk	Subtext/comment
Them	This will be easy.	I have a model that says this will be easy.
You	But it's Jim, remember. He always argues about things.	Add complexity to model.
Them	Oh dear, perhaps I'll leave it for now.	Revise model, muse about possibility and change decision.

Alternatives

Asking them questions forces them to think and decide. Giving them choice between several items limits the decision to what you want them to choose. In this, you can either offer things which are equally agreeable to you or force the decision by offering one good option and other unattractive options.

Who	Talk	Subtext/comment
You	Would you like the red one or the yellow one?	Offering them a choice to force a decision.
Them	The red one is nice.	I prefer red to yellow and will buy the red one.

What if

When you talk about the future, they also have to think more consciously about what may happen. Asking questions makes this even more effective. Talking about possibilities leads them to choose.

Who	Talk	Subtext/comment
You	What would you do if we lost power?	Ask them to think about the future and make a decision.
Them	Ah, well. We'd be in trouble. I guess we need a backup system.	Musing and formulating.

Involvement

If you get people involved in what you are trying to sell (or even in the sales process!) they will acquire a greater conscious interest in the subject and consequently engage more with you.

Who	Talk	Subtext/comment
You	Would you like to try this out?	Offer involvement.
Them	Ok. What do I do first?	Engaged and thinking about it.

Problem-solving

People often have goals that involve solving difficult problems. If you can help them to solve the problems that are distracting them, you may either be able to turn this to your purpose or otherwise create an obligation to listen to you with an open and attentive mind.

Who	Talk	Subtext/comment
You	Would this solve your problem?	Offer solution to identified problem.
Them	Yes! That's great. Thank you.	I owe you.
You	Could I take a few minutes to show you something?	Request repayment of obligation.

Deception

Lies and other deceptive methods also work at the conscious level, although the potential for discovery and resultant betrayal effects can make this hazardous. Nevertheless, bending of the truth is very common. People who are successful at deception are often convincing because they first convince themselves and so do not give away their deception with any body-language signs.

Who	Talk	Subtext/comment
You	Sorry I'm late. The train was late this morning.	Make an excuse.
Them	What happened?	I am suspicious.
You	There was an engineering overrun and they didn't put on the first train. The next one was really packed!	Imagine realistic excuse and then describe what you see in your head.

Bypass methods

Pausing to think carefully about what we should do is a luxury we cannot afford for every decision. For the vast majority of choices, we therefore use largely subconscious and intuitive shortcuts. This allows for a wide range of persuasive methods that bypass the conscious process, triggering short-cuts and influencing the subconscious without conscious realization.

Stress

If you provide too much information or otherwise raise the stress that the other person experiences, they will start satisficing (seeking *any* solution that will reduce their stress rather than seeking the best solutions that will meet their goals).

Who	Talk	Subtext/comment
You	Mary won't like that. You're boss won't like either. Let's just forget it.	Talk rapidly about multiple stressors.
Them	Good idea!	Anticipate stress. Accept stress-reducing solution.

Distraction

Our zone of focus is very small, as described in Chapter 12. Magicians and pickpockets typically work by distracting you one way into a small zone of focus while doing their business outside this area. If you can distract and occupy conscious thought then you will be able to use a short-cut method without them wondering what you are doing.

Who	Talk	Subtext/comment
You	What will Carl say?	Trigger musing.
Them	Hmm. He might be interested...	I'll have to think about that.
You	By the way, you are coming next week, aren't you?	Persuasive message.
Them	Mm? Yeah, sure.	I'm busy thinking. I'll agree to that minor request without too much worry.

Stimulating needs

While you cannot change needs, you can stimulate them, either appealing to what is desired or prodding what is not sought. Thus you can appeal to fear, greed, hope, etc. Stimulation at this basic level can cause an immediate response with little real thought.

Who	Talk	Subtext/comment
You	Are you interested in doubling your money with little risk?	Appeal to greed.
Them	Absolutely!	Agree with little questioning.

Arousal

If you stimulate emotions such that they enter an aroused state, then their emotional state will have an effect on how they make decisions, in particular replacing rational thinking with emotional reaction.

Who	Talk	Subtext/comment
You	Mike says you're stupid.	Trigger anger.
Them	What!! He's a fool!	I'm angry that someone thinks that of me.
You	Let's show him. How about if you join us next week.	Shape their thinking.

Heuristics

Use a rule of thumb that they will not challenge. A way of doing this is to reflect back to them the heuristics they have used in the past. You can also use heuristics that are common within an industry or social group. The rule you use can range from technical estimates to social evaluation and stereotyping.

Who	Talk	Subtext/comment
You	As you said last month, the test phase always doubles the time.	Use a heuristic they have already used.
Them	Yeah. I guess we'll need to extend the project timescale.	Agree with themselves, but without questioning if this case is special.

Conditioning

With a little time, you can use conditioning to program a specific response to particular stimulus, which you can then use in other situations. While this method may seem a bit primitive and perhaps the domain of animal trainers, it is surprising how programmed we often are.

Who	Talk	Subtext/comment
You	(as a competitor name is spoken) AAAH! Sorry I hit my bruise.	Repeatedly cause discomfort when competitor name is spoken.
Them	(jumping) What?	After a while, they will feel uncomfortable whenever the competitor name is heard.

Good reason

One of the social rules that we use is that, if a person asks for something which is not too costly to us and which sounds reasonable, then we are obliged to comply with their request. Psychologist Ellen Langer found that the best way to queue-jump at the photocopier was to say 'because' and give any reason, even silly ones.

Who	Talk	Subtext/comment
You	Can I go first because I am in a hurry.	Using 'because' but with weak reason.
Them	Sure.	Reason given, so agree without further thought or challenge.

15. Translating into Action

It is one thing to decide to do something and it is of course something else to make it happen. There are many ways in which we fail to achieve what we really intend and the act of turning what we mean into communication and action is fraught with difficulties, even for excellent communicators. Great care is therefore needed in this stage.

Words, music and dance

We have three channels of communication through which we interact with other people. We have *words*, the intonation or sounds we make (the *'music'*) and body language (the *'dance'*). What is surprising is that words can form less than 10% of communication, while body language often contributes over 50%. Having said this, words are still the core of communication, and one word can change the meaning of an entire conversation.

Fig. 15.1. Words, music and dance

Understanding language

Language says much about the person, the way they think in general and, and what are thinking now.

Formality

Language can vary significantly in formality, from abstract and objective to colloquial and subjective. Formal language suits such uses as management reports but is seldom suitable for persuasion. Informal language is more personal and seeks to connect the speaker and listener rather than create the separation of formal distance.

Informal language may appeal to the senses and to the particular preferences of the other person. It is relaxed and tuned and designed to persuade. Formal language, on the other hand, is created within strict rules and is often intended to impress.

Accuracy

What is said is always a serious distortion of what it intended. Words are little packets of meaning which are connected together as ill-fitting sentence jigsaws that have little chance of fully representing what is truly intended.

Being accurate can be a deliberate act of effort as the speaker struggles to express a deep meaning, thinking carefully about words and structures. Inaccuracy can be a careless thing, as the speaker uses whatever words come to mind in jumbles of internal conflict. Accuracy may sometimes be deliberately discussed or the speaker may try to create new truths by assertion and bluff.

Cultural codes

Culture is embedded deep within language and the words you use betray a great deal about where and how you were brought up. We each have a different set of preferred words and choose them differently for each situation.

Entire languages also contain culture and act to shape nations. German, for example, is a precise language that creates and suits correctness, while English is more ambiguous and is better aligned with fantasy and poetic imagination.

Figures of speech

We not only use language in a literal way, but also in elaborate and creative ways to create subtle new meaning. 'Figures of speech' are common such patterns that allow for a wide range of expression.

An effect of such adjustment is that we have to put more cognitive effort into understanding and hence pay more attention to it. When we link words together, we bring the ideas and meaning from one to the other. Hence the meaning of a word can be significantly extended.

Table 15.1. Comparative figures of speech

Word	Principle	Example
Metaphor	X is the same as Y	He is a dog.
Simile	X has a similarity with Y	He is as stubborn as a dog.
Analogy	X is very similar to Y	He is like a dog.
Metonymy	X represents Y	Talking to the press.
Synecdoche	A part of Y is all of Y	She is a real brain.

Repetition has a deep and comforting effect on us and appears in various ways across various communications as it beats out primitive rhythms.

Table 15.2. Patterns of repetition

Name	Principle	Example
Rhyme	Repeating ending	Looking fine, feeling mine.
Alliteration	Repeating beginning	Putting pen to paper.
Assonance	Repeating middle	Groove to the tube, dude!
Antithesis	Contrasting opposites	It was the best of times, it was the worst of times.
Triple	Three in a row	Faith, hope and charity.
Anaphora	Repeating initial phrase	We shall fight, we shall win.
Anadiplosis	Starting with previous final word	I love everyone. Everyone needs me.
Tautology	Repeating an idea	I seek success. I shun failure.
Polysyndeton	Repeating conjunctions	And I saw, and I ran, and I fell.

Implications for changing minds

Use comparisons to extend meaning and repetition to hammer home key points. Explore other figures for further use.

Distortion

Meaning can be deliberately changed by distorting the literal interpretation of a word. Such distortion can be accidental but may also be a deliberate ploy.

Table 15.3. Patterns of distortion

Name	Principle	Example
Hyperbole	Deliberate exaggeration	She's going to *kill* me.
Understatement	Deliberate downplay	She won't be pleased.
Litotes	Use negative to say positive	I am not unhappy.
Irony	Reversing meaning to say opposite	That was hilarious.
Paradox	Strangely reversed truth	Youth is wasted on the young.
Polarization	Take extreme positions	Nobody likes you because you always do that.

Distortion can be deliberate, as above, but may also be a result of inadequate musing or formulation. Preferences and bias lead to further such variation.

Simplification

It is impossible to give full detail of everything we mean and so we use gross simplifications, leaving things out and making sweeping, general statements. This makes what we say easy to misinterpret and much conversation is a system of elucidation of an original point.

Omissions often leave out people, using words like 'they' without indicating who 'they' are. Judgments and decisions made during inference and formulation are also seldom described and 'Who says?' or 'Why?' are often appropriate in response.

Preferences and bias can lead to generalization, where words like 'all' and 'every' are used and may indicate black-and-white thinking.

Implications for changing minds

Challenge distortion and simplification that indicate limited thinking. Use these yourself for deliberate effect.

Power words

Some words have a greater impact than others. Put anywhere in a sentence they will automatically grab attention and have a fairly predictable effect. Table 15.4 gives some typical examples. You can create more power words by identifying words that will trigger basic human needs (see Table 3.2). Fear and desire are the most common emotions as needs are threatened or anticipated. Hence, for example, 'dangerous' evokes fear and 'exclusive' creates desire.

Table 15.4. Typical power words

Word	Appeal to need for...
Deserve	Greed, identity
Easy	Control, laziness
Exciting	Stimulation, arousal
Free	Greed, laziness
Guaranteed	Safety, control
Healthy	Health, life
New	Control, esteem
Now	Stimulation, relief
Results	Control
Safe	Security
Sex	Propagating genes
You	Identity
Right	Certainty, belonging

'God words' are those which are unchallengeable and may represent ideals and aspirations. For example, talking about things which are 'profitable' in a company may prevent further discussion about potential issues with the subject.

'Devil words' are politically incorrect and typically betray careless bias. These include swearing and deprecation of sensitive subjects from religion to race. Organizations and societies also have devil words which indicate areas of discomfort, such as 'loss' or 'fail'.

Implications for changing minds

Understand the impact each word has and so choose them carefully for deliberate effect.

Intonation

It is not only *what* you say that is important, but *how* you say it. The music of intonation adds much meaning and needs careful attention.

You can change pitch, volume, speed, texture and much more, as in Table 15.5. Modulation is useful for adding interest to what you say as you increase and decrease the pitch of your voice. A flat tone sounds boring. As you change the intonation you tell the listener how excited you are, how important things are, and what you want them to think and do.

Table 15.5. Intonation and meaning

Intonation	Possible meaning
High pitch	Tense, visual thinking
Low pitch	Calm, sensory thinking
Increasing pitch	Becoming excited, uncertainty, questioning
Decreasing pitch	Becoming calm, certainty, commanding
Flat pitch	Unmotivated, disinterested, bored
Loud voice	Desire to be heard, seeking to dominate, anger
Quiet voice	Timidity, confidence
Talking quickly	Excitement, tension, visual thinking
Talking slowly	Calm, pensive, uncertain
Varying texture	Sensory or auditory thinking
Mixture of above	Expressiveness, multiple meanings

Emphasis

Spoken words are typically emphasized by saying them louder, lower or slower, with the contrast between surrounding words marking them out as special. Emphasis can also be added by such methods as pausing, repetition or using intensifiers such as 'very' or 'incredibly'.

By adding emphasis to what you say, you mark out particular words as having special meaning. In emphasizing, you are effectively saying 'pay particular attention to this word.' As with intonation, emphasis provides a subtext that adds meaning, which often gets noticed only at a subconscious level.

Body language

One of the major ways in which we communicate emotions is through signals. 'Non-verbal communication' is commonly called 'body language', and includes vocal sounds as well as body shape. When we are stressed, for example, tense muscles lead to stiffness, jerky movement and also affect vocal texture. Surface effects are reflected in visible changes in skin tone and hue, from blushing to 'goose bumps'. Table 15.6 shows some of the major body language patterns.

Table 15.6. Body language patterns

Pattern	Emotions	Symptoms
Closed	fear, anxiety	Crossed arms and legs. Drawing inwards. Holding oneself. Short, sharp movements.
Open	happiness, satisfied, confident	Relaxed, broad stance. Arms and feet separated. Wide movements.
Agitated	excitement, fear	Sudden movements, tense, red skin, animated face. Fast, speech with varying tone.
Still	calm, sadness, superiority	Stationary body, arms hanging. Slow movements and speech.
Managed	anxiety	Regulated (especially hands and face), fleeting mixed messages.
Uninhibited	naivety, relaxed	Wide movements, loose, aligned words and body language.
Attraction	love, desire, hope, anticipation	Leaning towards, reaching out, holding, enveloping, inclusive language.
Repulsion	hate, fear, disgust, shame	Leaning back, moving away, drawing self in, pushing away others. Contemptuous or fearful language.

As indicated above, much body language includes subconscious signals of emotional states, from skin tone to muscular rigidity. You can go a long way towards building empathy with others by noticing and understanding these signals.

Do note that it can be a trap to assume that another person is feeling something from a single signal. Body language often appears in clusters that are associated with a particular attitude or feeling, as in Table 15.7.

Table 15.7. Body language emotional clusters

Attitude	Emotions	Symptoms
Romantic	love, desire	Open, standing close, prolonged eye contact, touching, redness of skin, dilated pupils.
Dominant	pride, superiority	High, looking down. Instructing. Prolonged gaze. Invading others' space. Assertive.
Aggressive	anger, hate	Animated, agitated, shaking fist, 'claw hand', red skin, showing teeth, simulated attack.
Submissive	fear, anxiety	Small, lowered, withdrawn, closed. Quiet, timid voice.
Fearful	fear	Pale skin, tense, avoiding gaze, speech errors, sweating, fidgeting. Choked, quavering voice.
Relaxed	calm, happy	Open, smooth movements. Smiling. Slower speech.
Enthusiastic	happiness, excited	Animated, wide movements, smiling, mobile face. Rapid, louder speech with varying tone.
Depressed	Sadness	Drooping body, trembling lip, flat voice tone, tears.

Remember that you cannot manage all of your muscles and trying to do so only sends mixed messages that lead others to assume you are lying or concealing something.

Implications for changing minds

Learn to read body signals, both theirs and yours. Watch for non-verbal clusters and correlation between words and body. When they say something, closely observe how they physically change.

Observe your own body language to give clues to your subconscious state and then work on this internally. If you appear tense, for example, you could deliberately calm your thoughts (and then watch for your body to tell you that it has agreed with this suggestion).

Cognitive constraints

In practice we are constrained in how we can turn our thoughts into communications that others will happily accept. One of the things we worry about is the inference process of other people and in particular how they will judge us.

A way we avoid such problems is by conforming to values, social norms, regulations and other rule sets which people use in their evaluation of us. For this we use an internal censor or conscience which prevents us from using the wrong words and doing the wrong things.

We are also limited by the processing capability of the brain, and when we err in our communication, it is often because we are working in real-time and just do not have the time or ability to work out the best thing to say.

Bias

We all have deep biases which are often programmed into us when we are young, and can include politically incorrect preferences such as racial or gender bias which may be betrayed by the 'devil words' we use. A particular bias we have is between the 'in-group' of family, friends and colleagues and the 'out-groups' of anyone to whom we cannot easily relate.

Even though we may intellectually dislike this bias and attempt to avoid voicing it, it can easily result in subtle changes in our words and actions that may well be detected by those who have been sensitized to such thought.

It is notable that we also have bias about ourselves. Bias *against* ourselves can appear as positive modesty or unhelpful submission. Bias *towards* ourselves may include pride (which can be positive or excessive) and selfishness. Bias towards others (vs. self) may comes from a history of domination or rules that abhor self-promotion.

Implications for changing minds

Note the cognitive constraints and bias that others have that result in them limiting their ability to communicate. Read between the lines to understand the underlying motivators and thinking.

Changing minds and translation

Trying to persuade at this stage is too late. Decisions have been formulated and all you can do is to read the outer signs in order to discern the inner process and intent. This is a difficult and highly skilful activity, but done well will give you enormous advantage.

In terms of positive action in persuasion at this stage, if you can realize early their deep intent, you may be able to respond quickly to prevent them becoming entrenched by public commitment.

Matching formality

When the other person is formal, you may want to build rapport with them by using similar language, at least initially. You may then be able to wean them slowly into greater informality (if this suits you).

Who	Talk	Subtext/comment
Them	It is essential to complete this activity.	Formal language.
You	Indeed, I will complete it today.	Reply using same formality.

Questioning inaccuracy

When the other person says something that seems unclear in any way, for example if it seems distorted or over-simplified, then a simple response is to ask questions to get more accurate information. This process can help the other person understand what they mean.

Who	Talk	Subtext/comment
Them	I went there yesterday.	Incomplete data.
You	Where did you go?	Ask for specific information.

Testing understanding

Another way to help ensure you understand is to reflect back to them what you think they have said, paraphrasing with your own words.

Who	Talk	Subtext/comment
Them	I want a washer.	I need a washing machine.
You	So you want to buy a good washing machine today?	Check that they are not just looking for a washer for a nut.

Challenging bias

When the other person shows bias that you consider to be unfair or undesirable, you can always point this out to them.

Who	Talk	Subtext/comment
Them	Women just don't understand.	I have bias against women.
You	Excuse me, there are ladies present!	Defend the women present.

Hearing intonation and emphasis

Listen carefully to the music of what they say as there is often hidden meaning in the patterns of pitch, volume and other acoustic variation. You can use this to demonstrate a deeper understanding that others might miss and so develop a stronger rapport. A way of doing this is to initially match their pitch and then change direction.

Who	Talk	Subtext/comment
Them	I don't know what to do.	Rising pitch.
You	It's bad, I know. But I can help.	Rising pitch first to show empathy, then descending to calm them down.

Reading body language

As with intonation, body language will tell you a lot about how they are feeling. Watch for clusters and changes that happen in synch with what you and they say. Watch also for them trying to control their body, for example as they hold it still or move jerkily. Legs will often give away information when the upper body is held rigid.

16. State

At any one time we are in some kind of internal mental state which appears in the external attitudes we adopt and the moods into which we fall. Understanding this state is critical to effective persuasion.

In a given state we have a 'frame of mind' which acts as a cluster of mental patterns that act together to form a recognizable entity. In each state our motivators may be different in some way. Models, preferences, and even beliefs and rules may be bent to accommodate how we are thinking at the time. For example when I am in a depressed state, I may belief I am useless, while after winning a race I would likely feel on top of the world and believe I could take on and succeed in any challenge.

Because attitudes change our motivators they also change how we perceive things, how we make decisions and the actions we take. States are consequently very important for persuasion as different methods will work differently according to the varying mental state in which the target person is currently residing. You will therefore need to use differing approaches depending on whether they are happy, sleepy, bored, excited and so on. This also means you need to recognize the state they are in and decide a course of action, which can include waiting until they are in a state that is more conducive to persuasion or nudging them in that direction.

Implications for changing minds

Before you start to change the other person's mind first understand their mental state. Then use appropriate methods that will be most effective with the prevalent motivators. Also change your methods as they change their state.

Attitude

Attitudes are tendencies towards particular ways of behaving that are based on our perceptions and the meaning we create. These in turn is based on our internal motivators, from beliefs to preferences. Any single attitude is hence a state of mind. Rules are particularly important as these govern how we judge others.

We often signal our attitudes to others, helping them to decide how to act towards us, for example where gang members signal their hostility towards others, effectively saying 'stay away or suffer the consequences!' Attitude signals can come from what we say, how we say it, how we dress, our body language and so on. It can be sent in a single, brief glance or in a consistent style of behaving.

We have attitudes towards certain things and people that can be positive or negative and vary in intensity. Attitudes can also vary with context, for example our attitude towards our own children can be very different to attitudes towards other children. We also have preferences for attitudes and we each adopt some more than others.

Attitudes tend to persist over long periods and may be resistant to persuasion (think teenagers!).

Mood

Moods are emotional states that are generally based around a single emotion, such as happiness or anger, but which may include multiple others emotions, such as a depressive state which could include loneliness and boredom as well as sadness.

Moods are generally more persistent than individual emotions which go up and down more easily, but less durable than attitudes. We behave in 'mood-congruent' ways, for example in the way happy people smile and are more outgoing while people who are feeling pensive talk less and dream more.

Implications for changing minds

Understand the attitude and mood and how difficult these are to change. It is often easier to play to these rather than try to change them. Attitudes in particular can take a long time to change.

Temperament

A person's temperament around a particular area encompasses their long-term emotional state and attitude, about which this 'average' other emotions may go up and down. For example a person can have a sunny temperament with a higher than average level of happiness, where very little gets them upset or angry. Another person may be generally depressive with regular introspection and frequent negative moods.

Changing temperament is not easy and may seem impossible. The best you can do in many cases is to slowly shift the average, such as when a person gradually becomes more content across their life.

Emotions

While mental states can encompass many different variables, they are often associated with single emotions, such as happiness, anger, boredom and so on. These emotions tend to bring other emotions and different drives along with them, creating a complete state rather than a simple emotional change. Thus a person who is happy is more likely to believe the world is a fundamentally a good place when compared to when they are angry, when the world may seem threatening or bad.

Entering an emotional state often includes transitioning to a more aroused state, where the person is more alert and connected with the world around them. Many feelings can be seen in non-verbal body language, making this a useful signal to read changing emotional state.

Trance

A trance is a curious state where the person has a distinct focus and where they may ignore significant external stimuli. The idea of trance and hypnosis can be scary and have negative connotation for many people, but it is just another state.   Nevertheless due ethical considerations are appropriate wherever entrancement might occur.

To some extent we are always in some kind of trance as we focus on matters in hand or drift off into daydreaming. When we are musing, thinking internally of what might be, we are typically in quite a deep trance where we do not notice what is going on around is. We also fall into trance as we read stories, watch movies and listen to music.

Triggers

Different mental states are entered when some stimulus or cue triggers a transition from a previous state. Triggers also act to move a person out of a state. We thus flip from state to state either because of the events around us or through our internal musings.

Triggers are sometimes called 'hot buttons' when pressing them leads to emotional arousal. It is important to know what buttons *not* to press as well as which triggers will move the person to the state you are seeking for them.

Triggers can be both external and internal. Hence, while the person may change state based on events around them, such as what you say or do, they may also suddenly change when their musings make them realize something significant.

Triggers can sometimes be read from attitudes, where the potential change in state is indicated in the signals used ('If you do that I will get angry'). Triggers may also be found by discussion ('What do you think about...').

Anchors

Anchors are often familiar thoughts or items which keep a person in a particular state, such as the pleasure of reading a book or the exertions of playing football. It makes sense to anchor yourself in a pleasant state, but we can also become trapped in less comfortable positions, for example where an alcoholic gets stuck in a downward spiral.

Anchors are also important when moving a person to a desired state, in order to prevent them from drifting off elsewhere. Anchoring may be achieved by various means, such as repeating a key phrase, a subtle touch or some other sensory cue that says 'stay where you are'. Releasing anchors to allow further state change may just be 'letting go' or may be effected by a triggering action.

Implications for changing minds

Understand the triggers that move people into and out of states. Find what works best for each person, preferably before the main changing minds activity. Also find how to anchor and otherwise keep the person in an appropriate state before triggering them on to the next state.

Mindset

A simple discovery by Stanford professor Carol Dweck is that there are two ways to think about people and the world. You can take a fixed mindset or a 'growth' mindset. The impact of this choice is huge.

Fixed mindset

When you take a fixed mindset, you assume things are as they are, and cannot be changed. In particular you see people and their attributes this way too. A person's intelligence and general personality (including your own) are seen to be traits, fixed at birth, so there is no point trying to change it.

This mindset leads to classifying people as stupid or smart, friendly or nasty, good or bad. It leads to a view of failure as a bad thing. If you fail at something then there is no point trying to get better.

Children praised as being 'clever' tend to adopt this mindset. 'I am clever' cannot be changed. So they avoid difficult challenges where they may not seem clever.

Growth mindset

The alternative to the fixed mindset is to see things as variable, including personal attributes such as intelligence and skills such as being able to persuade others.

This mindset is hugely empowering. Now failure is an opportunity to learn. Your ability and success is driven by your actions, not fate. An additional benefit is that stress driven by a lack of control decreases.

Children praised for 'working hard' take the growth mindset. Seeing themselves as determined learners, they see the world as their oyster and achieve far more than those praised for cleverness.

Implications for changing minds

The implications for parents and teachers are immediately apparent. Praise effort, not just results. Talk about learning, not failure.

Adults, too, can change how they see the world and themselves. This mindset shift can be facilitated with careful praise, reflecting and encouragement. Mindset is belief, and belief is reality. By changing what you believe, you can change your world.

Hot and cold

Two very distinct states into which we fall are sometimes called 'hot' and 'cold'. We are so different in each of these two states; it is as if we are different people, with different rules, preferences and so on. This makes it very important in changing minds to understand and manage these.

Hot

In the 'hot' state, we are emotionally aroused and are largely driven by basic emotions and subconscious drivers. Short-term satisfaction of needs is critical and we are relatively unthinking in what we do or how we do it.

Persuasion-wise, this is not a good place for rational argument. A hot state can, however, be effective for gaining short-term compliance and emotional enthusiasm. Long-term change attempted here is at risk, and later, cooler reflection may annul any commitments made.

Cold

The 'cold' state is associated with rational thinking and considered decisions using sensible criteria. Choice tends to be slower here but, when made, decisions usually stick. This is a good state for logical persuasive methods and when you want them to carefully consider what you are saying.

Table 16.1. Hot and Cold differences

What	Typical hot	Typical cold
Emotions	Excitement, fear, delight, anger	Satisfaction, contentment
Goals	Satisfy immediate needs, reduce current discomfort, sustain good feelings	Complete task in hand, work towards long-term goals
Rules	Do whatever it takes	Look good to others, obey social rules

---

Implications for changing minds

If you want to get people to accept something in the short-term, get them aroused. For longer-term change cool them down.

State transition

Using triggers, we move from state to state in a sequence of transitions. These changes in state can be mapped using a 'state transition diagram' as in the example of Figure 16.1, where a person contacting a support engineer changes state depending on the response they get. Thicker arrows show easily triggered changes and bigger boxes show greater emotional arousal.

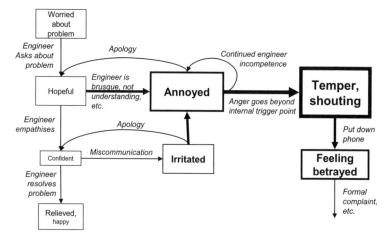

Fig. 16.1. State transition and emotional arousal

Implications for changing minds

This diagramming method can very useful for thinking through how people change state. By mapping out a person's known actions you can learn more about how they think and react.

The method is also useful planning as, if you can literally see where they might go, you can perhaps tread carefully, avoiding unwanted states. You can also plot a desired route, perhaps reaching your goal as soon as possible.

Path dependence

To get from one state to another is not necessarily a simple switch and the fastest route is often via a number of intervening states. The classic sales sequence of Attention, Interest, Desire, Action, for example is actually a set of mental states through which the sales person moves the person on the way to completing the deal rather than leaping directly to closing the deal.

Sometimes there is no alternative in changing minds but to go by the long route, gradually nudging the person one state at a time towards closure. However there may be many potential routes and sometimes a short-cut can be found by an exploratory approach rather than using a fixed formula, as illustrated in Figure 16.2.

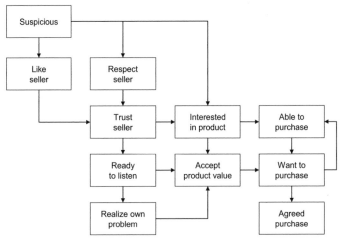

Fig. 16.2. Alternative paths to purchase

Implications for changing minds

Explore the possible paths that you can take, perhaps through early informal conversation. Find how eager or cynical the other person is. Test short-cuts along the way, but be prepared for a long and steady process through what may seem like irrelevant states, but which inexorably lead towards closure.

Changing minds and state

In changing minds it is important to take mental and emotional state into account, either playing to the state as it is (and how it changes) or acting to change it.

Be persuasive

Changing minds is best done from a confident, positive frame of mind in which you can empathize with the other person yet sustain action towards your own goals. You should hence start by moving yourself to an optimal persuasive state.

Think about a time when you were really successful in changing minds. What happened to get you into that state? How did you feel? What did you say to yourself? How did you see the world in general? Step into that state. Feel it. Listen to it. Be it.

State first

People are often more persuadable when they are in a positive state, so it makes sense to use a two-stage process whereby you start by moving them to a positive state and only then get on with the main business of persuading. Hence, for example you might work to cheer up someone who is miserable or distract a person who is being contrary.

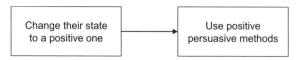

Fig. 16.3 Two-stage persuasion

Who	Talk	Subtext/comment
Them	Oh I've had an awful day.	In negative state.
You	Well now it's time to have fun!	Trigger positive state.
Them	You're right! Let's go out.	Changed to positive state.
You	Sure! Before we go, can I ask you for a little help?	Start target mind-changing.

States, like emotions, are infectious, particularly if you have already bonded with the other person. If you want them to be happy, you be happy. If you want them to be pensive, you should assume this state. If you go first then they are far more likely to follow.

Trigger phrase

Start a sentence with a short phrase before the main question that triggers an internal movement towards or into a desired state. Not being the main part of the sentence, the other person is less likely to consciously notice this phrase, although it still has an effect in moving them into a particular state of mind.

Who	Talk	Subtext/comment
You	Quick question, John, are you ready to start the process?	Hurry them so they do not pause to evaluate what you ask
Them	Yes, of course!	In speeded-up state.
You	Honestly now, what do you think of Jane's work?	Trigger state of truthfulness.
Them	Well, to be truthful, I think she's having difficulty.	Feeling need to tell difficult truths
You	Simple question, could you take over?	Get them thinking in simple, non-evaluative way.
Them	Er, yes of course.	In simple thinking state, not considering the detail

Provocation

Use a sentence that prods the person into an aroused, hot state. This may even be deliberately nonsense as the purpose is to get them into a particular state. Be careful with this as not only might they go into the wrong state but they may also be difficult to manage once they are aroused.

Who	Talk	Subtext/comment
You	I've had enough. I'm leaving.	Extreme reaction.
Them	What!! You can't leave now!	Shocked, angry.
You	Well, if you can't be bothered then I'll go and do it myself.	Give more detail.
Them	Hang on, I didn't mean it like that…	Fear, guilt.

Entrancing

People can be led into a semi-hypnotic and suggestible state by various means, such as boring them with monotonous drivel so they head off into a daydream state. Another method is to introduce a sudden shock that jars them out of their current state and then, as they are relaxing afterwards, encouraging them into an even more relaxed position. They may also be more suggestible in the uncertain position immediately after the shock.

External stimuli can also be entrancing. Music in supermarkets is designed to relax people into a buying state and the 'Gruen Effect', of cognitive envelopment and overload, is often designed into shopping malls in order to lead people into buying more than they might originally have intended. Clubs entrance dancers with alcohol, flashing lights and throbbing music. A man may be entranced simply by beholding a beautiful woman. Religions entrance followers with chanting and prayer.

Changing context

The surrounding context has a significant effect on the state into which people fall. You can change this environment in two ways: by staying in the same place and changing various things there, or changing location by going somewhere completely different.

One way of changing the room is by tidying up and removing distractions so they may focus more easily on you. Perversely, the opposite can also work by providing so many other distractions they only half-listen and are less likely to object to your arguments.

Going somewhere different is helpful when thinking is anchored by the current environment. For example to get people to be more creative it can be a good idea to take them out of their normal work environment, including changing cues such as dress, language and tools.

Part B:
People Together

In Part A, a detailed model of how we think was described. This, however, does not work alone as we are highly social animals and much of our interaction is with one another. This leads to a very tricky situation where one SIFT-3M system is faced with another one.

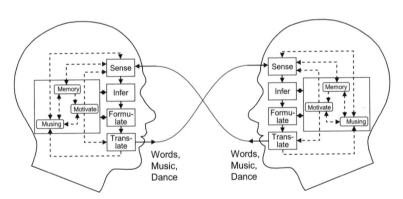

Interacting SIFT-3M systems

If the normal system inside one head is difficult and error-prone enough, then connection between different people is fraught with additional difficulties as people try to understand what others are thinking and to change that process. This gets even worse when groups of people interact together. It is perhaps amazing that we ever understand one another!

17. Relationships

Understanding individuals is difficult enough, but changing minds happens *between* people. When people communicate with one another, there is a constant stream of expression and interpretation (and, quite often, misinterpretation). We do make sufficient sense of what other people say and hence establish cognitive connection with them. Through this communication, we form relationships with others, bonding into liking and friendship with some, while avoiding or keeping a cautious distance from those we dislike or mistrust.

Theory of mind

In inferring the meaning from what someone else says and does, as well as in formulating how we will respond, we need some kind of understanding of that person. We hence develop a 'theory of mind', guessing what they are thinking and how they might react to what we say and do.

Implications for changing minds

When you seek to change someone else's mind, think about the theory of mind you hold about them. This may be significantly inaccurate, leading to ineffective persuasive efforts. The same applies in the reverse direction and if you find others treating you unfairly or with distrust, it may be based on their theory of mind about you.

Manage your own theories of mind by developing a rich set of principles based on a real understanding, then applying them flexibly, checking what works and adjusting accordingly. Manage the theories of mind of others either by fitting in with classic stereotypes or by deliberately and consistently breaking the classification they have applied to you, helping them build a more effective model.

The first few seconds

First impressions are terribly important. When we first meet other people, we quickly classify them as we match them up against the set of stereotypes and models we have. Then, once we have put them in a box with a nice clear label, if they ever try to climb out by acting in a way that does not conform with the label on their box, then we are increasingly inclined to push them back in. Of course they are also doing the same with us and, while focusing on judging them, we may find ourselves judged even more harshly.

As with other thinking, we use simplified models in our theories of mind which are not always a good representation of other people and can hinder our relationships with them. How good our understanding of them *really* is will be based both on the complexity of the models we use and our ability to classify them into the right model. If I have only a few simplified stereotypes that I use with little thought, then my classifications will be wildly inaccurate and my communications poor.

Implications for changing minds

Be very careful in the first few seconds. Deliberately send signals that say '*This* is what I am' to help them classify you in the way that you want. Also be careful about your own classifying of others. People are complex and it is very easy to get this wrong.

Reciprocity

The basis of any relationship is that each person gives things to the other and gets things back in exchange. Overall, this ends up in an equitable and dynamic balance as we give and take in due proportion.

There are strict social rules around reciprocity that obliges repayment of the help we give others. This also acts at the emotional level and if I give you a smile, you will likely feel obliged to smile back.

Implications for changing minds

Give in order to get. Give something to them that they appreciate then ask for what you want. Do not over-do the giving as this invokes annoyance when others owe you significant amounts.

Respect

Listen to youth culture and you may find the word 'respect' crops up surprisingly often, perhaps reflecting their desire for it. A basic human respect and acceptance of the other person and their rights is critical to any successful relationship.

The opposite of respect is contempt, which is one of the biggest predictors of any relationship breaking up. Where one person treats the other with contempt, even in a small way, any current friendship will likely erode.

Trust

Trust is the cornerstone on which relationships are built and which allows for delayed reciprocity and exposed vulnerabilities. If we trust someone, we do not have to check up on them or watch our backs. We know that they will keep their promises and will repay their debts.

When trust is given and then betrayed, the resultant backlash can quickly turn friendship into hatred and enmity. Trust is so important that it has a chapter in this book all to itself (Chapter 21).

Bonding

When a person likes another person sufficiently they will form an emotional attachment to them, such that the other person becomes an extended part of their identity. Respect and trust are tied closely to bonding, both leading to it and increasing further when the bond is created.

Note that this bonding need not be mutual, for example where a person attaches themselves to a leader or celebrity. Once formed, a bond tends to be broken only reluctantly. Bonding can lead to adulation and unquestioned obedience, even to the point of self-destructive actions.

Implications for changing minds

Respect others and show trustworthiness, seeking to create a bond between them and you. When they do this they will question your motives far less and easily accept what you say as truth.

Friendship

Friendship is a state of mutual admiration and support that includes a higher level of respect, trust and bonding than is experienced with other acquaintances. This state does not happen suddenly and Table 17.1 shows common stages we go through in the dance of revelation as we gradually trust and tell more on the road to friendship.

Table 17.1. Stages of Friendship

Stage	Detail
Orientation	Initial physical evaluation and stereotyping. Play safe with small talk and following social rules.
Exploration	Each steadily reveal more personal information. Build richer model beyond stereotype.
Affective	Talk more about private and personal matters. Compare values, beliefs, attitudes, etc.
Stable	Mutual understanding and sharing. Deeper trust and delayed reciprocity.

Friendship develops differently for each of us and may be experienced at different levels of intensity. We also seek different things from friendship, from short-term companionship to longer-term partnership. Whatever friendship is to us, there are some further factors beyond respect and trust that lead to friendship, as noted in Table 17.2.

Table 17.2. Factors which lead to friendship

Factor	Detail
Similarity	We like people who are like us in some way, from social background to having similar attitudes (in practice, opposites seldom attract).
Proximity	We grow to like people we see often (more so than 'familiarity breeding contempt').
Reciprocity	We like people who like us and dislike those who dislike us. We also share with those who share with us.
Appearance	We admire beautiful people, but our friends will be of similar attractiveness to us and wear similar clothes.
Competence	We like people who are good at what they do, but we do not like people who make us feel stupid.
Shared experience	We like people with whom we have 'been through the mill' together, sharing difficult experiences.
Knowledge	Just knowing more about the person makes most people seem more human and likable.

Love

Love is a much-misunderstood word that gets associated with romance and sex, but has a much wider scale. Psychologist Gerald Sternberg identified three components that lead to seven types of love:

- *Intimacy*: Closeness to, and liking of, the other person.
- *Passion*: Intense longing and arousal.
- *Commitment*: Readiness to do anything for the other person.

As Table 17.3 indicates, there are many forms of love, extending from simple friendship to the deep affection of lifelong partners.

Table 17.3. Types of love

Type of love	Intimacy	Passion	Commitment
Liking	X		
Infatuation		X	
Empty			X
Romantic	X	X	
Companionate	X		X
Fatuous		X	X
Consummate	X	X	X

Breaking up

Relationships and friendship do not necessarily last for ever nor do they remain at the same level of intensity. Love relationships typically settle down after at most a couple of years and friends may come and go with the cycles of life.

Relationships are a process of discovery about the other person, and initial ideals in the 'honeymoon' period may be shattered as the everyday humanity of the other person is exposed. Breaking up also happens when there is some form of betrayal, where one person breaks a promise or social rules are transgressed.

Implications for changing minds

Relationships are fragile things. If you want to sustain friendship while changing minds, you must consider the longer-term effects of your persuasion.

Conflict

When a relationship breaks down, then methods of peaceful and rational persuasion may not seem possible. When people fall out, they may enter a state of conflict in which they seek to coerce one another by forceful means. This is not changing minds.

There is a role for a persuader who stands between people in conflict and who may bring them to their senses by intermediary action. International peacekeeper William Ury has identified ten roles that this person may take, as described in Table 17.4.

Table 17.4. Ury's roles for the person in the middle

Conflict cause	Role	Action
Scarce resources	Provider	Help both get what they need.
Only know fighting	Teacher	Show each how to handle differences.
Separated by deep divide	Bridge-builder	Connect them so they may better understand one another.
Differing interests	Mediator	Bring them to the table. Represent each to the other.
Disputed rights	Arbiter	Be a fair judge who selects solution.
Unequal power	Equalizer	Defend the weak. Persuade aggressor to seek peace.
Injured relationships	Healer	Soothe hurt. Calm emotions.
Hidden atrocities	Witness	See and expose what is happening.
Fighting without rules	Referee	Set and police the rules.
Vulnerable being hurt	Peacekeeper	Separate warring parties. Provide safety for victims.

Implications for changing minds

Do not seek to persuade by force. When others seek to coerce you, describe what they are doing and refuse to play their game.

Where you can, use your persuasive ability to help others who are in conflict with one another.

Power

Power is the capability we have to achieve our goals, and it can take many different forms, as indicated in Table 17.5. In persuasion, it allows us to influence other people, convincing them to act in requested ways.

Table 17.5. Power

Source	Description	To increase power
Ownership	What I own I can control	Acquire personal ownership through purchase or exchange.
Position	Authority from job to direct others	Get promoted to positions of authority. Build your empire.
Gatekeeping	Ability to block access	Get to a position of control. Trade access for other forms of power.
Knowledge	What I do with what I know	Acquire and protect information. Give it out sparingly.
Skill	What I can do that you cannot	Constantly learn. Develop skills that others do not have.
Obligation	What you feel obliged to do for me	Do other people favours. Remind them of their obligations.
Trust	What I can ask of you because you trust me	Be trustworthy. Keep your promises and actively care for others.
Self	I can always choose my own actions	Remember your own ability to say no and choose your own path.

Power may take a considerable period to develop and may decrease over time if it is not sustained. It can be attractive as people seek the protection of the powerful. Excessive power, or power abused, causes fear and can lead to covert action to contain and drain it.

Implications for changing minds

Build your power. Use power to get more power. Conserve it carefully and use it sparingly. Let others see only enough of your power that they find you attractive and do not fear you unnecessarily. When you do use your power, make it count.

Games

In our interactions with others we often fall into ritualized patterns of behaving that have more to do with games that have strict rules than thoughtful and independent action. From simple greetings to complex and dysfunctional obsessions, we are regularly ensnared by internal and external rules and gameplay, for example as in Table 17.6.

Table 17.6. Some games we play

Game	Description	Why
Poor Me	Tell sob story. Make excuses.	Get sympathy. Avoid responsibility.
Drama Triangle	Aggressor attacks Victim. Rescuer saves Victim (and in doing so may become an Aggressor…)	Aggressor: feel powerful; Victim: feel hope, relief; Rescuer: feel superior, get thanks
Chase Me	A approaches B a little. B approaches A. A retreats. B retreats a little. (endlessly repeat)	'Thrill of the chase'. Win partner (this is the basis of much romantic activity).
Blame Game	Transfer responsibility and fault to others.	Feel superior. Avoid guilt.
Stop Me	A harms self. B tries to stop A.	A: Sense of control. B: Selfless righteousness
Got You	A traps and punishes B. B plays Poor Me or invokes Drama Triangle.	Righteous superiority.

Theory of mind appears strongly in the games we play with others as we try to second-guess what they will think and do. Ritualized games allow us to get this right more often as we invite and entrap them in defined sequences.

Implications for changing minds

Spot the invitations to play and do so only with conscious care. You can also use ritual patterns to trigger responses that lead others to think and act in ways that support your cause.

Communication and changing minds

When we talk with others there are many opportunities for changing minds (in fact some would say that is all we do). We communicate through language, which is a rich source of both misunderstanding and subtle persuasion. Here are some more methods you can use.

Sensory language

Sensory language uses words that evoke the five senses, making what is said appear immediate and realistic. It uses words like *see, hear* and *feel* to paint sensory scenes and hook the other person into a vicarious experience of what is being explained.

> It feels good to be here today and thank you for asking me to speak. As I look out across the order in this room and listen to the traffic outside I am reminded of the silence of the darkest jungles of Peru, where the scent of wild orchids suffuses the damp nights and distant drums warn of an ever-present peril.

Outcome language

Outcome-oriented talk connects with the needs and goals of the audience, appealing to such as deep needs for safety and higher needs for esteem, as well as connecting with the things they need to achieve in daily life.

> I know you are busy and need to go home soon, and I will take just five minutes of your time, after which I will remain for those who want to discuss this further. Let me ask you something now – will you be carrying a computer home with you tonight? Does the fact that people walk out of here every day with confidential data in their backpacks worry you?

Temporal language

Temporal language positions things carefully in time, using the past for what is finished, the future for what will be and the present for what is, now. With care you can leverage differences such as between the perfect tense (things completed) and imperfect (may still be open), or the dynamics of motion through time versus bringing things to a sudden halt.

> Now that you have done the things that needed doing and are working on what will be needed next, I want you to stop and think what you want now, this minute.

Their language

Listen carefully to the language that they use. Hear the common words they use (we all have them). Listen to the formality, the jargon, the speed and intonation. Then reflect this back to other person. You can even use their body language. Do not copy them like a parrot, but do match them subtly in what they say and how they say it.

> Them: Yeah, well you know I like to kick around on a Saturday night, see what's goin' down.
>
> You: Cool. So what'yer doin' t'morrow? Wanna hang around down the Roxy, like?

Enhancement

Nouns and verbs tell us what is happening to what. With the addition of adjectives and adverbs, we can enhance the meaning created. Thus 'house' can become 'beautiful house' and 'running' becomes 'desperately running'. Enhancement can also continue through further phraseology and devices such as metaphor and irony.

Do be careful when enhancing not to over do it. 'Purple prose' is the name given to overly florid language where meaning is obscured by decoration.

> Like a drunken elephant on an oscillating see-saw, he slowly wove his way down the street, desperately trying to maintain an impossible balance.

Storytelling

Storytelling creates a narrative that people find easy to appreciate and associate with their selves. Stories have characters that develop across a plot. They use various devices to hook you in and keep you interested.

> I knew a man once who, like you, was looking for love. He felt empty and anxious and tripped over himself as he tried to please. Until one night when he met Sarah. She was beautiful and had the biggest blue eyes you ever saw and when their eyes met something happened inside him.
>
> Can you imagine that? That's right, because when you meet the right person you know the right thing to say, just as you do with your best friends. What would you say now if you met your Sarah?

Focus

When you talk about many things, it can be easy for the other person to get lost in the jumble of ideas and models you put forward. On the other hand, using a sharp focus you can keep things simple for them and hammer home your argument, one clear point at a time.

> Now although this system does many things, I am going to talk first about sound quality, because that is what you want and because this system produces such a crystal clear sound it would make an angel cry. The sound stage is ethereal and the bass will shake the walls.

Emphasis

When you emphasize the things you say, you are effectively saying 'this is the important bit'. Emphasis highlights words and short phrases that may even connect together to give a subtle additional message.

Emphasis can also be added with body language, marking out important elements with movement and gesture.

> If you *buy* this *now*, I will give you another *10% discount*. Think about how *envious* your friends will be. I can see you *want* it. Do you want to *take* it?

Jargon

'Jargon' is the use of specialist and technical terms that enables abbreviated conversation between experts. Using jargon with non-experts will often confuse and annoy them, which is seldom of benefit. However, if you use an *occasional* jargon word, it will send a signal that you are more expert than them and hence they should unquestionably trust what you say. A quick explanation afterwards is usually enough to cool any ruffled feathers.

> The results show a bimodal distribution, with these two peaks that indicate there are two things we need to worry about.

A similar effect can be gained by using obscure words that demonstrate your expertise with the language. A large lexicon signals both linguistic dexterity and underlying intelligence that perhaps warn that an attempt at argument is likely to result in failure.

> That does rather obfuscate the matter. When things are not clear, customers will probably go elsewhere.

Distortion

Language is often used to distort the communication by consciously or subconsciously giving different degrees of attention to different things, for example:

- Exaggerating what is intended to ensure it gets noticed.
- Modestly downplaying a success.
- Overlooking the faults of friends.
- Leaving out things which may cause embarrassment.
- Framing failure in the past tense.

Vague language

When you speak in unspecified generalities, the other person will seek to create the unclear meaning, trying to complete what you say. In doing this, they will frame what you say in their own experiences and even put themselves into the empty frame of a person who is not named.

The last person who said things like that found that it had an unexpected, yet strangely pleasant effect.

18. Groups

When pairs of people get together, then the complexity of the individual is multiplied by the dimension of relationship. When more than two people connect, then the complexity multiplies further.

We crave group membership. Our need for a sense of belonging and to achieve recognition and esteem drives us to seek out and join groups, even at the expense of sacrificing some of our independence. Once accepted by them, our group work is just begun as we then seek to fit in, acquire power over others and boost our status.

We each belong to many groups, such as family, work teams and social circles as well as groups based around general characteristics such as nationality, ethnicity, religion, age, ability and so on. Membership of these can confer advantage and disadvantage, and we may consequently seek to change the groups to which we belong.

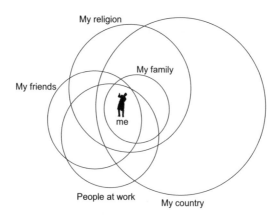

Fig. 18.1. We belong to multiple, overlapping groups

Boundaries

Groups have boundaries and whether you are in the group or outside the group makes a great deal of difference as to how you are treated by group members. Within the group, you are an 'in-group' colleague and are given significant levels of trust. If you are an 'out-group' person then you will always be viewed with a certain suspicion. The boundaries of the group are often well-guarded and any interloper is treated with caution or hostility and may be ejected or refused entry.

People in other groups help define our group. In being like others in our group, we are, by social definition, unlike those in other groups. Language supports this difference when we talk about 'us' and 'them', or 'we' and 'they'. In a word we separate our group from all others.

Other groups are also defined by boundaries, although our definition of their boundaries are often far less complex than their own. Hence we create stereotypes as simplified classifications. When groups fall into conflict, differences often become exaggerated.

Joining

Joining a group may simply be a matter of having the right personal attributes, such as age or country of birth. It may also be a serious choice and involve petition, acceptance and significant ritual. To join a company may need multiple interviews to determine your cultural suitability as well as your professional ability. Street gangs set recruits challenging and often law-breaking tasks to test their commitment and to lock them in.

Once accepted, there may be further induction and a trial period in which the new recruit is on notice of ejection if they do not meet required standards.

Implications for changing minds

Join or demonstrate membership of a group to which your target audience belongs. Show you have things in common and demonstrate your commitment. Understand and follow rituals. Then evoke the principles of trust, attention and obligation that group members owe to one another to change their minds (though do be careful not to attack group norms).

Team development

When a person is faced with joining a work team, they typically have a host of concerns in balancing personal and group objectives. While they want to satisfy basic needs and meet personal goals, they also need to fit in and contribute to the success of the team.

The first stage of forming a new group is hence very tentative and exploratory, with people seeking to understand others and how their needs, values and goals may be met. This then falls into the storms of conflict as people jostle for position and argue about group values and goals. Eventually the group norms become established and people find acceptable roles where they can function and perform effectively as a team.

Beyond this basic 'form-storm-norm-perform' pattern, other effects can occur, as in Figure 18.2. When teams fall into conflict, they 'deform' which may require the team to be re-formed, either through strong leadership or by a change in team membership. When the team comes to a natural end, people may suffer from genuine 'mourning' feelings when they leave.

Some teams avoid deforming and go beyond basic performing into a highly productive 'high performance' state. These teams are typified by intense internal focus both on team success and on a stretching challenge they have taken on.

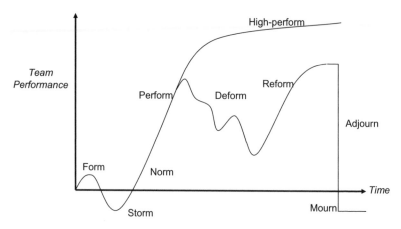

Fig. 18.2. Patterns of team formation and development

Staying

It is one thing to join a group and it is another to be successful within it. Remaining as a member first requires that group rules are obeyed, for example in supporting others and obeying leaders.

Groups often have a hierarchy of seniority with formal and informal roles and positions that demand increasing respect. Working one's way up the hierarchy to achieve greater status is an important activity for many. In a 'survival of the fittest' evolutionary scenario, those who achieve higher status get more choice in partners and greater chance of creating a hereditary legacy.

Physical challenges for position are rare in modern society although status in the group is typically achieved through useful expertise or social skills. Networking is a typical skill where a person has a wide range of contacts and friends they can call on in times of need, paying for this benefit by helping others who one day may need their help.

Leaving

Leaving a group happens in two ways: you either leave voluntarily or you are thrown out. Voluntary departure of a popular person may be accompanied by pleas to stay and rituals of departure including gift-giving and partying.

Being ejected from the group is an entirely different procedure and is something akin to a body's immune reaction. The unfortunate person may feel an increasing sense of isolation beforehand as the group ostracizes and emotionally sidelines them. They may be talked about behind their back and avoided as it is realized that they are not welcome. Some people will take the hint and leave, while others may need a more direct approach. Termination may also be a quicker affair, for example when a person transgresses critical group rules and is peremptorily ousted.

Implications for changing minds

Build your position in the group by networking and helping others. Demonstrate your value. If you meet stubborn opposition in your goals, the greatest power you can marshal against your detractors is your ability to get them sidelined or ejected from the group.

Roles

In a group of people, individuals may fall into one or more different action roles, depending on their own skills and preferences as well as opportunity and need within the group.

A brief summary of typical team roles are shown in Table 18.1. Remember that, as with other systems, these indicate preferences and tendencies whereby individuals can often function happily in more than one role. It is worth noting that in any such role a person may be helpful for the group but can also over-do the role such that it causes difficulty and decreases the chance of the team meeting its goals.

Table 18.1. Typical team roles

Role	Description	Implications
Driver	Seeks to lead people towards achievable challenges. Focuses on movement and direction.	Align them with you or be the driver yourself. Work together to move others in the right direction.
Builder	Seeks to create order and predictability. Designs and builds structure.	Work with them to help build a clear organization, but beware of it becoming unwieldy and over-controlling.
Socializer	Focuses on trust, relationships and harmony within the team. Listens and nurtures.	Use them especially in team building and maintenance. Beware of excessive focus on agreement paralyzing the team.
Researcher	Searches for new information. Analyses and experiments. Focuses on truth and learning.	Use them to help fact-based decisions. Beware of information for information's sake.
Thinker	Innovates, solves problems and brings in new ideas. Challenges current thinking.	Use them to stimulate thinking, but ensure you do not get stuck in the ideas stage.
Doer	Puts ideas into action and gets them done. Focuses on measurable results.	They are the workhorses of teams. Ensure they stay motivated and working on the right things.
Fighter	Defends group rules. Fights intruders and builds power of group vs. others.	Give them something to fight for and against. Beware of them opposing important change.

Group operation

As groups establish themselves, a number of other processes become established that enable the people to handle the standard types of situation that they may face. These include:

- *Rule-making*: One of the first things teams do is to establish rules for one another about how to behave and how not to behave. If this rule-making is not done deliberately, it will happen through informal conversation and effective punishments and rewards.
- *Communication*: Patterns of communication form within teams to share information, whether it is formal briefings or through individuals who acquire information-sharing roles.
- *Boundary management*: Rules and processes will exist as to how the group manages its boundary with the rest of the world. This includes how they interact with other groups, how they handle visitors and people who try to join the group.
- *Decision-making*: Groups decide in many ways, from long debates to structured meetings. Decisions may require consensus, where one dissenter can veto a decision, or autonomous action may be possible.
- *Conflict-handling*: Conflict within the group may be avoided, handled quietly or subject to open and vigorous debate.
- *Punishment and reward*: Groups motivate their members largely through attention and the harshest punishment for any group member is to be ignored or excluded. Rewards may also be in the form of being given desirable tasks and having access to resources.

Implications for changing minds

Take a leading role in building and managing group processes, whether this happens formally or informally. Be vigilant about the rules being broken or changed and why this is so, and respond appropriately.

Linkages

Groups become even more complex when you take into consideration the internal and external linkage between individuals, as illustrated in Fig. 18.3. These connections, which may be friendships or professional relationships, are *trust connections* which reduce transaction costs (the effort in any exchange) and increase the ability to communicate with and convince others.

Cohesion is the extent to which a group is strongly interconnected within the group and a highly cohesive group works well together on common goals. *Coupling*, on the other hand, is the extent of connections outside the team. There may be natural cohesion and coupling levels in business teams, for example in the high cohesion of design teams and high coupling of the sales teams.

Other team roles relating to connections include *gatekeepers* who are the sole connection with groups, *hubs* who connect with many others and *spiders* who sit in a control position the middle of a group. Groups may also have an 'inner circle' of persistent trust, where critical policies and decisions for the group are made by a select few, and outer circles of loose associates whose dedicated commitment is less critical.

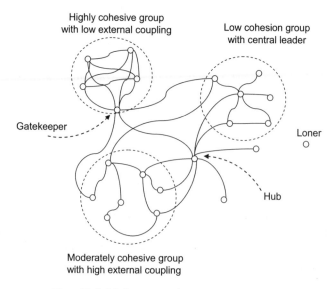

Fig. 18.3 Linkage and network patterns

Networking

Networking, while it has always been important, has become particularly important in recent years with dynamic, distributed global organizations and a lack of stability in organizations and jobs. Networking is also very important for sales people and independent people who need a good network in order to find new work. Hub roles within a social network include the following:

- *Collectors* gather information and keep it to themselves, using it sparingly and carefully.
- *Consultants* gather information but are ready to share it and are often the 'go to' person for many others.
- *Broadcasters* redistribute information they acquire to a wide number of other people.
- *Channelers* send what they learn to target people who may be interested in this information.
- *Introducers* do a lot of connecting other people together, increasing the density of the network.
- *Intermediaries* who act as 'go-betweens' without people who are interacting

The connection between people may be strong, with high levels of trust and obligation. Weaker ties through 'friends of friends' or even more distant connections can be surprisingly useful. An interesting discovery by researcher Mark Granovetter was that people looking for jobs were more successful by tapping these weaker connections. A lesson from this is that a close group of friends mostly just know one another and for new information you need to expand into the wider network.

A remarkable experiment by Stanley Milgram (which has been reproduced on the internet) showed the power of networks in that, on average, you can get to anyone in the world via six connection 'hops'.

Implications for changing minds

Work on your network constantly, seeking in particular powerful hubs who can help you. Contribute also as you can, building a wide obligation and a reputation as a person worth helping.

Spreading ideas

When new ideas or products are introduced to people within a group, these are often viewed with suspicion as they could disturb group harmony. Individuals therefore worry about criticism and about being ostracized. They also may be concerned about the cost and effort involved in changes.

A model derived from anthropology and often used in marketing is the 'diffusion of innovations' curve, as in Figure 18.4, which shows how different groups of people have different preferences around new things.

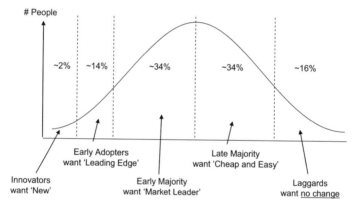

Fig. 18.4. Diffusion of innovations

Innovators are easy to get involved because they like anything new. They are also useful for getting Early Adopters engaged. These are the first test as they seek real value and are always open to persuasion.

The most difficult stage is in developing the Early Majority, who tend to view ideas and products used by Early Adopters as unproven and hazardous. This is often best overcome by a 'divide and conquer' approach, winning over one small group at a time and vigorously publicizing successes until things take off (typically when about 25% or so of the total population is converted).

The Late Majority will come along in time, once they are convinced that things are as cheap, easy and as risk-free as possible. Laggards can be problematic, and are best ignored (if possible), otherwise a coercive approach may be necessary.

Management and Leadership

Teams and organizations often have managers who provide the control and have responsibility for getting results by telling their subordinates what to do to achieve these. Organizations also need leaders who have visionary views of the future and inspire people to follow them. Table 18.2 shows the difference between managing and leading.

Table 18.2. Leadership vs. Management

Subject	Leader	Manager
Essence	Change	Stability
Focus	Leading people	Managing work
Have	Followers	Subordinates
Horizon	Long-term	Short-term
Seeks	Vision	Objectives
Approach	Sets direction	Plans detail
Decision	Facilitates	Makes
Power	Personal charisma	Formal authority
Appeal to	Heart	Head
Energy	Passion	Control
Dynamic	Proactive	Reactive
Persuasion	Sell	Tell
Style	Transformational	Transactional
Exchange	Excitement for work	Money for work
Likes	Striving	Action
Wants	Achievement	Results
Risk	Takes	Minimizes
Rules	Breaks	Makes
Conflict	Uses	Avoids
Direction	New roads	Existing roads
Truth	Seeks	Establishes
Concern	What is right	Being right
Credit	Gives	Takes
Blame	Takes	Blames

If a group does not have a leader, then they will often find one from within (this happens in the 'storming' phase). Groups may have unrealistic fantasies that their leader will rescue them and keep them safe. Leaders who fail in this impossible task may be vilified and rejected and another leader sought.

Changing groups

Groups are a lot harder to change than individuals as each person may worry about being ostracized or ejected if they break the unwritten group rules. Leaders in the group can be particularly problematic as they have achieved their position and gathered their power through the status quo of the current system. Any revisions of the system may threaten their position and hence they may well vigorously oppose any change.

Social leaders

Social leaders are people who others look up to and who have unofficial positions of influence within groups. You can tell them because whenever something questionable is proposed, people will look at the social leader or say they want to talk with them first.

If you focus your attention on getting these people bought in to your proposals then they will be your friends in converting other people to your cause.

An approach by some commercial companies that sell fashion items is to give free products to social leaders, based on the premise that this demonstrates the clothes as being 'cool'.

Diffusion management

Ideas and ways of behaving 'diffuse' through groups and large populations as individuals tell one another about ideas and see the successes of people who act in new ways.

The trick here is to understand the different needs of each group, from Innovators and Early Adopters to Laggards and address these differently. Overall, adoption of ideas, products or actions in any group can be speeded by ensuring that:

- They have high relative economic or social advantage.
- They are compatible with current motivators or previous methods and systems.
- They are not difficult to understand and use.
- They are easy to try out.
- Their benefits can easily be observed.

Join the team

The best way to change groups is often from the inside, so indicate you are a linked to others by highlighting similarity or joining as a *bone fide* member, then use the established communication channels such as email distribution lists, newsletters and meetings to spread your message and change minds. It also helps to make friends and form alliances, particularly where there are factions and people with different views and who may hence oppose you.

Gossip and grapevine

A common way that thoughts spread through a group is via informal conversations at the water-cooler and other gathering spots.

A neat trick is not to actually say anything is detail, but to leave as much as possible to the imagination. This can help avoid you appearing as a trouble-maker. In any case their vivid imagination will be much more effective than your limited words.

Burning platforms

One way to move a group of people is to make it impossible for them to stay where they are. A person standing on a burning platform will jump, preferring probable death to certain death. Likewise when it is certain that the status quo cannot be sustained then people will be forced to change.

Create a crisis. Declare a state of emergency. Make a mountain out of a molehill. Make denial and the sticking of heads in the sand difficult or impossible.

Vision

The counterpoint to the burning platform is the attractive vision that excites and motivates people to want to achieve it. A vision is a *motivating view of the future*. To motivate, it must be memorable and to be memorable it must be short. To make it more realistic, it may be phrased in the present tense and should be specific. 'Rule the world' visions are both clichéd and common. For example:

We are the destination company for top MBAs.

This deliberately provokes the question, Why? The answer is because MBAs seek successful companies where they will continue learning.

Plant

Have a person who is a plant (ally, collaborator, spy, etc.) within the group who can give you information and support your cause within group settings. This works best when their friendship with you is not known to others in the group. They may even speak against you at times to conceal their sympathy, but on balance and in critical situations will help you achieve your aims.

Common enemy

If there is one thing that unites a group of people, it is a common enemy who threatens to break them up, harm them or otherwise disrupt their way of existence or break their beliefs and values.

It is generally not a good idea to be that enemy, although it can be done if you do not mind being the 'bad guy' and have someone else who can rescue the group and lead them to safety.

New manager

Appoint a tough new manager who has a brief to make the change happen. Without established relationships, they will find it easier to force changes. Likewise in the reverse direction, people may well be less inclined to feel betrayed by someone with who they have built up the social capital of trust and obligation.

Leadership

Even better than internal influence, the best way to change a group is to take charge. When you are the leader, you may well have the power to change the rules. Leaders who do this are either brought in for the purpose, for example in business restructuring, or creep up the hierarchy in effective disguise only to show their true intent when they reach the top (Mikhail Gorbachev in Soviet Russia comes to mind here).

Leaders cannot do whatever they like as followership is a voluntary position. Subordinates do as they are told, but followers buy into your vision and into your charismatic personality. Paradoxically, leaders must follow their followers and be careful not to lead where nobody will follow.

Part C:
The Core Process
for Changing Minds

So far we have been looking at minds and how they work. Now we get to the heart of changing minds, bringing it all together into the underlying pattern found in all methods of influence and persuasion.

In some senses, this is the holy grail of changing minds, the unified theory that brings together all other systems. Of course it is neither magic nor religion, but it does provide a basis for understanding changing minds as a single discipline.

This model differs from other methods in that it has a critical focus on visceral feelings. You *experience* trust, tension, closure and commitment as felt emotions and persuasion has a great deal to do with managing these feelings. Of course there are cognitive and active elements, but if you can manage how others feel, then you can change their minds.

19. The Core Process

Many jobs, as noted earlier, have changing minds as their core discipline. Whether you work in sales, negotiation, education or a host of other fields, your job may well be largely based around getting other people to think, feel, believe or act differently. Each discipline has its own set of knowledge on how minds may be changed, and each is a treasure trove that both confirms the core principles and adds individual nuggets of wisdom that are equally applicable in other areas.

The Core Process model for changing minds is based on cross-disciplinary research that seeks commonality and extracts those core principles that form the underlying pattern of all persuasive techniques. The basic process is shown in Figure 19.1 and elaborated in following sections and chapters.

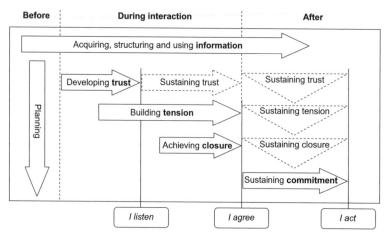

Fig. 19.1. The Core Process for changing minds

Information Management

The first and overarching element of the Core Process for changing minds is the management of information, starting before you meet the other person and continuing through and following all interactions. Changing minds requires communication, and good communication requires good information.

Information is power, which includes the ability to delight, surprise and satisfy the other person. It means understanding how they think and being able to expose any deceptive tricks they may play on you. It enables you to set realistic prices and make valued concessions.

Some information is more powerful, and digging for details, though tedious, can bear sweet fruit. Other information can be made more powerful and its value increased through proving its truth or combining it with complementary data.

The bottom line about information is to seek it out, organize it and use it with care for maximum effect. Chapter 20 elaborates on this and shows you the detail of how to manage your information.

Trust

From the moment you meet the other person, and often from some time before, one of the uppermost questions in their minds (and likely yours, too) is 'Can I trust this person?'

Trust is the lubricant of relationships and without it they grind to a halt. If I trust you I will listen to you and accept your proposals as honest and trustworthy suggestions. If I do not trust you then you will persuade me of nothing.

In persuasion there needs to be sufficient up-front trust-building to open the gate to realistic and credible exchanges. This can be seen in simple rituals, such as greetings, that signal a shared understanding of social conventions.

Once the conversation has started, trust continues and increases in importance, as any sign of dishonesty, unreliability or other betrayal of trust can result in a collapse in the relationship, with minds that head in the opposite direction to the desired change.

The bottom line about trust is to build and nurture it, because it is easily lost. The subject of trust is extended and developed in Chapter 21, where methods of building trust are explained.

Tension

Although all other parts of the model are important, the heart of the Core Process is in the building and management of tension.

Tension is felt emotionally as an arousing internal pressure. This can be negative, such as the tensions of fear or anger. It may also be more positive, such as in the tension of excitement or desire.

Retail selling is the classic tension-building discipline, with the sales person piling on the pressure of reasons to buy now and carefully handling the internal tensions of 'objections'. Other disciplines, from teaching to storytelling also make significant use of tension.

Tension can be dysfunctional when our bodies become unable to cope with the endless internal stress we experience in the modern world. If we do not manage our own tension then we may experience an emotional breakdown, with a weakened immune system and consequent further illnesses.

The bottom line for tension is to know its effects and hence to make good use of it. Tension is discussed in more detail in Chapter 22.

Closure

The other side of tension occurs where the tense bowstring is released and emotions snap into the released state of closure. In changing minds, closure is the "Aha!" of realization of a lesson learned. It is choosing to follow the leader. It is the decision to buy. After the discomfort of indecision, it is often a blessed relief.

Note that closure is something the target person does, not something that is done to them. Although sales people use 'closing techniques', personal closure is an internal process.

In contrast to developing trust and the long, slow build-up of tension, closure is often a sudden change. This may even be accompanied by involuntary outbursts and physical changes, which can be useful signals for the alert observer.

Closure usually feels good as the brain rewards us for relieving the tension with a shot of the body's natural opiates. When you close you may feel excited, pleased, grateful or comforted.

A key in managing closure is to see it happen rather than keep pushing. Closure is described in more detail in Chapter 23.

Commitment

In a number of situations when you are changing minds, reaching closure is the end of the road. Getting a single decision or 'aha' is all that is needed and no further interest goes beyond this point. In many other cases, the initial closure is just the first step on a longer journey, in which the maintenance of that closure is a significant issue.

For example, in business sales, initial closure may simply be intent to purchase, with the signing of the contract after further discussions. Between the agreement and action, there may be many opportunities for the enthusiasm of the initial agreement to wane.

Even in one-off retail sales, the 'buyer's remorse' of a customer who later regrets their purchase is not a good advertisement for repeat sales and recommendations. Customer post-sale perceptions are often important enough to warrant continued efforts to assure their loyalty.

Changing minds and the Core Process

This Core Process is different from other methods of persuasion in the way it focuses on how people are feeling. To be successful in using it you need two abilities. First, by using the methods in this book, you should be able to invoke trust, tension, closure and commitment. The second skill can be more difficult, as it is to know when you have been effective by reading those emotions. If you have limited empathy this requires closely observing and understanding of body language.

It can also help in developing skills to explore a wide range of persuasion disciplines. The Core Process is useful here as a lens to help understand the underlying common patterns used in such diverse situations as teaching, storytelling and selling.

Skills come in particular through deliberate practice and open understanding. The more you deliberately act to trust, build tension and so on, and are also able to identify the results of your action, the better and more skilful you will become. This can be done in small ways, such as getting a stranger in the street to help you or negotiating a discount on a purchase from a market trader. As you get better you will build your confidence and so improve further.

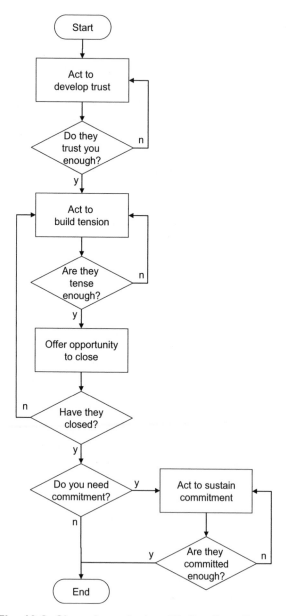

Fig. 19.2. Changing minds with the Core Process

20. Information Management

Information is the lifeblood of persuasion. If you know nothing about what the other person wants, then you cannot make any meaningful exchange. If you do not know what power they have and how predisposed they are to using it, then you will effectively be working with your head in a noose. And if you do not know yourself and what you really want, then you may well drive a poor bargain.

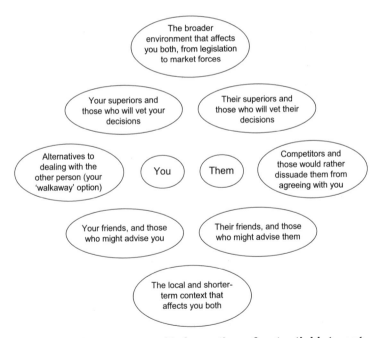

Fig. 20.1. Some areas of information of potential interest

The nature of information

Data, information, knowledge and wisdom

Data and information are not the same. Data is raw words or numbers that have no meaning as yet. When the data is taken and organized, it can be interpreted and informed meaning extracted from it. In combination with other information, this leads to a fuller knowledge that gives richer meaning. From this understanding, wisdom is needed to determine appropriate words and actions.

Truth and FOG

Information you are given can have varying degrees of truth, and significant work may be needed to verify it and hence develop trust in its truth. For example, things may be true only in some circumstances or information may be incomplete.

A simple acronym that is useful when examining information from other people is 'FOG':

- Facts are empirically proven, with clear evidence.
- Opinions are often offered as facts, yet are unsubstantiated.
- Guesses are acknowledged opinions or creative ideas.

The most common of these is opinion, and information is frequently based on a viewpoint or position. Understanding that viewpoint, and what is *behind* it, can give you very useful additional information.

Locus

Where information resides and where it travels can itself be significant additional information. Like the tree in forest falling when nobody is there, information in a library that nobody accesses might as well not exist. On the other hand, hot news that travels around the world in minutes has a very different effect.

The nature of how information is passed from person to person is very important. It can be passed by word of mouth, from one person to another. It can also be broadcast on global media that many people regularly view. What you or others do can significantly affect this.

Locus is important for power. Potent information held close may be of significant value, as might public information spread far and wide.

The value of information

Like material things, information can have highly varying value, ranging from being relatively worthless to being immensely valuable nuggets of gold. Information often has different value to different people, which can be very useful in negotiations. Knowing the value of information, both to you and to others, is therefore important.

Information and power

Power held is the potential to act in ways that will achieve your goals. Information enables your choices and may also be used in persuading others, for example where knowing a selling price empowers purchase negotiations.

What, when and who you tell who can have weak or strong effect. It can constrain, distract, shock, direct or otherwise influence their perceptions, choices and actions. As with all things, understanding is a great moderator of action.

Information and re-use

Like a joke, much information can only add value once, at least for each person, which makes it important to get the timing right when you do use it. Used too soon and it loses power. Used too late and it may fall flat.

In the way that comedians re-use the same joke in many individual live performances before telling it on television, information may have its power multiplied by constraining where it is used, at least before a more general broadcast.

Information and time

Like the daily news, the value of information may have a limited life. If you use it today it can have significant impact, but if you wait until tomorrow you will gain less from using it. Information may also go up and down in value over time or only be useful at certain times, for example information about holiday destinations is only of value when people are booking their vacation.

This changing value can lead to an effective information economy, where you might 'buy low and sell high' – or at least be able to take advantage of known cycles.

Before you start

Before any work to change minds begins, you need to consider what information you will need. This should include, for both you *and* the other person:

- How the person thinks, feels and reacts.
- What is really needed and what may be requested.
- How one person views the other person and predicts what they will say and do.
- What persuasive strategies and tactics may be used, and how they will respond to opposing approaches.

In some forms of changing minds, such as advertising, you will never be face-to-face with the target people. In these situations you do not have the luxury of immediate feedback as your audience consumes your message. In other direct contexts, such as public speaking, communication is still largely one-way and feedback still limited.

The effect in all such cases of reducing interactive information is to increase the importance of prior research. Marketing is a rich discipline you can plunder and offers many tools and techniques such as:

- Studying customers in their native habitats, observing patterns.
- Doing experiments by disturbing those patterns and finding further patterns in the responses.
- Giving them samples of products or services and observing what happens.
- Doing experiments in controlled surroundings, seeking to isolate specific patterns of cause and behavior.
- Asking questions, either interactively or through written questionnaires, to determine internal perceptions and constructs.
- Seeking available third-party information to reduce the need for the above expensive and time-consuming work.
- Using information gained to segment customers into groups that will be treated in different ways.

Understanding the person

The early part of this book describes a basic psychology, which becomes very useful in managing information about the other person. If you can understand how they think and feel, then you will be much better able to change their minds. Although minds are not directly visible, there are many clues in what is said and done.

The chapters on motivators (Chapters 2 to 9) can be very useful here and Table 20.1 offers a few questions to which you can seek answers.

Table 20.1. Understanding their motivators

Motivator	Things to discover
Needs	How much do they need to be in control? How delicate is their ego? What self-esteem? How important (or not) are their relationships with others? How do they seek arousal? What stimulates them?
Emotions	How emotionally stable are they? How rational? How generally happy or depressive are they? To what extent are they empathetic about others?
Beliefs	How firmly do they assert things and assume truth? What sense of duty towards others (or not) do they have? What rights do they think they have? What are the unspoken things they expect?
Models	How do they classify you? How do they think they can get what they want? Do they see 'one right way' or take multiple viewpoints? How are they approaching their problems?
Rules	What actions do they consider good and bad? What are their rules for you vs. for themselves? What are their rules about breaking rules? How do they prioritize and make choices?
Preferences	How do they handle uncertainty? To what sense do they pay most attention? How friendly and gregarious are they? How organized and logical are they? What attention to detail do they give?
Goals	What do they say they want? What unexpected things would delight them? What are their life goals? What are their work objectives? What are the problems they face?

Discover their whole SIFT-3M process

Beyond basic motivators, the whole process of sensing, inferring meaning, formulating action and translating this into action is a landscape to be discovered, along with how effectively they remember and what goes on in their background musing. If you understand their mechanisms of thought you can apply levers to modify this process.

Uncover their tensions

While you want to create a motivating tension in the other person, they already have many tensions that drive their lives that may obstruct and distract from the tensions you want to create in them.

If you know what is motivating them now and how the tensions acing on them are operating, you have information which you can use both to resolve current tensions and also perhaps replace them with tensions that direct them to your purpose.

Uncover potential tensions

Beyond the things that drive them now, there are a host of things that may drive them in future to achieving their life goals, from unrealized work problems and risks to financial and time constraints.

Once you have identified those things to which they are most sensitive, then you will be able to apply gentle pressure to achieve the greatest response. The heart of persuasion lies in the management of existing and potential tensions and these are covered in more detail in Chapter 22.

Understand their context

People do not stand alone. If you have to persuade somebody of something then they may also need to persuade others, such as when a person needs agreement of a partner when buying a car. If you do not know who else will have to be persuaded (and what will persuade them) then you may be on a losing track.

Even if further agreement is not needed by the other person, do remember that others will judge the person you persuade on how sensible they were to be persuaded. To make matters worse, the person will try to guess how those others will judge them and will agree or resist your advances based on this (potentially false) impression.

Know yourself

Knowing the other person contributes a great deal towards managing the relationship. Even more importantly, if you are a stranger to yourself, then the relationship has little hope. Just as you need to understand the other person it is also critical to understand yourself, objectively perceiving the full SIFT-3M process.

Self-image

First consider how you view yourself. When you complete sentences beginning with 'I...' you are often using your beliefs about yourself. When you say 'I know that' you are framing yourself as intelligent. 'I like my work' creates a professional association. 'I hate...' says something about your preferences or values. Two key (and often intertwined) elements of perception that are critical for changing minds are your perception of yourself and your perception of other people. As Figure 5.1 shows, combinations of these can lead to very different actions which can have a significant impact on persuasive situations.

Projected image

What we know of ourselves and what we show to others is not always the same as the image we try to project. We feel parts of our selves are vulnerable to attack and so try to hide them, perhaps through bold aggression. We also feel ashamed of other parts or that the other people would not understand, so we strive not to show them.

What we are prepared to show and what we project varies with the context and who else is there. In this way we effectively wear different masks as we communicate with others.

Fig. 20.2. Projection and reception

Reflected image

How others see you is often very different from the image you intend them to perceive. Understanding this can be a surprising and difficult process, both for those who are honest enough to tell you the truth, and even more so for you. To see yourself as others see you, you must first have the courage to ask (and in a way that encourages and enables a candid reply), and then have the fortitude to listen objectively, without trying to defend yourself from possibly uncomfortable news.

What you may well find is that different people perceive you in very different ways. The initial impressions you give people may change when they know you better, and still differ from those the understanding of those few who know you very well. The context is often a significant factor in this: for example, when you play different roles in work and at home.

Four selves

Psychologists Joseph Lufts and Harry Ingram described four selves, based on what we share and hide, and things to which we are blind, As in Figure 20.3. These selves are of different size and importance, leading to open, naïve, secret and mysterious personas that correlate with larger public, blind, private and undiscovered selves.

	What you see in me	What you do <u>not</u> see in me
What I see in me	**The Public Self**	**The Private (or hidden) Self**
What I do <u>not</u> see in me	**The Blind Self**	**The Undiscovered Self**

Fig. 20.3. Johari Window

Knowing yourself includes knowing that there are parts of yourself that you do not know, and being ready to listen and explore these. It also means considering what parts of yourself you should expose or hide, based on how it will help your purpose rather than simply based on personal preference.

Know what you are selling

Surprisingly often, we try to convince others about things where we are not really convinced ourselves or where we have a limited understanding and are basing our conviction on simple faith. When others ask 'why', we are then stymied. It is hence important to be able to reason logically about what we have to sell.

Features and benefits

One of the things a sales person learns early on is the difference between features and benefits. Both are important, but if you show off the features of the product before the customer has decided what they need, then all you will get is objections. Features are product-based, while benefits are customer-based. Benefits are what they will gain from owning and using the product. Features enable benefits to be achieved, but you cannot assume that the other person will be able to make this connection. Benefits can be practical, for example keeping warm. They may be emotional, such as pleasure in aesthetic design, or social, such as the status enhancement that the product may endow on its owner. This gives a much wider scope for persuasion than simple features. The emotional and social elements are powerful tools that hook into deep human drivers and can bypass rational objections.

Demonstration

If you are selling something, knowing its features and benefits may not be enough. You may also need the skills to operate it, demonstrating how easy it is to work and how wonderful the benefits are. Words are good, but experience is better.

Questions and objections

The other person may have questions to ask. It is well worth spending time beforehand musing about what these might be and what you can say that will not only answer their questions, but engage and enthuse them.

It is also helpful also to know what objections the other person may have with regard to accepting your suggestions, and what you may say to allay their fears and so turn rejection into acceptance. Good information management limits objections and resistance, but you should still always be ready.

Questioning

One of the best ways of gaining information is to ask for it. A common problem, however, is that we are often unsure what to ask or how to best phrase our questions.

Curious Kipling

The basic attribute you need in questioning is curiosity. Know that you do not know and be interested in finding things out. Rudyard Kipling wrote a short poem that gives six very useful questions you can use at any time to find out more:

> I keep six honest serving men
> (They taught me all I knew);
> Their names are What and Why and When
> And How and Where and Who.

Table 20.2 elaborates on these, giving a number of examples of how they may be used to elicit information.

Table 20.2. Kipling questions

Question	Discovers	Examples
What	Facts, actions	What is wrong? What shall we do? What is stopping you?
Why	Cause and effect, rationale	Why did that happen? Why are you upset? Why not do it now?
When	Timescale, plans	When did it happen? When will you finish it? When will you be ready?
How	Method, process	How did you do that? How does it work? How will you fix it?
Where	Location, locus	Where is it delivered? Where does it go next? Where did you see it last?
Who	Person, responsibility	Who will do it? Who are you working with? Who else would know?

Closed and open questions

Closed and open questions are very different and achieve different goals. A closed question leads to a short answer, such as 'yes' or 'ten' as it seeks agreement or simple facts.

> What is the name of your wife?
> Are you ready to move now?
> How many children do you have?

Open questions seek more information and encourage the other person to speak for significantly longer. They are therefore useful for eliciting deeper and more complex information.

> How did you manage to sell so many?
> Can you tell me about your company?
> Why are you upset?

Closed questions are good openers to conversations as they are easy to answer, though too many may seem like interrogation. A useful formula is three closed questions that guide thinking, followed by the one or two open questions that get you the detail you want.

Probing

After initial questioning, you may want probe for detail in certain areas, as in Table 20.3. Be careful here about appearing too aggressive, asking leading questions or otherwise risking reaction or false replies.

Table 20.3. Probing questions

Question	Discovers	Examples
Purpose	Intent, objectives	Why did you say that? What was it all for?
Relevance	Usefulness of information	Why is that important? How would that be used?
Completeness	Missing information	Before that, what did you see? What else happened?
Accuracy	Truth, fact	Are you sure about that? How do you know that is true?
Evidence	Examples, reality	What have you achieved here? Can you give me an example?
Meaning	Inference, formulation	What did you mean by that? Do you see what I mean?
Evaluation	Judging, assessment	Do think it will work? Would you say she is capable?

Listening

Questioning is not very useful if you do not hear the reply. While listening is an obvious need, few do it really well. One problem is that we do not need all our mental capacity to hear the words and so start to think of other things, only half paying attention and hoping to pick up later the gist of the things we missed. We then ignore what we do not understand, add bias and misinterpret what we hear. To make matters worse, we signal bored disinterest and may interrupt the other person before they are finished. When they do the same, conversation becomes a competition and very little useful information is exchanged.

Active listening

Active listening involves putting significant effort into the listening process, actively seeking to understand the other person. Active listening can include:

- Attentive body language, facing the person, looking at their face, leaning in, perhaps holding chin in 'musing' manner.
- Signals of approval and interest with nods and small noises ('mmm', 'uh-huh' etc.).
- Checking that you understand by paraphrasing what they say. 'Now, can I just check that I've got it. What you effectively saying is…'.
- Showing respect for the person and their views, even when you disagree with them.

Empathic listening

Sympathy involves expressing concern for the other person, and is usually helpful. Beyond sympathy, if you can empathetically feel what they are feeling, then you can build a greater understanding of one of their most important motivators. To develop empathy, watch their body language and listen to the tone of their voice. Then connect these with what happens and what is said.

Whole-person listening

Beyond empathetic listening you can seek to understand their whole SIFT-3M process. This requires an extraordinary degree of attention and much practice as you seek to understand the finer detail of how they are thinking and feeling.

Research

Outside of one-to-one conversation, much useful information can be gained from various additional forms of research. When you are researching organizations, for example, much secondary research done by others may be available, such as through websites and industry reports. Information on individuals and more specific situations may require a more personal approach and can use such primary research methods as surveys and interviews.

Depending on the importance of the situation and the time you have available, this can be a deep and significant research (for example in international negotiations) or a quick ask-around.

Strategy

After you have acquired information, the next question is how you will use it. A critical question is the extent to which you share the information, including what you will...

- ...openly share up front, perhaps to build a trust or indicate your initial position.
- ...exchange for return for information that they hold.
- ...slowly reveal to reduce overloading the other person or giving them the wrong impression of you.
- ...never give them, perhaps because it will harm you or the relationship.

Strategy also includes making a range of decisions about your approach, such as:

- Where and when you will meet the other person (eg. their territory, yours or neutral ground).
- How you will develop your argument with what information and persuasive methods.
- How collaborative or competitive you will be.
- How quickly you want to reach a conclusion and whether this must be in one session or whether it can wait.
- What you will do if you do not change minds as planned, such as when negotiations not reach a satisfactory conclusion for you.

21. Trust

Trust is utterly fundamental to human relationships and even more so for persuasion. If I do not trust you then I will be suspicious of all attempts at changing my mind. If I believe that you may harm me or take unfair advantage, then I will take defensive action. And if you prove unfair in practice then I will seek compensation or even revenge.

In changing minds, trust is a gateway, as the less I trust you, the less I will pay attention to your efforts to build tension and create closure. Conversely, the more I trust you, the more easily I will accept what you say as true and the less I will ignore you or spend time in checking up on you.

It is consequently important when seeking to change minds to spend time up-front in bonding, establishing rapport and otherwise building trust. This can include highly ritualized activity, as in greeting and small talk. In complex situations where you will be asking them for more than they might easily give, then deliberate and time-consuming action is often needed to create sufficient trust.

Once enough trust has been established to start the proceedings, the need for trust does not go away. To sustain the relationship, trust must be maintained in all words and actions, and the chances of breaking down of trust must be minimized.

A reason that we need to think about trust is the remarkably deceptive capability of the human animal. In evolutionary battles, trickery can be at least as effective as force. However, detection skills have evolved alongside our deception skills and we are constantly on the lookout for treachery. Which all points to my need to earn your trust before you will pay any real attention to my persuasive arguments. Trust is an essential, a basic foundation on which all interaction is based.

The nature of trust

To manage trust, the first step is to understand its purpose and the way that people use it as both a barrier and an enabler of interaction with others.

Predictability

To enable us to live safely, we have a deep need to be able to predict the future. Trust helps us in this prediction by determining what others are likely or unlikely to do. If I trust you, then given any situation, I may not know exactly what you will do, but I can at least be certain you will not cause me any serious problems. If I trust you to fulfill a promise, I need to be able to confidently predict that you will keep your side of the bargain.

Rapport

When I trust someone, I feel a sense of rapport with them. A bond is established between us and I feel a certain closeness to them. In effect, I have attached our identities together such that, in some ways, we feel like a single person. Rapport is experienced as a sensation, a warmth when thinking about and being with the other person.

Establishing rapport is synonymous with building trust and the extent to which you are able to create this connection will have a significant effect on your ability to change minds.

Variation and context

When I trust another person, then I can trust them in two ways. First, I can blindly trust them in all things, no matter what proof I have. If they say 'trust me' then I trust them. There are not many such people, and these are generally limited to family and a few good friends.

The second type of trust, which I use with most people, is to first have a basic level of trust, based largely on my beliefs about people. After this, it will depend on the situation. For example, I always lock my car but will trust a person I ask in the street to give me accurate directions.

When you are seeking to change minds, you are likely to find yourself in the 'suspicion box' of the other person where, before you can begin persuading, must prove your worth.

Transaction cost

Trust, or lack of it, has a cost. During interactions with others, we have the choice as to whether or not we trust and blindly accept what the other person says is true. If trust is neither complete nor blind then there is a *transaction cost* in the efforts to predict the other person's actions or otherwise hedge against possible lack of trustworthy action. A general rule is 'the less the trust, the greater the transaction cost.'

Within changing minds there is always some transaction cost on both sides. While this cannot be eliminated, the overall cost can be minimized with up-front investment in, and subsequent maintenance of, trust. In this way, trust is a desirable state that most people will seek.

Trust boundaries

A group or society is defined by its boundary and how people think, look and behave either side of that line. A key element of this boundary effect is trust. If I am a member of the group I will trust other members more and non-members less. Groups are thus defined by their trust boundaries. Within the trust boundary, the transaction cost is much lower and is one of the key benefits of social grouping.

When changing minds, it can be very helpful and is often necessary that you gain access to one of the other person's trust groups. Entry to a trust group does come at a price: to be accepted as a member, you are expected to follow what are often strict rules. Failure to comply is likely to result in punishment and/or ejection, as described in Chapter 18.

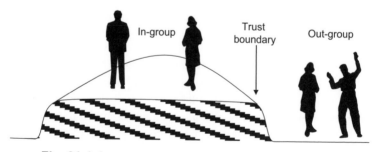

Fig. 21.1. In-group, out-group and trust boundary

Social capital

'Social capital' is to relationships and society what money and financial assets are to countries and companies. When people are trustworthy and help others, the net social capital increases. When they call on trust to ask for help and particularly when they are untrustworthy, then social capital decreases.

Your personal social capital, which equates to your ability to call on others for help, is effectively the sum of all things you have done for other people, less the sum of things others have done for you, plus the 'social credit' you can get. The social capital in a group is theoretically the sum of all trust, and practically proportionate to the amount of social credit an average individual can acquire.

National and organizational trust

Francis Fukuyama, in his study of national economic success and trust, identified how the size of our trust boundaries and the social capital within them are key predictors of success. If I trust my employer then I will be loyal and work hard. If I identify with my nation, I will be friendly and collaborate with people I hardly know.

Nations with a high level of social capital tend to thrive, with large organizations that people will join and trust. At the other end of the scale, where a population has been taught to distrust (often by a selfish and cruel hierarchy) economies are constrained by the unwillingness of people to trust one another and widespread poverty may result. In such environments, the trust boundary often stops with the family and organized crime may thrive as a surrogate for a distrusted state. It is also noteworthy that once a population has learned to distrust, it may take many generations before they learn to trust again.

In a similar way, organizations which adopt harsh and coercive management methods have a low-trust environment in which people succeed by political manipulation and with little thought of the effective cost to the company. Individual reward and punishment, if not moderated by wise leadership and rules of human decency, can lead to disloyal employees and high internal transaction costs.

If you are seeking to change minds in an environment where trust has been destroyed, then the best approach is often to work with individuals and small groups, and even then be prepared for a long period of trust-building.

The Structure of Trust

Given the importance of trust in changing minds, let alone the success of entire economies, a key question is 'How do people trust one another?' If I can understand this, I can take actions to build trust that support the process whereby you will trust me.

Figure 21.3 shows the overall structure of trust that we will explore, identifying ways in which you can develop and maintain trust. We use very different strategies for determining trust in the short term, when we do not really know whether to trust, as opposed to the longer-term, where the real trustworthiness of the other person may be discovered. Much also depends on the character of the person doing the trusting.

The truster

The nature of the person doing the trusting has a lot to do with the trust they will give. While some people will blindly trust a stranger, others are paranoid in their universal distrust. Between these extremes, most of us take due caution, as in Figure 21.2.

Fig. 21.2. The trust spectrum

This is partly driven by our beliefs about people. If I believe others are selfish, then I will not trust them. If, on the other hand, I believe people are fundamentally kind and caring, then I will give trust more easily.

Giving trust means taking a risk, as the other person could take advantage of that trust. If I have a preference for lower risk then I will be less ready to trust others.

Trust is also moderated by power relationships. If I am more powerful than you, then I will trust you more easily because I know I can take revenge if you betray me. If you are more powerful, however, I will be cautious as you may harm me without fear of redress. In a reverse of this, we often admire and respect powerful people and so may blindly trust them, based on this naïve view.

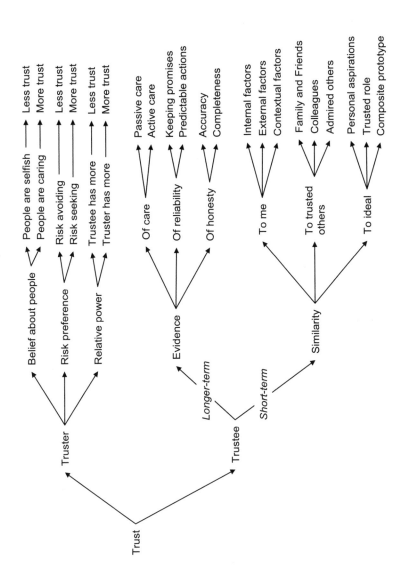

Fig. 21.3. The Structure of Trust

Long-term trust

In our experiences with others and our quest to know if we can trust them, we seek to discover how reliable they are, what personal integrity they have and the degree to which they care about us. In this way, long-term trust is based on practical *evidence* that we gather about the trustworthiness of other person.

Reliability

In order to stay safe and achieve our goals, we constantly predict what will happen next, particularly in the actions of those around us. If people do what we expect them to do, then we feel a sense of control and are able to confidently plan and take action. We label people whose actions are predictable as being reliable and we will consequently increase our trust in them.

The perception of unreliability (and hence lack of trust) increases in a non-linear fashion. If I make one or two mistakes, you may easily forgive and forget. However, after further mistakes you will rapidly classify me as unreliable and my good reputation will be lost.

Keeping promises

If I tell you that I am going to do something and then do not do it, then you will consider me unreliable and next time you will not fully trust me. Therefore, if I want to retain your trust, then I must always keep my promises.

The first secret of keeping promises is not to make them unless you fully intend to keep them and are confident that you have the time and ability to do so. If you are a 'yes-person' who hates to say 'no', then you are also likely to be unable to keep all of your promises and consequently seen as unreliable and not trustworthy.

The next thing to consider is whether you fail to meet promises simply because you forget. The human memory is notably unreliable and you need to ensure that you do not get a reputation as unreliable simply because of memory failure.

Carefully manage your promises by writing them down and using time management methods to keep yourself on track, for example by keeping a 'to do' list that includes notes about what is promised to who, and by when.

Managing expectations

A problem can occur when the other person believes that you have promised one thing when you believe you have promised another. Sadly, no matter how unfair this is, they may still end up not trusting you as you confidently deliver something that they do not expect (and miss delivering what they do expect).

The trick here is to manage perceptions so they continue to expect what you know you can deliver. Expectations management usually comes in three stages:

(a) *Set the expectation*, ensuring that the initial promise is fully understood. Be careful about detail, for example where 'tomorrow' may mean first thing or last thing tomorrow. After any exchange in which commitments are made, it is usually a good idea is to summarize and test the agreement.

(b) *Maintain the expectation*, for example by giving the other person regular progress reports. Without this maintenance, their memory of what was promised (and hence expectation) may distort. Be careful about changing a promise: you may be allowed to modify it a little, but multiple changes will erode trust.

(c) *Confirm delivery to expectations.* When you complete your promise, repeat the original agreement as you demonstrate how what is delivered is what was promised. This says 'Look, I have done what I promised', prompting them to agree and increase their trust in you.

Following instructions

Reliability is also demonstrated when you carry out instructions given to you. This is very similar to promises, but has a subtly different slant.

When you make a promise, you are in control. You can choose whether or not to make and break the promise. When you are told to do something, typically by your employer, then your choices are sharply less and their expectation is more specific. If you succeed they will be satisfied, but are unlikely to be delighted. If you fail, they may not only be disappointed, but also rather annoyed.

As with promises, it helps to clarify what you are being asked to do and then, when you have completed it, confirm this with the person giving the instruction.

Following rules

Outside of explicit promises and instructions we are bound by explicit and unwritten rules which we are trusted to follow, and so can lose trust if we break them.

Explicit rules include national laws and company policy. Breaking these can result in defined punishment. Breaking unwritten rules, including professional ethics, group norms and social morals, can have equally dire results, such as social rejection.

The implication for changing minds is to know and follow the rules, including group norms that may conflict with your personal values.

Integrity

Integrity is rare blend of honesty, alignment and selflessness in an admirable mix that is easy to trust, but can be hard to find. If you can show a strong integrity it will sharply increase the trust that people place in you.

Honesty

Trust and truth are close bedfellows. Someone who is always honest will be trusted. In a study by researchers James Kouzes and Barry Posner of over a million people about the characteristics of their most admired leaders, honesty came out at number one, ahead of vision, foresight and a host of other admirable traits.

Politicians are sometimes accused of being 'economic with the truth' when they do not lie but do conceal things simply by not talking about them. They may also embellish and stretch the truth as far as they dare. Honesty with integrity includes telling the whole truth and nothing but the unvarnished truth.

Honesty with selfless integrity also includes telling the truth even if doing so causes the teller harm. In practice, as with other selfless acts, this can be surprisingly powerful at creating trust.

Where concealment occurs, whether it is deliberate or otherwise, then people have to guess whether what is hidden contradicts what is visible. Full openness and transparency, even at the price of sacrificing short-term gains, will go a long way towards achieving a higher level of trust. Concealment still often happens for various reasons, but should always be done with full realization of the social risks being taken.

Alignment

Integrity has a great deal to do with alignment between a person's beliefs, values and their behaviors. This does not automatically lead to trust, as a person can believe that it is a 'dog-eat-dog world' and have aligned values and ways of behaving that you do not find trustworthy. There should be alignment between their motivators and yours, typically including common morals of respect, support and so on.

Integrity in alignment is particularly evident in situations of stress and conflict, where many of us may revert to stress values that are based more on self-preservation than altruistic trustworthiness. Given the right situation, a surprising number of us would steal or even kill to keep ourselves or our families safe.

People who are aligned are generally very focused. Effective sales people align themselves between their products and their customers. Likewise, teachers align themselves with the learning styles of their pupils, the syllabus and their own desire to teach.

Selflessness

We all have a natural concern for ourselves and, in our wondering about whether to trust others, we may suspect that they are so driven by selfish concerns that they will not merit our trust. Selflessness is an attribute of integrity that includes values that put other things above personal concerns. Typical selfless values include 'being professional' and 'helping the weak'.

It is little wonder, then, that we will seek out and trust a truly selfless person – yet we find such a concept so incredible, we may be initially suspicious of someone who seems to embody this ideal. Only with enough evidence and possibly a trial or two will we thaw and give our trust with confidence.

An archetypal selfless character is the white knight, who faces and defeats the fierce dragon in order to rescue the helpless maiden. The same pattern happens in the real world, for example, where a manager of a team that has been fired helps all of her people find alternative jobs before looking out for herself.

The implications of all this for changing minds is that if you want people to trust you, then you can do a lot worse than developing a real sense of integrity. Done well, it will not reduce your desire to change minds, but it might affect how you want to change them.

Care

The final dimension of long-term trust is care. If I think you care about me then I will be more likely to trust you. A leader who shows concern for his or her followers is more likely to be trusted than one who just commands the action.

Passive care

The first form of care is passive. Simply put, if you turn away from me, I will not stick a (metaphorical) knife in your back. Passive care is a 'do no harm' approach and trusting someone not to harm you is a big step for many people. Harm in this sense could include such as:

- Selling me something I do not need or which is defective.
- Asking me to do something I will later regret.
- Spreading hurtful gossip about me.
- Telling others things that I told you in confidence.

Passive care means *not* doing this sort of thing. We all understand the human selfishness and ability for deception and coercion that we know others have and fear that it will be used against us. If we can have the confidence that they will not use this potential to harm us, then we will increase our trust in them.

Active care

Beyond the 'do no harm' of passive care is a more dynamic state of active care. Whereas in passive care we will not stab a person whose back is turned, when we reach active care we will take positive action to save them should somebody else attempt to harm them, maybe even to the point of sacrificing ourselves to save them (although this pinnacle of martyrdom is admittedly rare).

Active care is seen where a retail store provides free help to its customers, for example in packing and carrying goods, or where a manager takes time to ask after an employee's ailing relatives.

In changing minds, create trust by vigilantly seeking situations where you can demonstrate active care. Active care puts you in the position of rescuer, a heroic role where you are cast as the selfless white knight. Rescue is also a part of classic persuasive 'Hurt and Rescue' pattern (Chapter 25). This can lead to the double benefit of simultaneously persuading and building trust.

Short-term trust

A problem we face in many situations is that we do not have the time to gather evidence to determine whether the other person is trustworthy, yet we are faced with a short-term decision as to whether we should trust them.

We face this situation most times we buy something. We do not know the sales person from Adam, yet we must decide whether to believe their spiel. To handle such situations, we need a short-term short cut to help guess their trustworthiness. The key that we use for this is *similarity* to us or others we trust.

The immediacy of interaction with strangers usually means we do this comparison at a subconscious level. Our assessment therefore comes out as a feeling that we like (or dislike) the other person, although we might be hard-pressed to say why. Although this works well in many situations, it is also a weakness that may be deliberately exploited. From the smart and smiling salesperson to the stern policeman, there are many situations where our trust buttons are being pressed without our knowing, and where real trustworthiness lies more in the manipulator's personal values than in the methods they use to gain our trust.

Similarity to me

I believe that I am good, right and trustworthy. If you are like me then I will assume that you, too, are like this and I can trust you. Even if we are not *that* good, I know that I can predict what you will do and hence will trust you more than others. In this way, we look for hints that others are like us, from our deep drivers to events in our past.

Similar internal drivers

I will trust someone who thinks like me. If they have similar beliefs, values, mental models, goals and so on, then I can easily predict how they will behave and know they will do the 'right thing'.

We cannot see inside people's minds and so we guess these inner drivers by watching and listening to them, where much information can be gained by attending to the 'words, music and dance' of speech and body language. In practice this is very difficult, yet we frequently make quick assessments of these important factors and base our trust on our rough readings far more than any hidden reality.

Similar external appearance

The dilemma in assessing someone for internal similarity is that we may have limited interaction with the other person with which to make this assessment. We may also be unsure of the assessment we have made, and so will look for more evidence.

The easiest evidence is in appearance: if they look like us on the outside, then we can assume that they are probably also like us on the inside. Thus we base trust on the flimsiest of visual evidence, such as age, gender, height and clothing.

This drives much of the way that social groups dress in similar ways. Students, street gangs and business people all have uniforms that signal 'I am like you – trust me!' As an easy thing to copy, external appearance is also a method commonly used by those seeking to persuade. If you look like your target audience, then they will often listen to you. If you look different, then you may be shunned.

Similar ways of behaving

If you are like me in the things you do, then I may take these as external similarities that reflect internal similarities and hence trust you more. The simple cognitive leap is 'If you *act* like me, then you must *be* like me'. Similarities in the way we behave includes mannerisms, language usage and hobbies.

We all belong to various groups, in and out of work. In work, we have departmental groups, professional groups, team groups, etc. Outside we may be supporters of football teams, on school committees, etc. This sense of shared belonging creates trust boundaries and we will trust others within these limits.

Historical similarity

Much may be inferred about beliefs and values from our past, including such as religious, academic and social histories. Even if the other person claims to be an atheist, if they were brought up in a Christian society, they are likely to have largely Christian values.

If you went to the same school, college or army regiment, then I will assume you had a similar formative cultural experience and therefore we both think in the same way. In particular, studies have shown that shared experiences and living in close proximity are strong predictors of friendship and trust.

Similar to trusted people

Another similarity used in short-term assessment of trustworthiness is to compare the other person with someone who is already trusted. As with other short-term methods, this applies both to deciding who to trust and deciding who not to trust. If you look like a person I know who is not trustworthy, then I will treat you with undue caution.

Similar to friends and family

We trust most those who are already close to us, who we know from long-term experience and who are within our trust boundaries. If the other person is similar in some way to these trusted people, then we will also tend to trust them.

Thus I will trust more a woman who reminds me of my sister or an older man who looks or acts like my father. I might also be suspicious of a person who reminds me of a cousin I do not like.

Similar to colleagues

If the person in question is similar in some ways to people in my broader trust groups, whether they are colleagues at work or fellow members of my church, then I will trust them more.

If the other person is to be trusted in a particular role, then we will compare them with trusted others in the same or similar role. If I have worked with an engineer who I liked, then that person may become the ideal against which I compare all other engineers.

Similar to admired people

There are some people who are not like us, but who nevertheless we admire and with whom we would like greater similarity. These include leaders who inspire us, musicians who amaze us and performers who enthrall us. Hence if I am particularly taken by a rock star who is critical of the government, then I may start to appreciate others who are similarly critical.

In wanting to bond with an attractive other person, we attach our identity to theirs, hoping that what they have might rub off on us. This connecting of identity then leads to trust, as we see them as 'similar to me'. It is then just one more overlapped step to connect with the person who is similar to the admired person.

Similar to ideals

Where direct comparisons are not available or not helpful, then we may still use constructed models of the ideal 'prototype' person against which to compare the other person.

Although some of the ideal attributes that people seek are predictable (integrity, care, etc.), others may be unique and linked into our history, for example a person with an authoritarian father may like being controlled. The best way of learning people's ideals is usually through observation of how they respond to different other people.

Similar to personal aspirations

While we have a projected self which we promote as a nice and wonderful person, we also know our own limitations and less-than-perfect thoughts and deeds. We often, if we can admit it, have an ideal self, a person that we aspire to be. The more the other person reminds us of this ideal, the more we will trust them.

Young children look at their own reflections and see an idealized perfection. To see this ideal of a perfect 'me' in another person can create a powerful and curiously narcissistic admiration.

Similar to trusted roles

There are many roles in society for which we have a relatively fixed level of trust, including doctors, police, managers, postmen and so on.

We know that we are talking to one of these people because of the symbols and other cues they use, from uniforms to attitudes. Unfortunately, this is a pattern that confidence tricksters use. By taking on the symbols, language and deportment of a trusted role, they can quickly get their victims to relax and trust them.

Similar to composite prototype

Just as we build stereotypes that we press onto people so we can pour scorn on them, we also construct *prototypes*, or idealized other people. Thus I might have a prototype for a partner, manager and so on. Prototypes are often composites of all the best people we have known or dreamt of. Like Cinderella's slipper, we then try to fit the prototype on everyone we meet. Experience tells us we may never find a perfect fit, but even a partial fit sends the other person way up in our trust ratings.

The hysteresis of trust

Hysteresis is a natural principle that is seen in situations from room-temperature thermostats to patterns of trust and betrayal, where change, up or down, is delayed until a 'trigger' point is reached.

As Figure 21.4 shows, from an initial state of distrust, although a person may be trustworthy, trust is not given for a while as the truster seeks long-term evidence. Once given, trust may be sustained even when trustworthiness slips, as we tend to forgive our friends for minor misdemeanors. As the other person finds that they do not need to be so trustworthy, their attention to it gradually slips until they go too far and the trusting person flips over from trust to an outraged sense of betrayal. This is usually a one-way trip and the betrayer may face a long period of re-earning trust.

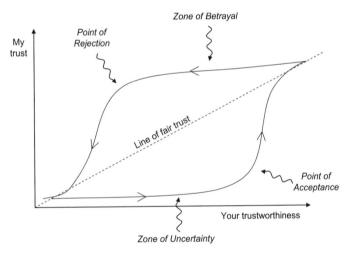

Fig.21.4. The hysteresis of trust

This pattern is often seen in marriages, for example where a man takes his wife for granted, largely ignoring her until one day she explodes. It also happens in companies which take advantage of the trust that customers place in their brand. Cost-cutting leads to erosion of quality of products or services. This seems to go unnoticed and continues until a point of betrayal is reached, at which mass desertion and other serious effects occur, from widespread negative publicity to highly damaging lawsuits.

Betrayal and justice

When trust is given, we expose our vulnerabilities to others and otherwise make it easy for them to take advantage of us. If they break the trust we give them, we feel betrayed and will typically become angry, often vociferously so, and may rail loudly at or about the betrayer.

Reparative justice

A betrayed person may seek *reparative justice,* where a price is put on , repairing and restoring trust. This may be dictated by the betrayed person, particularly for a more serious transgression, such as when a romantic relationship has been damaged by one person having a dalliance with someone else.

The betrayer may be able to restore trust particularly if they offer apology and some form of restitution, such as a gift or increased attention. For example a restaurant that spills food may present the affected person with a complimentary bottle of wine.

Retributive justice

When angered beyond reason, the betrayed person may not be so easily be bought off and may seek the disproportionate revenge of *retributive justice,* where the betrayed seeks to return even greater hurt to the betrayer.

This may be framed as a reparative act, such as when a slighted wife demands her husband make amends by buying her a dress, but becomes retributive when punishment is sought, such as when the wife deliberately buys a very expensive dress.

We can be a vengeful species and our laws allow for significant retribution when social trust is betrayed. From capital punishment to significant fines, we may seek public revenge on those who betray us.

Risk management

An injured person may well back away from the betrayer, seeking protection from future harm, for example by taking some kind of mitigating action or preparing some contingency to guard against further untrustworthy action. Such protection is damaging, as it dramatically forces up the transaction costs within the relationship.

Fair and foul play

When we want something, it is not only important whether or not we get it, but also whether or not a fair allocation process is used. Children naturally know this when they shout 'It's not fair!' as much as a persuasive plea as a statement of discontent. Hence we seek both the *distributive justice* that gives us what we want and also the *procedural justice* of fair play.

Figure 21.5 shows possible responses to combinations of procedural and distributive justice.

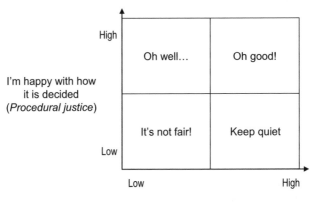

Fig. 21.5. Procedural and distributive justice

When the outcome is satisfactory and it was arrived at fairly, then we feel the results are deserved and we are content. If, however, we think that the process of decision unfair in some way, then many of us will not complain, although we will likely still feel somewhat guilty about the unfair benefits we are gaining.

When the decision does not go our way, then of course we are unlikely to be happy with this allocation. Yet, provided we can see that a fair process was used, we will usually accept the decision. If, however, we consider the process of decision to be unfair, then we will likely be tipped over into the anger of betrayal and seek distributive or retributive justice.

Detecting lies

The flip side of detecting truth is detecting lying, and being able to spot the tell-tale signs is an essential skill in any interaction. The good news is that very few people can lie without their subconscious sending some kind of signal. What happens is that a tension gap appears, for example between their preferred self-image of being honest and their actual dishonesty (or even their desire to succeed in their lying and their fear of being found out). This causes distortion in the translation of their intent into both verbal and non-verbal language. If you can spot the clues, you can identify the lies.

In children and some naïve adults, the signs of lying stand out as obvious beacons. Most of us who lie, though, work hard to suppress these signals – but with around 600 muscles in the body, 45 of these in the face and with many dedicated to expressing emotions, it is nigh on impossible to conceal lying.

Psychologist Paul Ekman discovered that when people lie they often show fleeting 'micro-expressions', which appear as very brief changes in facial expression, typically a grimace, as the subconscious expresses its distaste at the lie. General physical tension and stiffness may be a clue, including the resultant jerky movements, particularly in the lower body, which liars often forget to control.

There are yet a few people who believe so vehemently in their own lies that they see them as truth and hence show no giveaway signs. Interestingly, a disproportionate number of these people end up in one of two professions where this ability is a clear asset: selling or acting. Fantasists who totally believe themselves, though they may speak convincingly, often give themselves away through the inconsistency of their stories. It is no coincidence that a key method used by the police is to ask for the person's story at different times and in different ways. Another trick is to get the other person to tell their story backwards – this will be more difficult for the liar, who will hesitate more as they have to keep replaying their story forward to keep up.

Generally, lies are indicated through signs of stress or through the increased thinking that is needed to sustain the lie. The latter is more reliable, as stress may appear due to many other reasons.

Table 21.1 shows a wide range of signs of lying you can seek. A particularly powerful method is to link these with significant speech, for example how they change when you ask them probing questions.

Table 21.1. Signs of lying

Liars...	So they...
...are often worried about being caught or feel guilty, and are therefore tense.	...speak in a higher pitched voice. ...hesitate. ...make speech errors. ...move jerkily.
...do not remember what they say happened	...say things which are inconsistent. ...miss out irrelevant detail.
...make up stuff.	...hesitate as they think about what to say.
...are worried about what you might ask.	...talk a lot to use up the time. ...get 'emotional' to try and put you off. ...go along easily if you change the subject.
...are worried about what they might say.	...use language carefully. ...pause to think before answering. ...give short answers. ...use a monotonous tone.
...fear eye contact will give the game away.	...avoid eye contact. ...blink more often. ...rub their eyes more. ...wear dark glasses.
...fear being detected.	...say as little as possible. ...try to get away or change the subject. ...parrot back your words with a denial.
...try to control body language.	...hold the body rigid. ...leak signals then cover up fast. ...smile with the mouth but not the eyes.
...cannot control body language.	...send conflicting signals with different body parts. ...have eye pupil dilation. ...shrug and grimace. ...give the game away with lower-body signals. ...fidget, with hands and feet.
...feel threatened.	...attack, defend or deflect. ...place barriers in front of them, from arms to books.
...need time to think.	...repeat the question. ...adjust their clothing. ...ramble on about inconsequential things. ...have slight delays in speech-body alignment.
...know about the above and over-compensate.	...appear too relaxed. ...keep a 'frozen face' to avoid leakage. ...stare. ...go too rigid. ...go into excessive detail. ...show no discrepancies at all.

Creating trust

Trust is a critical gateway to persuasion and needs constant work to develop and sustain it. This chapter has already covered many indicators for how to achieve this which are summarized very briefly in the table below.

Table 21.2. Trust-building summary

For	Strategy	Tactics
Short-term trust	Show similarity	Act, talk, dress or otherwise appear to be similar to them, people they trust or to their ideals.
Long-term trust	Give evidence	Be honest, telling the truth. Only make promises you can keep. Actively show that you care about them.
Repair	Apologize	When you fail or cause anger, immediately apologize and otherwise seek to make amends.

In addition to this, there are some additional methods that lead to trust.

Trust them

If you trust others before they trust you, then you imply that you like them and are ready to take the risk of the relationship. This reduces their risk and so makes their decision to trust easier.

By trusting first, you also create a reciprocal dynamic whereby they feel obliged to trust you in return. As with all giving, this should not be done to excess, as it can sometimes cause anger at the perceived enforcement of obligation.

Show vulnerability

If you expose a weakness to them, such that they feel they could take advantage of you, then you are effectively trusting them. This again creates a reciprocal obligation.

Leaders often use this method to effectively say 'I am human, like you', thus making use of the similarity rule. An important point here is to show the weakness in an area that is not particularly important. This avoids scorn and uses contrast to highlight strengths in other areas.

The Ben Franklin method

Ben Franklin was known to build trust by asking others for a little help in something inconsequential. The principle here is that people will not refuse a small request as this would seem mean. They then have to explain their generosity to themselves, which they do by concluding that the other person is good, liked and hence trusted more.

Professional trust

People who come together to make a movie have little time to get to know one another. In what has also been called 'swift trust' the necessities of the job lead them to trust each other's professional ability. In effect, the job of the producer is as a trust designer, selecting a crew who will be able to work together as an effective and instant team. Likewise professional people brought together to do other jobs must quickly get on with the work and hence trust one another's ability.

Reference

One of the most valuable sales leads is the *reference*, where a friend connects the salesperson with you, effectively telling you that you can trust them. Similarly, many people would choose a plumber who was recommended by a friend rather than taking pot luck in the telephone directory.

Liking

We trust people who act as if they like us. Be kind and generous. Smile and show you are happy in their company. Show interest in them and their lives. Accept them as they are and avoid criticizing them, particularly about personal things.

Shared experience

A method used by armies to bond troops together is to put them through gruelling exercises. Any shared experiences lead to trust and shared difficulties lead to quicker and deeper trust, particularly where people are dependent on one another.

Ask them

As well as getting them trust you, you need to trust them. This means you should say and do things which will encourage them to be more trustworthy.

A simple approach to increase their honesty is to ask them if they can be trusted (be as apologetic as necessary). Of course they will say yes, but then having stated their position of trustworthiness they will feel they have to act consistently with this, otherwise they would feel guilty and self-recriminating about their dishonesty.

Use intermediaries

If they do not fully trust you, or you do not fully trust them, then you can make use of a trusted third party. This can be a useful approach when there are significant things at stake and any untrustworthy act by the other person could cause significant problems.

Third parties can take a number of roles, from owning the process of negotiation (and enduring both follow the rules) to making decisions that cannot be made by the parties together.

Allow reversal

Another way of creating trust is to allow agreements to be reversed after they have been made. This is seen in shops that have money-back returns policies and financial companies that have a 30 day cancellation policy to allow for 'cooling off' and to compensate for over-zealous sales people.

When parties know that they can reverse the deal, they are more likely to agree to it. Yet having agreed to it, it would be inconsistent of them to reverse the agreement, so in practice most people do not reverse, even if they really would like to do so.

22. Tension

Think of a time when you were in a heated discussion. Or perhaps when you were buying something expensive. Or maybe when you were enjoying an exciting movie. Did you feel some form of tension in each, perhaps as you worried about succeeding or maybe anticipated a satisfying outcome? Tension is the basic psycho-physiological motivator that drives us to pretty much everything we do. We feel a force, a need, and hence become tense and so act. This tension thus leads us to buy the expensive item or stay in the movie seat, gripped by the storyline as we wait to find out what happens next.

Tension and its application is at the heart of changing minds. Like the tension in a drawn bow, it seeks the satisfaction of release and motivates us towards this closure. Changing minds means managing the tensions that other people experience, turning them up and down like dials on a control board and so directing their motivations. This is not as easy as it might seem as people experience multiple simultaneous tensions and their actions are driven by a combination of these. They also may generate new tensions in reaction to our attempts to manipulate them. Managing tension is more of a subtle dance than a simple progression towards closure.

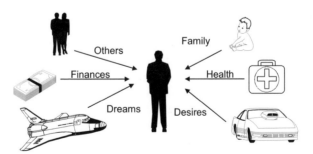

Fig. 22.1. Multiple personal tensions

The nature of tension

Understanding tension is the first step to managing it. It is hence useful to start with the detail of what tension is and how it happens.

Bodily tensing

Tension is not just a state of mind – it is actually felt in the body as a result of muscular contractions. When we are tense, we are *literally* tense. When we feel tense, we are clenching muscles in various parts of the body. For example we often store tensile stress in the abdomen (the 'knot in the stomach') or the shoulders (often leading to a stiff neck), although we can become tense anywhere or everywhere.

This visibility of tension can be useful in changing minds, where it can be an unconscious signal from the other person that shows you are having an effect. Look for changes in response to your words in such as:

- Rigid, raised shoulders.
- Limbs held rigidly, maybe at odd angles.
- Clenched hands.
- Jerky movements (often small).
- Rubbing of the tense areas.
- Holding the body tight.
- Changes in skin tone.
- Rise in voice pitch (tension in vocal chords).

Cognitive dissonance

Psychologist Leon Festinger studied a cult who believed they were going to be saved from a doomed earth by aliens on a particular night. He described the odd state they entered when this did not happen as *cognitive dissonance*. This is characterized by the tension we feel when we hold two incompatible thoughts in the mind at the same time, or when our thoughts and actions or experiences do not align. We consequently seek consistency as a basic need.

Festinger's cult reduced their dissonance by assuming their faith had saved the world. They also reversed their secretive past in telling everyone about this, so reducing the dissonance that they might be wrong by seeking more believers to reassure them of their faith.

Cognitive gaps

Cognitive dissonance occurs when there is a *gap* between two thoughts that causes discomfort. Managing tension may hence be viewed as *gap management*. Tension leads us to search for a solution to close the felt gap, as illustrated in Figure 22.2. We first feel the tension, then the need to reduce it and so search for an effective solution.

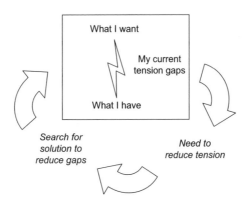

Fig. 22.2. Tension gap process

Motivators

Disturbance of basic systems is at the core of tension, which itself is at the core of changing minds, as in Table 22.1. This provides many deliberate routes by which tension can be created.

Table 22.1. Motivator gaps

Between...	...and	Example
Needs	Reality	I need company. I am alone.
Beliefs	Experience	I believe aliens do not exist. Then I meet one.
Actual emotion	Desired emotion	I feel sad and I want to feel happier.
Rules	Experience	I must arrive on time. I am late.
Rules	Other rules	I must not steal but I must feed my family.
Models	Experience	I think people are motivated by money, but you are working late for no extra pay.
Goals	Achievement	I have to complete this work today. It is lunchtime and I have only done a little.

Gap size

If I am very poor, then my desire for money may be much greater than if I am comfortably off. The size of the gap therefore has some predictable relationship with motivation, although this may well be non-linear. For example as I approach an anticipated event, tension rises sharply towards the end, particularly after a trigger zone is reached, such as one week before the event, when I pay increasing attention.

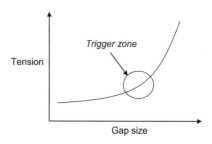

Fig. 22.3. Tension changes as gap size increases

Gap flexibility

Some gaps are easily moved, while others are rigid and unchangeable. For example some people may be open to financial negotiation while others have a very fixed view of price and payment.

When a gap seems inflexible, it may be because it is not well understood. If the *causes* of the inflexibility can be discovered, then these may be addressed or bypassed. Hence if a fixed perception about the reliability of a car comes from reading a review, a contrary review may be shown, or guarantees offered.

Often, when a gap cannot easily be changed, it is because there is another gap acting to prevent the change. Thus my desire for the car might be easily increased, but my fear of what my partner would say holds me back from agreeing the deal.

Gap sensitivity

For some gaps, a small change in size may result in a significant change in tension, particularly if the person is prone to anxiety or a trigger point is passed. For example just hinting that someone else might want the car might lead to a significant increase in desire.

Multiple gaps

We are constantly affected by many motivational gaps that can cause more problems as they simultaneously pull in many different directions. 'I'm being torn apart!' is a familiar description. If I see a nice car, then I may well develop a cognitive gap between not having the car and having the car, although this may be opposed by gaps such as having money and not having money, or having a happy partner and having an angry partner.

We have *systems* of tension gaps that we seek to keep in balance. So if I like Jane but hate tennis, yet Jane loves tennis, I may well seek to reduce the imbalance felt by trying to persuade Jane against tennis.

Gaps also appear across several motivators, for example if I see a well-dressed beggar, my model of beggars is challenged, and I feel values-based tension as to whether I should give him anything.

There are two common strategies that we use to handle the confusion of multiple gaps: multitasking and prioritizing. In multi-tasking, we slice up time, doing a bit of each job at a time, like the stage performer trying to keep many plates spinning at once. With prioritizing we just do the most important things first. 'Important' may be theoretically logical, but is usually where most tension is felt. A common pattern is running from pillar to post, doing just enough to reduce tension until a bigger gap pulls you onto something else.

Multiple opposing forces can also lead to stasis, paralyzing us into indecision. For example, when doing one thing makes you feel guilty about not doing something else, you might end up doing nothing.

Fig. 22.4. Multiple tensions

It is useful in changing minds to know the other person's pattern of response to multiple tensions. Will they try and fit in your request, then never complete it? Will they put it on the list of things to do? How do they prioritize? What priority would your request receive? How might this change?

Gap polarity

Gaps have polarity in that they can be negative or positive. When you think about going on holiday, you experience the positive tension of excitement. When you think about paying for it, the tension around affordability might be negative. This is the basis of the pain and pleasure of Chapter 25 and also leads to complex interaction of multiple gaps and 'tension systems'.

Interestingly, polarity affects different people differently, with some people being motivated first by negatives, while others are more motivated by the positives. These are quite different in effect: negative motivation creates 'push' away from something undesirable, while positive motivation creates 'pull' towards something desirable. This is very significant for changing minds, and it is worth testing the other person on an unimportant subject before deciding whether and how to use the positive carrot or the negative stick.

Positive motivation has many benefits, but can be more difficult to apply, which is why many people opt for the more coercive stick. A problem with this is that negative motivation causes an avoidance strategy where the other person, seeking to escape the pain in any way, may well not move in the desired direction.

Emotions

Many emotions can be traced to unfulfilled needs, and hence can be seen as indicators of gaps in motivators: fear shows a safety gap, frustration a control gap, desire as a goal gap, confusion as a mental model gap, and so on.

Table 22.2. Tension-creating emotions

Positive	desire, intrigue, interest, curiosity, excitement, hope
Neutral	surprise
Negative	fear, dislike, anger, envy, jealousy, disgust, shame

In changing minds, this makes emotions a useful signal of not only the presence of tension but also the cause of that tension. When you are persuading others, you need feedback to know the effect you are having. Beyond the visible tensing of muscles, emotion can be detected in the many signals of non-verbal language, from redness of the face, to the sound of the voice, to the way hands are used to accompany and shape words.

Time

Tension gaps often have a temporal dimension, in which the gaps are between past, present and future, as in Table. 22.3. In changing minds this is useful as you build gaps between what was, what is and what might be.

Table 22.3. Time-base tensions

Between...	...and	Example
Past freedom	Present responsibilities	I was happy when I was young, free and single. Now I have a family.
Present problems	A better future	I am heavily in debt. I dream of winning the lottery.
Past stability	Future uncertainty	A young man is leaving the security of home and is worried about how he will cope.

Tension also has a varying effect across time. Sudden tension acts as a shock and has the destabilizing effect of a punch, while each increment of a steady increase in pressure is easier to accept, yet eventually still overwhelms. Both these effects are used in stories, where occasional shocks accompany the steady rise in tension towards the climax.

Things that caused tension yesterday may well cause less tension today as more current thoughts and concerns occupy our minds. When tensions are painful, we note that 'time is a great healer' and even debilitating grief fades, although sometimes too slowly.

Emotions may be located in time, as Table 22.4. Surprise is felt when present events are not as expected. Anger may be at past events that did not meet previous expectation. Hope may be for a different future. Different emotions also cause directional movement, creating pull and push towards and away from things.

Table 22.4. Time-focus of emotions

Past	Disgust, shame, pride, surprise, anger
Present	Love, happiness, sadness
Future	Hope, fear, desire

Stress

Tension and stress are strongly related but they are not identical. Stress has the negative connotation of damaging discomfort, while tension includes the positive thrills of anticipation and excitement. Tension can thus be pleasurable as well as unpleasant, which means it can be used both as a carrot and a stick.

Search for a solution

Depending on the tension felt, problem-solving may be a leisurely and logical search or a more urgent seeking. As shown in Figure 22.5, without tension we have little motivation and are ineffective. As tension increases, our actions and decisions become more focused and effective. However, if the tension increases above a certain level, we become increasingly desperate in our search for a solution and we enter *satisficing*, where we start grasping at straws as we search for *any* solution that will relieve the unbearable tension. Eventually, if tension is not resolved, we collapse in emotional breakdown as our bodies can no longer tolerate the stress.

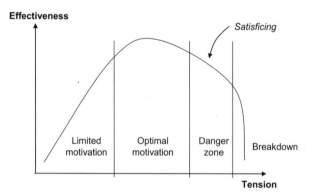

Fig. 22.5 Increasing tension

Satisficing is used in all kinds of persuasive situations, from military interrogation to children nagging at their parents in a toy-shop. The principle is simple: pile on the pressure until they are sweating, then tell them what you want, with an implied or explicit indication that this will release the tension. Note that this is something of a sledgehammer technique, creating temporary compliance rather than a more lasting conversion.

Fight or flight

The classic effect that excessive stress causes is a 'fight or flight' reaction, where a person experiences a threat and is driven either to fight back or run away. The adrenaline rush gives us energy and anger or fear takes over to drive us into attack or headlong flight. We may otherwise freeze, like a rabbit in the headlights of an oncoming car.

If your tension-creating actions lead to this response, then rational discussion is no longer effective and you will need to handle the physical effects of their extreme state.

Stress values

When people are responding to high levels of stress, their desperation may lead them to acts that are against their normal values. This is handled at the time by the taking on of a different set of 'stress values', for example as in Table 22.4, where self-preservation becomes pre-eminent and even harming others may become acceptable.

Table 22.4. Some normal and stress values

Normal values	Stress values
Unselfish, others first, win-win, be fair, keep the peace	Selfish, me first, win-lose, fight hard, dirty tactics, criticize

A dilemma then occurs as the person cools down and re-adopts their normal values. Faced with the cognitive dissonance of the gap between their normal values and what the have done, they are faced with the choice of abject apology, and perhaps some form of reparation, or else justifying their actions. The former route is the higher integrity action and, although it may result in short-term loss in status, it will help to restore trust. Sadly, however, few of us are heroes and we often take the coward's way out, typically blaming the victim for starting the altercation and even deciding that 'they deserved it'. To sustain this view we will typically stereotype the other person, de-personifying them as we reduce them to worthless 'things'.

This may seem awful (as we judge it with our normal values) but it happens surprisingly often. In the formation and sustenance of groups, individuals are often encouraged to de-personify and criticize out-group people. Although 'them-and-us' may be good for group harmony, and can be used in internal group persuasion, if you want to change the mind of an out-group person, then a greater acceptance of their different beliefs and values is necessary.

Coping mechanisms

When stress levels are frequently high and short-term satisficing is not always possible, then we may adopt some kind of coping, as in Table 22.5. These may seem dysfunctional and sometimes they are very much so, but they generally allow us to survive in some semblance of normality and put off resolution to a later, more convenient time.

Table 22.5. Coping mechanisms

Mechanism	Effect
Aim inhibition	Lowering sights to what seems achievable.
Avoidance	Avoiding situations that cause discomfort.
Compartmentalizing	Cognitive separation of conflicting thoughts.
Conversion	Emotional stress turns into physical symptoms.
Denial	Pretending event did not happen.
Displacement	Shifting of intended action to a safer target.
Intellectualization	Moving real issues to conceptual, harmless world.
Passive aggression	Agreeing, but then avoiding compliance.
Projection	Putting your bad feelings into other people.
Rationalization	Creating realistic but false explanations.
Reaction formation	Over-acting in the opposing direction.
Regression	Going back to a child-like state.
Repression	Subconsciously hiding uncomfortable thoughts.
Sublimation	Redirecting 'bad' energies to more constructive acts.
Suppression	Consciously holding back unwanted thoughts.

Freud called these *defense mechanisms*, describing the response in terms of the Id (the lower self) taking over from the normal Ego. Many therapeutic interventions are aimed at addressing such compulsive symptoms. While this book does not delve into therapy, it is a rich field for changing minds that you may want to explore.

In persuasive situations, people may well take advantage of the weaknesses of various chronic coping behaviors. If you find yourself giving in to demands too easily, then, hard as it might seem at first, facing up to these and getting help in sorting out your subconscious issues can give you a massive boost in your ability to change minds. Particularly if you are a business leader, your deep mental issues may well be holding you back or damaging the people around you.

Managing attention

Before you can manage tension you must first gain the attention of the other person and then sustain and direct it in ways to control their experience of tension. As discussed in Chapter 12, this requires action that plays to their senses and stimulates basic drivers.

Motivators

Attention is gained by addressing motivators in various ways, from challenging models to breaking rules or threatening basic needs. Chapters 2 to 9 offer many routes by which you can control their focus.

Arousal

The simplest way to grab attention is with some provocation that gets the other person emotionally and hence physically aroused, from physical action, to language that shocks them or otherwise provides sufficient stimulation. Done well, arousing them gets instant interest. Done badly, it may evoke anger and aggression that can be difficult to manage.

Amplification

Attention may be guided by increasing talk on one subject while suppressing or attenuating attention in other areas. Advertisers know that if you keep promoting something then even if it is not noticed at first, eventually it will get through, particularly if you exaggerate points of potential interest.

Distraction

Magicians call it 'misdirection' as they get you to look one way while doing their tricky stuff elsewhere. You can do the same, keeping attention away from areas you do not want them to explore, while simultaneously waving red flags in areas of interest.

Contrast

In all the noise of everyday life, we learn not to pay attention to many of the stimuli around us. Those that stand out most, contrast sharply with their surroundings and can be visual, auditory or linguistic in nature.

Teasers

Teaser adverts gain attention by showing something where the subject is unclear. Stories do the same thing, starting off a line of action and then switching to other strands before concluding them all only at the very end of the tale. Given our need for certainty and completion, we pay close attention until we realize what the advert is about, or how the story ends. Likewise, you can gain and sustain attention by teasing and keeping things incomplete and uncertain.

Surprise

We are surprised when something happens that we are not expecting, and can result from a physical shock or a verbal revelation. Such surprise can be pleasant or unpleasant, for example when we receive good news or bad news.

Beyond the effects of arousal, the fact that we did not predict what happened leads us to attend to it in order to learn more about it so we will not be surprised next time.

Them

One of the simplest attention-getters is their name. It is a close part of our identity and we attend to its every utterance. There is a world of difference between 'Excuse me' and 'Excuse me, Sam'.

They are also more likely to sustain attention if they are the subject of conversation. If you put others at the focus of your attention, then they will give you their attention.

Fragmentation

People often drift off from attention to you when they are bored or when what you are saying is too much for them to take in at once. You can therefore sustain their attention by feeding them smaller mouthfuls that they can digest one at a time.

Each piece you give them needs to contain sufficient provocation or stimulation to grab their attention, then sustained and brought to a satisfying conclusion that makes them value their interaction with you. If they consider you interesting and valuable, then any time you speak they will attend to you in expectation of something to which it is worth paying attention.

Managing gaps

As discussed above, tension and motivation is driven by the gaps between what we perceive and what we want. From this understanding, we can build a process for managing gaps and so increase or decrease tension to drive the person in the right direction, as in Figure 22.6.

1. Identify current gaps

The first stage of gap management is to find out where the other person is now, discovering the current gaps that are driving them. This is what a salesperson is doing when they ask about such things as business performance and current problems in supply management.

Possible research on current gaps can be highly variable and is quite situation-dependent. Often, it is feasible only to gain a superficial knowledge of current gaps, such as when a customer approaches a salesperson in a retail store. In such cases a few, well-chosen questions can be very revealing.

In other situations, more detailed research is both desirable and possible. If you are going to ask your manager for a raise in pay, then you may consider their pressures at home and at work, of needs unfulfilled and goals not met, or perhaps demands from both superiors and other subordinates.

2. Understand how they handle tension

While looking at current gaps, also look at how the other person has behaved around these, seeking to understand their gap-handling strategies.

Do they have lots of things on the go at once? Do they focus on one thing at a time? What is their satisficing threshold? How do they handle multiple tensions? Are they run ragged trying (and largely failing) to do everything at once? Do they seek compromise? How do they prioritize their choices? What motivators affect these (beliefs, preferences, etc.)? What is their decision process?

If you can see how they respond to tension -- and particularly multiple, conflicting tensions – then you can use this understanding in deciding how you should act around them. This knowledge will put your hands on the levers that will move them and enable you to selectively and effectively control the impact of the gaps you manage.

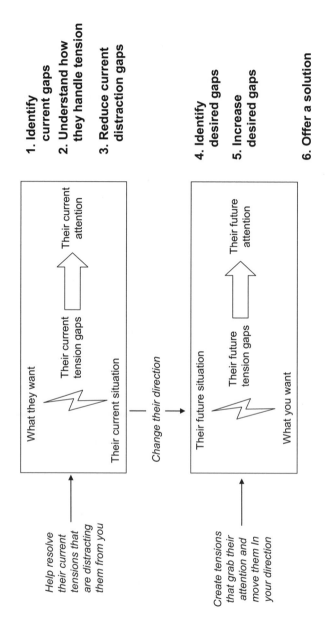

1. Identify current gaps

2. Understand how they handle tension

3. Reduce current distraction gaps

4. Identify desired gaps

5. Increase desired gaps

6. Offer a solution

Fig. 22.6. Gap management

3. Reduce current distraction gaps

Before you start levering open the target gaps, it is often a good idea to do something about other competing tension gaps. If the other person has a lot of other things on their mind, they will not hear even the most eloquent of your arguments as they focus on current goals and other, more immediate problems. But having already identified these current gaps, you can now set about reducing them.

Sometimes you can remove the cause of distraction, particularly if you have power in this direction, for example where a father sends other children out of the room and moves toys away in order to gain the attention of an errant child.

A good way of removing distractions is to change the context, moving the person away from them, for example taking a workmate out for a drink, away from the demanding thoughts of the workplace to a comfortable environment where they have nothing to do but sip and listen.

When they are busy with legitimate work that cannot reasonably be eliminated as a distraction, the best approach is often to help them with that work or otherwise speed up the process so they will have time to work with you. This may mean rolling up your sleeves and pitching in. You may also lend your power, for example to get more people involved or in removing roadblocks and delays.

Working to reduce tensions that distract the other person not only wins you time and attention – it also gives an excellent opportunity to build trust by showing active care in how you are interested in them and are seeking to help them.

One of the best ways of reducing current gaps that are distracting the other person is not to remove the tension but to subvert it to your purpose, turning it from a distraction to a desirable gap. This may be done by reframing the situation or their goals as needing them to collaborate with you. For example, if a couple inherit a sum of money and one wants to build an extension to a house and the other wants to go on exotic holidays, the first person may suggest that extending the house will allow them to rent out rooms and hence create an income for many more holidays.

4. Identify desired gaps

Almost independently from looking at the current situation, you can look to the future, at the gaps that you will need to have in place for the other person to change their mind. A simple process can be used to help you identify these.

1. Start with your goals. Clarify what you want to achieve, if possible in a simple statement. For example, 'I want Sam to go out on a date with me.'

2. Next, translate your goal statement into ways the other person should behave. What will you be able to see that will prove to you that their mind has changed? What body language? What words? What actions?

3. Then go inside their heads and identify the tension gaps that will drive those behaviors. You might well find multiple tensions that may have some effect. Keep all those that you might be able to influence.

4. Prioritize target gaps, selecting those that will have the best and most reliable effect for the minimum effort.

Prioritization can be a simple estimate or may use a more rigorous process of multiple weighted criteria and detailed cost/benefit analysis, where 'cost' is the likely difficulty for you in creating the gap, and 'benefit' is the likely efficacy of the resultant gap in moving the person towards closure.

In choosing gaps, consider at what stage different gaps may be used, for example what to hold in reserve if initial persuasive efforts do not work and what gaps will be targeted in what sequence in order to steadily increase tension.

Table 22.6. Identifying desired gaps

Step	Example
1. Your goals	Convince business managers to help with change
2. Success criteria	They 'walk the talk', giving proactive support
3. Effective gaps	Career aspirations, business goals, CEO criticism
4. Prioritization	Start with business goals, using CEO as escalation and career success as final reward.

5. Increase desired gaps

When you have made space in their busy tension schedule for the tensions you want them to feel, it is now time to crank the handle, levering open the target gaps in order to build up the desired tensions. Within gap management, building tension is a critical activity as it is this which leads directly to the desired closure.

There are many methods of increasing tension, as discussed throughout this book, although generally they work at the fundamental level by stimulating motivators, for example as in Table 22.7.

Table 22.7. Creating tension through motivators

Motivator	Building tension
Needs	Threaten or offer to satisfy needs.
Emotions	Evoke emotions by stimulating other motivators.
Beliefs	Challenge beliefs. Discredit references.
Models	Show models as inadequate. Offer new ones.
Preferences	Deny preferences. Offer ways of meeting them.
Rules	Challenge rules. Show that *they* break them.
Goals	Block or offer ways to satisfy goals.

Curiously and usefully, the other person may actually welcome your re-increasing of tension. Most people have a preferred level of tension, and your having reduced their current tensions has bizarrely created another gap between actual and preferred tension. For example, if you reduce the workload of a person with a strong work ethic, they will immediately start fretting about not having enough to do.

6. Offer a solution

The final step is to offer a solution that resolves the tension you have built, and hence reaching final closure. Done well, this will result in them biting your hand off and being grateful for your support. Done badly, it will result in resistance and objections as they perceive you as manipulating them. A trap in this is to offer the solution too soon, as sales people who thrust products at unready customers will know. 'Softly, softly, catch the monkey' as they say.

Note: Achieving closure is covered in detail in the next chapter.

Building tension

Beyond the direct addressing of motivators, there are many further principles that may be used to increase tension. Here are just a few:

Appeal

Appealing to others puts you in the position of supplicant. This puts them in a position of power, which means they could say no. But if asked nicely, most people will usually follow social rules that demand we help others.

If you have built trust with them, declining your request would go against the rules of friendship. And if you have helped them already, refusing you would go against social rules of exchange and repaying kindness. The thought of transgressing social rules creates a powerful tension that makes appeals difficult to refuse.

Assertion

If you assert something to be true, while this does not make it true, it does cause a problem for others as if they are unsure of your truth they are faced with the prospect of arguing with someone who appears to firmly believe it is true. This puts them in the situation of facing the double bind of either:

(a)   winning the argument and causing you to lose face, or

(b)   losing the argument and being embarrassed.

Causing others to lose face is unacceptable in many cultures while losing an argument is also shameful. Many people faced with this double tension will, as long as your assertion is not too outrageous, accept it quietly.

Assumption

If you *act as if* something is true then this gives the other person the dilemma of either accepting it as true or challenging you. Many will accept the truth, sometimes because you seem more sure than they feel and sometimes because they do not want to cause any embarrassment.

Sales people often use assumptive methods, for example asking how you want to pay before you have said you want to buy the product.

Authority

When the other person believes you have a formal position of authority, then challenging you would be breaking social rules about hierarchy and superiority, so they are likely to comply with little questioning.

It is also against the rules to challenge a person in a position of authority, which makes this tension popular with confidence tricksters who adopt the symbols of authority, from sharp suits to police uniforms. They also make significant use of assertion and assumption, making it particularly difficult for their victims to challenge them.

Challenge

When confronted with a challenge of some kind, the gap between not having an answer and having an answer spurs people to seek an answer. The opportunity to look good in the eyes of others also creates a motivating tension.

Dare them. Present them a puzzle. Show an opportunity. Present them a problem. Ask for their help. Or otherwise issue a challenge.

Confusion

We have a need to understand and explain what happens around us, as not to do so means we are not in control, which is both personally threatening and socially embarrassing. Confusion hence creates a scary tension and, just as a drowning person will clutch at a straw, so also will a confused person gratefully accept any reasonable-seeming explanation that comes their way.

Learning is often preceded by confusion. It is a canny teacher who deliberately creates this state in order that the student will easily accept a new concept.

Dependence

Power and persuasion often stem from a tension where I am more dependent on you for something I want than you are dependent on me to give something in return.

The power of parents is based around dependence, as often is the power of managers in companies, where their subordinates depend on their managers for reward, continued employment and promotion.

Evidence

When the other person believes something that you know to be untrue, then, if you present them with undeniable evidence, they will experience a tension between their belief and what they see before them. Evidence is thus a powerful tool for persuasion.

Courts of law are based around the production and examination of evidence and many lawyers have forced a dramatic confession by confronting the accused person with an accumulation of apparently overwhelming evidence.

Exchange

There is a social rule that says if I do something for you, then you are obliged to do something in return for me. This is based on the principle of social capital, where not to pay back a kindness is to take unacceptable advantage of others.

This approach is sometimes used by gypsy women who give you a sprig of heather then ask for money. Coupled with an additional tension of the implied threat of being cursed, many people pay up.

Exchange may also be a negotiated agreement, where simultaneous consent is given that if I give you *this*, then I will get *that* in return. Negotiators will often build tension here by painting what they are giving you as being particularly desirable and simultaneously downplaying what you have to offer.

Expectation

Expectation happens either when we predict something will happen or when we are told something will happen. Expectation appears as a tension gap between what is and what is expected. When managing expectations, you manage tension.

Framing

Framing says 'Let's look at this another way', typically by changing the model through which the situation is being understood. As models lead to meaning, which leads to tension, changing the model changes the tension.

Therapists often use reframing to help their clients see what appears to be a tense and threatening existence in a different and more positive way.

Interest

We all have things in which we have a particular interest and which provide the tension gaps that currently motivate us. If something is presented that may help to resolve these gaps then a secondary gap appears, in the desire to have the solution to close the initial interest gap.

Interest may also be stimulated by provoking curiosity, hinting at possible intellectual or material gain. Providing incomplete information opens a tension gap that prompts them to seek more detail.

Investment

If you can get the other person to do something, even something relatively small, then the fact that they have made an investment means they have to justify this to themselves or face the tension of acting without reason. When the investment is small, they cannot conclude it was some exchange, so typically decide it was because they like you or for some other intrinsic, personal reason.

When asked to do something more significant, they then have to act consistently with their past actions in order to avoid a further tension around appearing to act in an unpredictable and illogical way.

This method is used by people who get you to sign petitions to save the world. They know then that you are more likely to support their cause in future situations.

Logic

When a person presents something to you that seems reasonable and has a logical set of inferences and conclusions, then it is difficult to deny it. To assert against logic is to declare yourself illogical and unreasonable and hence a potential threat, which may be attacked.

People in debates often use logical arguments to support their case, whether these discussions occur informally or in formal settings, such as public and political arenas.

Offer

If you simply offer the other person something that is desirable in some way, then they will feel the tension in the gap between not having and having what you are offering. The offer is a basic component of sales and negotiation and even children will offer 'to be good' to get their parents to buy them a desired toy.

Opening

Like an open wound, something that has not reached closure will continue to fester and demand attention. So if you start talking about something but do not finish it, it will create tension in the other person.

Storytellers use this principle as they switch from scene to scene and back, building multiple unfinished story strands that escalate excitement, only to be drawn to a magnificent conclusion in the grand finale.

Passion

Emotions are infectious and if you are passionate about your subject the other person may feel a tension between their emotion and yours and so become passionate to close that gap. If they are not initially enthusiastic, they may also want some of the good feelings you are experiencing and so also become keener.

Leaders use passion when they expound their visions of the future and invite their audience to join them in the quest to build a better tomorrow.

Questions

Asking questions can be a powerful way of creating tension and was famously the core method used by Socrates for making his students think and learn. Questions can highlight a lack of knowledge or may cast doubt on what was presumed to be existing knowledge. The gap between not knowing and knowing stimulates curiosity or anxiety. It can also challenge a self-image of being knowledgeable.

Repetition

If you make a single appeal which does not work, the tension the other person feels will probably wane. Thus repetition keeps the tension active and escalates it as the person is reminded of the lost opportunity, or otherwise has their discomfort sustained.

Advertisers use repetition in showing you the same advert time and again. They may also continue the theme in different media so you are reminded at every turn, from television to web to billboards. Repetition is also a basis of trance, and music or other regular beat can be used for subtle background reinforcement.

Scarcity

When things are plentiful I can get them in my own time and when I need them. If, however, they become scarce, I project forward and imagine a time when I want what is unavailable. I then berate my future self for not getting the desirable item when it was available and so provoke my current self into acquisitive action.

Shops use scarcity when they have sales, sending the message that there is a limited time in which you can get one of the last few items at a bargain price.

Story editing

We all tell ourselves stories that explain why we do what we do, even if we do not realize we are doing this. Changing this story has proved a powerful method and has been successfully used in changing the lives of errant teenagers who seem destined to fail in life.

Threat

The basic component of the threat is an evocation of discomfort (often via fear) about a future event that may or may not be controlled by the persuader (for example, when buying a house, you could point out a forecast of house price depression). To create fear, link the other person's action or inaction to something undesirable.

Although using threats might seem immoral, they are surprisingly common and parents, managers and partners regularly threaten negative consequence if compliance is not achieved.

Vagueness

If someone tells you something but with gaps in the clarity and detail of what they are saying, then the tension caused by the incompleteness and uncertainty of what they are saying will lead you to guess at what they really mean, filling in the gaps yourself.

Therapists use this method when they talk vaguely about what another client thought and did. Their current client, without noticing what is happening inserts themselves into the story and so goes along with the healing storyline.

23. Closure

The ultimate goal of changing minds is just that: a changed mind, where changing one aspect of the target person's thinking causes a cascade of different thought, culminating with an internal change or decision you are seeking. Although information, trust and tension are all a part of the journey towards changing minds, they are not the objective. The critical point is where closure is achieved, where the mind actually changes in the intended way.

Closure as described here is not the same as closure in sales, where 'closing techniques' are used by the sales person to nudge you towards reaching for your wallet. In many sales situations the sales person is not really worried whether or not you have reached a true cognitive and emotional closure – their primary concern is that you sign on the dotted line as soon as possible so they can claim their commission and move on to the next customer. This is not true of all sales people, of course, and the best exponents really do change minds as they know that this is the basis of customer loyalty and that loyal customers will return again and again, as well as taking time to make persuasive recommendations to their friends and family.

Moving other people to closure is sometimes easy, for example when you have something they want or when your request is not a big deal for them. Asking a person at the dinner table to pass the salt does not need use of strong persuasion and is unlikely to lead to debate. Likewise offering to do the ironing will seldom lead to refusal (unless of course your ironing skills lead to creases rather than smoothness). The discipline and skills of changing minds and reaching closure really come into their own more and more as the likelihood of an easy closure decreases.

The nature of closure

As the ultimate goal of changing minds, closure is important to understand, yet it is easy to miss or misunderstand. It therefore needs care in mastering the subtleties of this tricky step.

Resolving tension

Closure occurs as the *resolution of tension*, as in Figure 23.1, and is usually experienced as a pleasurable sensation such as relief, comfort, etc. Whereas tension often happens as a gradual escalation, closure is a sudden change, as in the release of a coiled spring. The experience consequently tends to be felt more strongly and is clearly visible to the vigilant persuader.

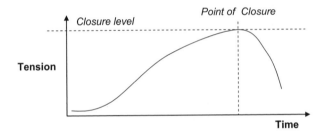

Fig. 23.1. Tension and closure over time

Changing state

There is a distinct mental change in a person when they switch from tensing to closure, which also usually includes a significant change in state, for example from anxious and jumpy to happy and relaxed.

Managing closure means working at this boundary, carefully pushing them over the edge so they let go of the tension and are enveloped by the experience of closure.

An internal process

Closure is an internal, cognitive and emotional process that occurs when tension is resolved. It is what happens within a person, not what is done to them. As such, you can only ever influence it indirectly.

Levels of tension

The tension level required for closure differs by situation. For example although on a diet I am easily persuaded to have some chocolate, though it would take a lot to persuade me to go rock climbing.

Three common closures

Closure is not simply about agreement. If you know what closure you want, then you can target your interventions. Here are three basic ways people close when you seek to teach or persuade them.

Aha

'Aha' is the closure of learning. It happens when the penny of realization drops and we make sense of things and fit new facts and concepts into our memory and system of mental models.

'Aha' is the closure that all teachers seek as they offer new ideas and knowledge. It is also useful in other areas of persuasion where you need a person to understand before they agree.

Yes

'Yes' is the closure of full agreement. It is the closure of deliberate choice, where a person voluntarily makes decisions and commits to action. This is the closure that managers and sales people seek. 'Yes' is also the main closure that is needed when you want to change a person's beliefs or other deep systems, and so is sought by priests, philosophers and other purveyors of truth.

When a person says 'yes', do ensure they mean it. Many use 'yes' to mean 'OK' or even 'I understand'. If you think you have only a tentative yes, check for real agreement with more detailed questions.

OK

'OK' is not the same as 'Yes'. An 'OK' in closure is an acceptance. It is the agreement of the person who capitulates, giving in to pressure and going along with what is proposed, just to release some tension. Accepting something that is not believed or wanted adds new tension, but this is less than the tension being felt before the closure.

'OK' is the closure sought by those who seek temporary compliance, who want action now and have little concern for a future where the coerced person might exact some revenge.

SIFT-3M closure

With a closer eye on detail, closure can occur in various ways across the SIFT-3M process, as indicated in Table 23.1 and Figure 23.2. These closures are described further in sub-sections below. Chapters in Part A can also be referenced for detail and methods for closure in these areas.

Table 23.1. Closure in SIFT-3M

Closure type	Example
Sensation	Something sought is detected
Inferential	Something not understood is understood
Formulation	Something important is decided.
Translational	An idea is expressed satisfactorily.
Motivation: Needs	Something feared is deflected.
Motivation: Belief	A belief is formed or accepted.
Motivation: Model	A model is accepted, created or changed.
Motivation: Preference	Comfortable choices are made.
Motivation: Goal	Something wanted is achieved.
Musing	A possible scenario makes sense.
Memory	I finally recall what I was thinking about

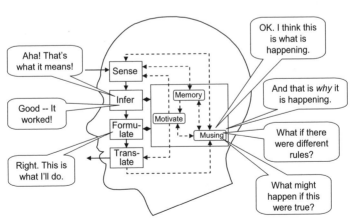

Fig. 23.2. Closure in the SIFT-3M process

Sensory closure

Sensory closure happens when we suddenly notice something, often when we have been consciously looking for it. When we want to sense something, from hearing a person across a room to detecting anything which is red, we send a signal to our senses to look (listen, smell, etc.) for that thing. This makes it 'jump out at us' when we detect it.

In changing minds this effect can useful when you want the person to 'watch out for' something. In doing this they may miss a remarkable number of other things, which may also be desirable.

Inferential closure

In the process of inference, meaning is usually achieved quickly and subconsciously as existing internal mechanisms close on 'obvious' interpretations. Inferential closure often occurs as a two-stage process: first when a prediction of resolution is made, and then again when there is confirmation that actions taken worked as expected.

Another set of tension and closure occurs when the basic inferential process fails and the tension of confusion and not understanding occurs. This is effectively resolved either through the closure of learning, or through the less effective closure of coping mechanisms such as denial and delusion (although these deflections of full closure can lead to later tensions of persistent psychological problems).

Formulation closure

Closure occurs in the formulation process where you decide what you will do and say next. This is often done using heuristic short-cuts. More important and difficult decisions are likely to be made through a conscious process of considering and choosing different options.

You can gain quick closure by offering easy answers and methods that help the other person avoid the effort of thinking. Where they need to think, you can offer prioritized criteria and rational arguments.

Translation closure

Translation closure involves the choice of how to turn intent into words and actions, which can be a tricky step. It is one thing to decide to do something and it is often another and potentially difficult process in deciding exactly how you will do it without causing misunderstanding or criticism.

Needs closure

When needs are stimulated or threatened, we often react strongly and closure is felt powerfully, for example when a threat is removed or desire satisfied.

Needs are fundamental motivators and most of what we do can be linked to satisfying them (and hence gaining needs closure). Understanding the dynamics of this can be the basis of powerful ways of gaining closure. See Chapter 3 for more details.

Belief closure

When we are trying to understand something where our models are inadequate, we often need to create or extend beliefs in order to explain and handle this new concept. For adults, this is a rare event and requires that we either make assumptions or believe another person.

Getting others to close on a belief is rather tricky as it requires that they believe *you*, as well as the point in question. See Chapter 5 for more details.

Model closure

We view the world through complex internal mental models and building new or changed models literally changes how we think and understand. Beliefs and models interact in complex arrangements and closure happens when the whole system is restored to harmony.

As with beliefs, changing models can be a painful and confusing process and may be resisted and achieve full alignment, it may be necessary to change several models. A common approach is to reframe, effectively saying 'Let's look at it another way'.

Preference closure

Preferences often work along a simple spectrum with comfort at one end and discomfort at the other end and we often use avoidance and approach strategies to move downhill towards a more acceptable state.

Any significant movement towards the comfortable end of the scale is likely to bring some sense of closure as anxiety takes a step downwards. For example when a person with a low risk preference manages to avoid taking on a hazardous piece of work, they feel the closure of satisfaction and relief.

Goal closure

When we achieve a goal, we feel some degree of satisfaction, from basic content through to delighted elation. The emotional level of satisfaction closure experienced is usually related to the importance of the goal and the effort required to achieve it.

There is much opportunity for goal closure in changing minds, either in closing their distraction gaps by satisfying current goals, or setting goals for them that moves them in the desired direction.

Musing closure

Closure also happens during the background process of musing as we engage in more leisurely games of figuring out what is actually happening and why. We also play 'what if' games as we mentally try out different models and project them into our understanding of the world to see what might happen.

It is common to see people nodding and smiling when they are thinking about something. This is a typical sign of internal closure as they make sense of something, select an option or otherwise make a decision.

A way of encouraging musing closure is to talk to yourself as if you are musing out loud. If you have connected with the other person, they will follow your musing and may adopt it themselves. It can sometimes be more effective if you seem to be changing your own mind rather than trying to directly persuade a person.

Memory closure

Closure in the use of memory typically happens where we remember something, bringing it to mind. It is the 'ah, yes' satisfaction when that annoying word that was on the tip of the tongue eventually finds its way to short-term memory.

Memory closure increases with effort, and the harder something is to recall, the greater the satisfaction we feel when we drag it out from the depths of the past and games such as 'Trivial Pursuit' have been very successful by finding an effective balance where questions are largely recalled only after some mental exertion.

The ability to recall is related to the way items are stored. Good teachers not only teach facts, they also teach ways of remembering that help the other person bring things back to mind when needed.

The emotions of closure

Despite the apparent rationality in inference and decision-making, all closure is emotional: at the point of understanding or decision, you feel *something*, whether it is the 'aha' of learning, the relief of a threat removed or the satisfaction of choosing.

Emotions of tension have a motivating force, pushing you into action. Emotions of closure (Table 23.2) differ in being shorter-term and disappearing shortly after being experienced. This can cause a problem where you want the other person to act after closure, and is taken up in Chapter 24 which discusses how you can sustain commitment over a longer period.

Table 23.2. Emotions of closure

Emotion	How it is created
Resignation	Realizing there is no alternative other than something that may not be desirable.
Completion	Finishing of significant period or activity.
Delight	Unexpected achievement of needs or goal. Or finding a way to easily achieve goals.
Realization	Understanding a thing not understood before.
Gratitude	Being helped in achieving goal.
Relief	Removal of threat.
Satisfaction	Expected achievement of needs or goal. Or reaching a decision to act.
Sadness	Realization that goals will not be met.

The emotional high of closure is a common reason why people move into persuasive professions. Consider the lawyer's delight at cracking the defendant or a key witness. Or the sales person's high at signing the deal. Or the teacher who finally gets an idea through to a difficult and reticent teenager.

Changing minds may be viewed as the management of emotions, from developing the comfort of trust to provoking the emotions of tension, followed by the elicitation of the emotions of closure. For example, I evoke desire by showing you what you have not got, then encourage the satisfaction of choosing to buy it.

The release of attention

One of the effects of tension is that it grabs the torch of attention. Tensions of desire, fear and any other incompletion cause us to pay close attention, lest we miss an opportunity or fall prey to disaster. Attention, like time, is a finite resource. Closure releases trapped attention so we can shine its light elsewhere. For example families of someone murdered may gain closure on the capture and conviction of the killer and so feel able to get on with their lives.

By helping people to gain closure on their current tensions, you can release their attention to these. They then will feel more able (and more obliged) to pay attention to you and what you have to say.

Body language of closure

Emotions show clearly in body language and the release of emotions at the point of closure is often highly visible as the body transitions from the physical tightness of tension to a more relaxed posture. Table 23.3 describes some of the body language of closure. Spotting transitions such as these can be easy and very helpful for the observant persuader.

Note that closure is a *change* in mental state and hence you should look for non-verbal transitions, including vocal changes such as lowering of pitch as the vocal chords relax.

Table 23.3. Body language of emotional closure

Emotion	Body language
Resignation	Sagging body, lowered head, sighing
Completion	Shift in body structure and position, raising or lowering head, short nod
Delight	Animated face and body, eg. punching of air, followed by relaxing of body
Excitement	Anticipatory animation and body tension, talkativeness
Realization	Raised eyebrows, opening eyes, nodding
Gratitude	Smiling, hugging, shaking hands
Relief	Slight sagging of body, smiling
Satisfaction	Small nod of head, releasing of body tension
Sadness	Slowing of body movement, sagging body, down-turned mouth, still face

Anticipation

Closure happens not only when a triggering external event actually occurs. As we forecast future events, we put ourselves in possible futures and experience what we might feel there, including feelings of anticipated closure. When we come back into the present moment, we bring some of those emotions with us, which can result in us reaching a state of closure purely through imagining what it would be like after a decision is made.

In persuasive contexts this can lead to tricky situations, for example where a sales person uses projective methods to get the customer to imagine what it would be like beyond closure. A surprise effect that also often happens is that the sales person *also* closes. In their enthusiasm to develop a close relationship with the buyer, they empathize so closely that they either lead or follow the buyer into a state of closure. If the buyer actually does close, then this is not a problem. However, the smart buyer will see what is happening and reverse the game. In what has been called the 'Quivering Quill', the buyer holds back just as they are about to sign the deal. The sales person who has themself closed then becomes a nervous wreck and will make significant extra concessions in order to complete the deal.

The final approach

Working up to the point of closure may include particular and specific activities that can be different for each person as we each enact our preferred process. If you can understand the detail of how a person understands or decides then you can shepherd them through these last few steps.

For example:

- A person buying shoes may walk around the shop, returning to the shoes increasingly often, trying them on twice, staring at them and then fingering their wallet.
- A student learns by writing increasingly shorter summaries.
- Someone decides by staring at the ceiling and talking to themselves (as visible by slight movements of their lips) then nodding slowly as things make sense.
- A person likes to see something demonstrated and then gets excited as they realize how they can make use of it.

Information-seeking

When people are faced with something that is uncertain, they seek information. This allows them to infer the thoughts of other people then disagree and challenge points that do not align with their needs and goals.

Information seeking also appears later, when the people have mentally closed in agreement and are seeking detail which they can use to turn the decision into reality. This can be seen in meetings, where discussion turns from argument to practical detail as people converge and close. Information-seeking that follows challenge can hence be a useful signal you can use to identify when people have reached internal closure.

Direction of movement

When you are moving them to tension and closure, consider the direction and distance of movement and the ways you can achieve this.

Building emotion encourages reactive decision based on values, desire or otherwise how they feel. Decreasing emotion opens the door for logic and reason, and is often important if you need to get more powerful and longer-lasting understanding and agreement.

Moving them inwards takes them away from outer concerns and may encourage more self-oriented thought. Moving them outwards makes social concerns more important.

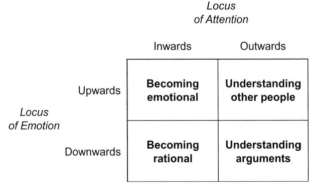

		Inwards	Outwards
Locus of Emotion	Upwards	**Becoming emotional**	**Understanding other people**
	Downwards	**Becoming rational**	**Understanding arguments**

Locus of Attention

Fig. 23.3. Ways to move them

Many closes

In a persuasive situation there is seldom only one closure. Although you may be primarily interested in the single closure that achieves your goals, there may well be many closures along the way. For example, the preacher seeking the goal of changing a basic value may need closures on other beliefs and mental models as well as decisions such as to keep listening and to accept the preacher as truthful.

It is a common trap for would-be persuaders to focus only on the final decision closure and to ignore all of the other closures that are needed. The result of this is that they get stuck in a mire of objections and resistance (it does not help either that many commercial approaches are based on an assumption that only one close is needed).

Adaptation

A key element of changing minds is to discover the optimal sequence of closures and hence design a parallel sequence of tension vectors that drive the other person down the oft-twisting path to the ultimate goal. Information management is a key factor in this action, initially in background research that creates a 'best-guess' plan and subsequently in learning and adjusting the plan in real time.

Real time adaptation of persuasive strategies is not unlike the physical real time action of soft martial arts such as Aikido and Tai Chi. The fundamental skill is a finely-honed sensitivity to the other person, feeling both their current position as well as the tensions that signal their momentary intent. A core ability of a skilled persuader is in sensing the dynamics of emotional and cognitive position and hence guiding the other person through an unfolding series of closures that inexorably lead towards your intended goal. The ultimate achievement in changing minds is that the other person believes that they 'did it all themselves' and that your roles was merely peripheral. This pinnacle was defined around 2500 years ago on Lao Tsu's classic Tao Te Ching verse on leadership:

> The very highest is barely known by men,
> Then comes that which they know and love
> Then that which is feared,
> Then that which is despised.

Achieving closure

After developing tension, there are a number of approaches and methods by which you can move the other person towards and achieve the desired closure.

Directing attention

A basic principle of achieving closure is in managing the other person's attention. By controlling the conversation, you can, for example, direct their attention away from areas that will prevent you achieving the closure you want.

Whatever you talk about will direct attention. For example, if a parent tells a child not to do something, then they are actually directing attention towards doing that thing. It is therefore generally better to talk in positives (unless, of course, you really do want the other person to think of the negative).

Whoever is talking can control attention. It would therefore seem useful to talk most of the time. The problem with this is that if the other person is not interested in what you are saying then your talk will *reduce* their attention. It is often better to talk less and listen more, making subtle use of your talk time to nudge attention in the right direction, for example by judicious use of questions.

Managing goals

Goals are the things we set ourselves to achieve, and by which we reach the pleasure of a satisfying closure. For example I may go to the shops to buy shoes for tomorrow's wedding or want my son to go to bed now without fuss.

If you can discover their goals, then you can frame what you want others to do as a way of achieving their goals. You can also get them to create new goals by stimulating their basic needs, either by threatening them or by offering opportunities to satisfy those needs.

An important consideration here is the effect of positive and negative stimulation of needs. Positive opportunities may attract them, but also may not. Negative threats always cause a reaction, but this can be unpredictable and undesirable.

Whichever method you use, you must, of course, gain trust for it to be most effective. It is also very useful to discover their preferences. People with a low tolerance of risk, for example, will ignore opportunities and react strongly to mild threats.

Managing interests

Interests are more general than goals, tending to sit between goals and needs. For example, when I have the goal of my son going to bed, my interests may include his health and general future, while my deeper needs include control, love and low stress.

Interests are particularly useful in moving to closure in the way that many goals are simply expressions of a higher interest. If you can find the interest, you may work at that level or move them to another goal that satisfies the same interest. For example, a teacher may conclude that a child not doing evening homework has an interest is spending time with friends. The teacher could point out how being made to do homework in school break periods would be even worse for the child's social life, or perhaps show how working harder in class leads to less time doing homework.

Managing interests often involves uncovering the broader purpose of the other person and then showing how your solutions will satisfy that purpose. In this way, specific demands they make that do not meet *your* purpose and interests may be circumvented.

Managing assumptions

In moving towards closure, it is impossible to know all the facts and we regularly make many assumptions. By managing the assumptions in the conversation, you are effectively controlling what is real and true, and hence shaping decisions.

One of the most common sales techniques is the 'assumptive close' where the sales person acts *as if* you have already decided to buy and there are only a few details left to clear up. For example, they may ask you if you prefer 'the red one or the yellow one', or may ask if you are paying by cash or credit card (before you have decided to buy).

Assumption can be done in large, assertive leaps or it may be used as tentative experiments. Whichever way you use it, do ensure it has worked. Sales people often do 'trial closes', where they may take assumptive action, but pause and watch to see if the other person goes along with the assumption without question.

Assumption also occurs in complex sentences when you make multiple assertions without pausing to see if the other person agrees, for example 'After we have gone to town and had coffee, we must check that our tickets have arrived before we get the train to London.'

Signals

Closure can be approached by sending (and reading) signals that indicate you are willing to make compromises in order to reach agreement. A typical signal would be to say that you 'don't normally' reduce your price (and hence signal that in this case you may well do so). A signal, if spotted, may cue a returned signal or even a concession of some kind, and hence move the negotiation a step closer to closure.

Signals can be made with voice tone and body language as well as with plain words. A hesitation or tremor in speech can signal uncertainty, as can body turns and face-touching. Showing uncertainty is usually undesirable, yet, in signaling, you can show your readiness to move while retaining proper dignity.

As well as a readiness to move, signals can be used to telegraph messages about non-moving and consequences. When an aggressor squares up to the other person and stares into their eyes, then a clear message of impending violence is sent. Likewise the firmness in a parent's voice tells a child that they have gone as far as they are going to go.

A significant social benefit of using signals is that it allows people to save face. Social rules generally say that a signal may be ignored, while if something is spoken then it must be recognized. Tentative offers can hence be safely made using a signal, in the confidence that no offence will be caused or taken if it is ignored.

Packaging

A common problem in negotiating is that the things being exchanged are of different value, making an agreeable closure difficult to achieve. A way of addressing this is to build a 'package' of items into a complete offer for which you require some equitable package in return. Packages may also be used to increase the value of what is exchanged. For example a manager offers more money and promotion prospects to an employee in exchange for longer hours and more responsible work.

The point of a package is that it is an all-or-nothing agreement. Either the whole package is agreed or nothing is agreed. Care is needed here, as some people may close on what is offered, ignoring the fact that it is conditional (the crafty negotiator, however may take advantage of this).

Asking

A very simple way of reaching closure is to ask for it, for example where a sales person asks 'Are you ready to buy now?' You can also ask more subtly, for example 'How are you feeling now?' and watching for non-verbal signs of readiness.

Sometimes people are hovering near to closure and just need a nudge to push them over the line. It is as if they feel unable or unwilling to make a decision, perhaps afraid that *you* are not ready for them to close. The cause of this can hark back to childhood days and parents who gave commands by asking ('Are you ready for bed?').

Asking questions also helps you acquire information that will help you understand how ready they are for closure. Good information management is an important part of closing.

Answering

When people have open questions in their minds, then providing an acceptable answer to those questions creates closure. The simplest way to find out if they have any outstanding questions is to ask them.

Rehearsal

By getting them to close on a number of relatively trivial points, you are effectively rehearsing the final closure. As they become more used to feeling the pleasure of closure, then the idea of a closure on a more significant point becomes more attractive and less worrisome.

For example a process of asking question and eliciting or providing answers provides a form of rehearsal for closure on a more important question. Sales people use rehearsal when they do a 'trial close', testing whether the customer is ready to buy the product. A way of causing thoughts of closure is to ask 'What if..' questions.

Silence

Nature abhors a vacuum and when you say nothing you create a tension in the other person that they can only (and easily) close by speaking.

Hence, for example, when a sales person asks for closure, the next step is typically to say nothing, piling on the tension that encourages movement to final agreement.

Legitimizing

Sometimes people feel unable to make a decision and that others must be consulted before closure can be reached. Depending on how real or imagined this is, you can either help them get agreement from others or otherwise remove or circumvent this blockage.

For example when a customer says they will ask their partner, the sales person may say 'What do you think they'll say?' and then guide an imagined conversation that leads to closure of the other person.

Escalation

When people are resisting closure, you can steadily increase the tension. This can be done slowly, carefully bringing the person to boiling point without them noticing, or more suddenly, pushing them past any sticking points.

Escalation may also involve bringing other people into the equation whereby the person may be embarrassed or coerced, for example where a teacher involves the head of the school or parents. Often the threat of such actions is enough to bring the other person to their senses.

Shock

When the other person is stuck in mental position, a short, sharp shock can be an effective way of jolting them out of their frozen state and readying them for the next stage. Shocks can also move reluctant people into final closure, although great care must be used with this method as it can result in reactions of fight, flight or other unwanted action.

Incompletion

When things are left incomplete and unfinished, we seek the closure of seeing them complete so we can turn our attention to other things. Using incompletion can be as simple as not completing sentences (so they must finish them) or starting to write out a sales form, so they will want to see it completed. Leaving many relatively small things incomplete can lead to an unbearable escalation of tension that in turn may trigger a major closure.

Retreating

Sometimes when people are feeling pressured, they will effectively push back and deliberately avoid closure as their sense of control is threatened. If the person looks like they are cornered, you can pile on the pressure in the hope that they will crack, but it can be much better to show concern by backing off and giving them time to think. This increases trust and an exchange dynamic where they move to closure in gratitude, particularly if this allows them to save face.

Retreat can also be used by approaching the person in a friendly way and then backing off. Many people, once they trust and feel a bond with you, will then follow you and also step into closure, perhaps in fear of otherwise losing the connection with you.

Objection-handling

A common situation occurs where you know what is needed but they do not. If you are identifying with them (in a good trust-building style), then you may start to assume that what is obvious to you is also obvious to them. What they see, however, is that you are acting as if something is true about which they may well be unconvinced. Telling them they have a problem is likely be ineffective here, as it just creates a tension between their certainty and your assertion. This is typically how objections to selling occur, for example where a computer salesperson launches into an enthusiastic description of benefits before the customer has even considered that they might need a new computer.

Handling objections is typically done first by understanding the objection and then by seeking a closure agreement that if the objections can be overcome then the deal will be complete. For example 'If we can address your concerns about finance, will you buy the car today?' Objections are then creatively addressed, for example when the sales person offers payment terms that overcome short-term cost concerns.

Objections may also be addressed in other ways, including:

- Dismissing them as irrelevant.
- Decreasing their priority or importance.
- Turning them around and showing them as a benefit.
- Writing them down as a list and visibly crossing them off as they are addressed.
- Postponing them so they can be addressed after closure.

Closing techniques

Sales people have a wide range of methods that nudge the customer towards closure, just a few of which are in Table 23.4. Note that a number of these may not gain lasting commitment and are hence inappropriate when the relationship or repeat sales are important.

Table 23.4. Sales closing techniques

Close	Action
Adjournment	Give them time to think. Say 'next time'
Alternative	Offer a limited set of choices (eg. two items)
Assumptive	Act as if they are ready to close
Balance-sheet	Summarize the pros and cons
Best time	Emphasize now is the best time to buy
Bonus	Offer delighter to clinch the deal
Companion	Sell to the influential person they are with
Conditional	Link close to resolution of objections
Doubt	*You* doubt, *they* persuade you!
Embarrassment	Make not buying embarrassing
Handshake	Offer hand to trigger automatic response
Hurry	Go fast to prevent them thinking of objections
No hassle	Make it very easy to buy
Now or never	This is the only time they can buy
Price promise	Guarantee to beat any other price
Puppy	Play on cuteness
Quality	Sell on quality, not on price
Standing room only	Show how others are queuing to buy
Summary	List all the reasons to buy
Testimonial	Show happy customers
Valued customer	Make them feel special
Ultimatum	Show bad things if they do not buy
Yes-set	Get them saying yes beforehand

24. Commitment

The problem with closure is that, like an ill-fitting door, things do not always stay closed. People who had bought the car, understood the lesson or agreed to support a change, suddenly or slowly regress to a state of uncertainty or regret. In fact there is a name for it: 'buyer's remorse' is what customers feel when the euphoria of the bargain dies down and they find themselves with a turkey. In some countries there are 'cooling down' periods when people can decline a previously-agreed offer, typically in purchase of financial products where there is no risk of 'soiled goods'. Many retailers also have a returns policy that, while it encourages early closure, can also lead to a later, and potentially costly, return of the product.

For some persuasion this is the subject's problem, not yours, for example when you have their money which they cannot claw back. In fact you may never meet them again and hence be safe against their anger and resentment. In practice such situations are rare and ongoing commitment is important, either because you will want to change their minds again or because the initial point of closure is not the end of the transaction. For example there is often a gap in creating organizational change between agreeing to the change and implementing the change. Likewise there is a gap between being taught a principle in the classroom and applying it in examinations or the outside world.

The bottom line in many persuasive situations is that the story does not stop after closure, and that there is more important work to do to ensure minds stay changed. This is the work of commitment management and can require at least as much effort as the original sale, particularly if the closure was not particularly strong. 'Pay now or pay later' is an appropriate adage, as good work in trust, tension and closure can make work in commitment easier. The reverse, of course, is also true.

The nature of commitment

The first step in managing commitment, as with other factors, is to get a good grasp of its deeper nature. When you know how it works, you will be better able to reliably manage it.

Shallow and deep commitment

Post-closure commitment is sometimes solid and firm, unshakable even in the face of disconfirming evidence that indicates the decision might have been wrong. Sadly, such strong buy-in is relatively rare. After the tense excitement of closing, doubts easily creep in and the certainty starts to unravel, as what made sense at the time now appears to be less reasonable.

Shallow commitment is often fragile and easily leads to wavering, indecision and retreat. A person with shallow commitment may well fear the criticism of others and be swayed by contrary arguments. You may easily get to initial closure with such people, but they just as easily float back into an unconvinced state or be otherwise persuaded to another new position. Shallowness can be a feature of personality where some people fear significant commitment, perhaps anticipating failure as they lack confidence in themselves or others.

Deep commitment, on the other hand, is robust and does not waver, even in the face of doubts or criticism from others. A deeply committed person may well be a visible advocate, loudly trumpeting the benefits and defending against doubters.

Deep commitment is often based on a clear and complete understanding that truly knows the reasons and appreciates the benefits. It may also come from an unshakable faith in the source of the subject in question. Thus a person who believes I am a real expert will commit fully to what I say in my area of expertise. To doubt one thing you are told by such a reference person is to doubt everything they have ever told you, which few are prepared to do.

Clearly, deep commitment in changing minds is a good thing, yet it is not always easy to gain. To get commitment that is deep enough for your purpose often requires significant and ongoing commitment on *your* part that in some ways can be a critical part of the ongoing persuasion. When others see you are in it for the long term, they are more likely to decide to join you.

Head, heart and hands

In gaining full commitment on something, you need not just logical agreement but also emotional buy-in and practical action. Closure may initially be gained in one dimension, but for sustained commitment this has to extend to all three. Commitment may hence be viewed as a triple-closure process, as in Figure 24.1.

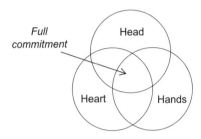

Fig. 24.1. Full commitment = heads, heart and hands

Single closure is not enough. If closure is a rational 'head' decision then a lack of emotional buy-in can easily lead to later problems ('It makes sense, but I don't really want it'). A simple 'heart' closure can also fail ('I want to do it, but it doesn't really seem worth it.') And a commanding 'just do it' approach that get only compliant 'hands' closure can lead to both cognitive and emotional rejection.

The sequence of head, heart and hands can be done in any order, as Table 24.1. The best sequence varies with individuals. Some prefer to be emotionally excited first, others need to start with reason while others again are happy to get on with it and make sense as they go along. It is important when starting with hands not to give significant rewards for this as it can lead to a rationalization of working only for the reward.

Table 24.1. Head, heart and hands sequencing

Sequence	Thinking process
Hands → Head	I am doing this, so there must be a good reason.
Hands → Heart	I am doing it, so I must feel good about it.
Head → Heart	This makes sense, so I feel good about it.
Head → Hands	It makes sense, so I'll give it a go.
Heart → Hands	I like the idea so I'll give it a go.
Heart → Head	I like it so it must make sense.

Loyalty

Loyalty is an emotional state of bonding whereby a person becomes attached to another person or to some thing. For example I can be loyal to Coca Cola, local stores, my country, my wife and so on. This attachment affects the person's decision such that they will support and defend people and things to which they are loyal to an extraordinary degree.

In business, beyond satisfied customer you can create loyal customers who come back time and again. The best customers, however, are advocates who tell others about how wonderful you are, as in Figure 24.2. Friends are like this too, and good friends will stick up for you when others are critical. This level of passion and commitment does not come free and you also need to work on a reciprocal commitment that bonds you together.

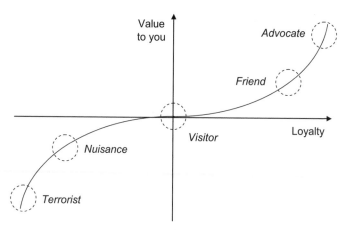

Fig. 24.2. Loyalty and value

Customers (and 'friends') can also be disloyal, turning against you with commitment to harm rather than help you. Sometimes they may just be a nuisance, though at worst they can appear as 'terrorists', who actively seek to hurt you.

This negative commitment can be created by your actions in the same way that you can create positive commitment. If you betray a friendship or act in a way that contradicts social rules then they may seek retribution for your 'sins'.

The perniciousness of reward

It might seem an easy thing to gain commitment if you can place a juicy carrot at the end of the road. But simple rewards are not that easy. If you offer money or some other reward then people will often shift their attention away from the real goal and towards the reward. You may hence *reduce* the internal commitment you seek to increase.

Money is an extrinsic reward. Bonuses and commissions easily lead to actions that maximize personal financial benefits while having unexpected and unwanted effects elsewhere. What you really want is the more motivating intrinsic reward of them feeling good when they think of reaching the final goal.

Rewards can work, but only circuitously, as what really counts is what I tell myself when I ask 'Why am I doing this?' A small reward can be effective as I cannot justify my action as being only for this and must therefore conclude that I wanted to do it anyway. Larger rewards can work, but only if they align with a professional pride that equates a high fee for a job well done. The best advice for motivating people at work is generally to pay them a fair wage and then work hard at creating a deep intrinsic motivation that bonds people to the ideals and leaders of the organization.

Lessons from brainwashing

After the Korean War, a number of American prisoners-of-war returned with a conviction that communism was better than capitalism. Their experiences were studied carefully and the term 'brainwashing' given to the treatment that had led to the methods used to build commitment toward communist ideals.

A key thing the communists did was to give small rewards for incremental moves in the right direction, such as for talking about the benefits of communism and then for signing a statement to this effect. To create internal justification for their actions the prisoners gradually became advocates of the communist philosophy and cause. This was coupled with an intense immersion that included long lectures, 'friendly' interrogation, isolation from alternative viewpoints and detailed confessions.

What also happened was that when the brainwashed soldiers returned to America, their brainwashing gradually wore off. Values and beliefs are very deep structures and even intensive methods can be insufficient to irreversibly change them.

Lessons from cults

Some religions and cults create fanatical devotion by using various methods, including:

- A generally social and caring environment.
- Trivialization and demonizing of external unbelievers.
- Intensive correction activity for those who waver, with ultimate expulsion should this 'penitence' fail.
- Demonstrations of faith that strengthen the organization and weaken personal ability to resist, including personal sacrifices, financial contributions and missionary work.
- Personal attacks that destroy identity and create guilt.
- Requiring confession and relinquishing one's former life.
- Secret knowledge only available to inner circles.
- Study and work levels that lead to exhaustion and further weakening of any potential resistance.
- Rites of passage that cement entry to inner circles.
- Always a next level to which people must aspire.
- Unquestionable spirituality, knowledge and authority of inner circles, with one ultimate central authority.

In other words, there is a constant pressure and desire to get to the next level which promises much, yet actually leads to greater striving towards the next level again. This non-stop effort is driven by the pull of the promise and hope of power, spirituality, accolade, salvation and other gains that play strongly to deep needs. It is also driven by the fear of wasting the sunk cost of all the striving so far, plus the fear of rejection and subsequent loneliness and hardship.

Lessons here that are applicable for creating commitment in the 'real' world include to:

- Make the ultimate benefits of commitments clear and desirable.
- Provide a constant stream of benefits that are paid for by demonstration of commitment.
- Let them see how commitment is comfortable and any lack of commitment is not.
- Deal with non-commitment justly, but robustly.

Lessons from the military

How do armies convince sane people to put themselves in mortal danger, even to charge into a hail of bullets and certain death? Does a person do this out of national pride? Seldom, in fact. Armies make a big deal about honor and dishonor. Heroes are worshipped as gods while cowards are incarcerated and expelled as vermin. On top of that they create powerful human bonds by forming small groups and then putting them through difficult training experiences in which they are interdependent for success. Soldiers seldom put themselves in harm's way out of a pure sense of duty – they do it more for their comrades and to avoid the shame of cowardice.

Military lessons for commitment include:

- Creating strong bonds between people through shared and difficult experiences.
- Socializing loyalty and comradeship.
- Celebrating the heroes. Punishing and reviling the traitors.

Lessons from business

Commercial and non-profit organizations are also very concerned with commitment. Businesses do use financial incentives, at base a salary that is predicated on the exchange of defined work for money. They also use 'golden handcuffs' that reward today's performance in the medium term future, for example with share options that cannot be cashed in for several years. Careless use of financial incentives do lead to dysfunctional actions such as sales people who offer deep discounts or hold up sales in order to ensure they get regular bonuses for meeting artificial targets.

Businesses also work hard to attract and keep people by paying attention to such things as leadership style, operational culture and physical surroundings. Companies that win 'Best company to work for' awards attract more applicants and can pick the cream of the crop.

Companies also pay significant attention to sustaining customer loyalty and work on the whole purchase and ownership lifecycles, as well as manufacturing processes, to be the supplier of choice.

Lessons from business for general commitment include balancing of financial and emotional incentives that give people what they need and constantly remind them that looking elsewhere would be a futile and unworthy activity.

Sustaining commitment

Critical tasks in managing commitment lie in the process of *sustaining* and *strengthening* it, which can be the hardest parts of the persuasion process. Gaining closure is the start of commitment and can be relatively easy in comparison to the potentially long slog of keeping people engaged, interested and committed.

Social position

One of the things in life that is of constant concern is what others think of us. After any closure we therefore may easily worry about what others might say. For example if I have agreed to buy a car I might still worry about criticisms from friends and family and the effect on my status in these groups.

By making things socially desirable, the commitment of people involved is increased. If staying committed makes me look good and backtracking makes me look bad, then I will sustain my commitment.

Affirmation

After closure, people often want to be reassured that they have made the right decision – so tell them this. Start by agreeing what you have agreed and cementing the initial closure with congratulations, smiles, nods and other affirming body language.

Then provide further ways of telling them that they have done well in their decision. When a person buys a car they feel affirmed when they see similar cars, adverts for the car, approval from other people, positive magazine reviews and so on.

Evidence

When a person has signed up to some activity which they may feel might not work out as planned, they may back out. This is typically what happens in business change, where managers retract their support for an initially-interesting improvement activity.

By providing a non-stop stream of evidence that things are going to happen as planned, for example by giving regular updates on progress, they will be reassured and more likely to continue their commitment. Evidence that other people have made the same decision as them and have already gained a benefit will also likely sustain commitment.

Trial

When people are told that something will work in a certain way, for example when a sales person talks about how effective and easy it is to use a vacuum cleaner, then the customer might be justifiably cynical. If, however, they can try it out themselves, then the evidence of their own experience will build stronger commitment.

Confidence

The confidence we have that any commitment will bring eventual reward is based on a combination of our self-confidence and the confidence we have in others. When achieving the final goal requires our own skill and determination, then we must believe in ourselves and our abilities. And when we are dependent on others to help us reach our ends, then we will watch them carefully as we seek confirmation or otherwise, that our trust is justified.

Sustaining commitment therefore requires constant attention to the confidence of the target person that expected and desired goals will be achieved. Confidence-building examples include where:

- A teacher sets tests before the real exam as much to build confidence as ability.
- A presenter at a conference mentions her qualifications and experience at the start of the presentation.
- A sales person congratulates the buyer on a wise decision.

Involvement

When people are involved with something, even in small ways, they will develop a sense of ownership and belonging and so will build internal commitment. For example a business manager who is involved in planning a change is more likely to go along with the work than a manager who has the change presented to her or him.

Consistency

When a person says they are going to do something then they are more likely to do it, for not to do so would be to show inconsistency between words and actions and hence appear less trustworthy and socially less desirable. The more you can get people to show their commitment, particularly to others, the more that commitment will become real.

Consequences

A common way of ensuring commitment is to make the consequences of not fulfilling the commitment very clear. These consequences are usually negative and uncomfortable, such as when a mother who wants her son to complete a promise to accompany her to town, points out how he would be lonely if he stayed at home.

Positive consequences for staying committed may also be used, such as where the mother suggests her son might meet friends if he goes to town. Negative and positive consequences used together have a 'push-pull' double effect.

Linking

When a commitment is linked to other commitments, then reneging on the commitment would also damage those interests. For example if a person borrows money, based on the assumption of continued employment, their commitment to working increases.

For example, a private school may secure the commitment of a parent to their child's education by encouraging them to put the child's name down for an exclusive university. The parent cannot now back out of paying school fees without damaging the chances of their child going to the target university.

Inoculation

A simple method of sustaining commitment in the face of likely criticism works in the same way as a medical inoculation against a virus. The process is to help the person rehearse responding to weak criticism (which you provide). For example:

> You: 'What would you say to a person who said you 'look stoopid'?
> Them: 'I'd tell them they are stupid not to buy one too!!'
> You: 'That's right! And how would that make you feel?
> Them: I'd be amused and feel good.

When they find they are not troubled by this and can respond to weak criticism, they gain confidence and translate this into the ability to respond to *any* criticism.

Part D:
Putting it together

The Core Process of changing minds described in Part C is the essence of any persuasive situation. At the heart of this sequence, trust, tension and closure appear many in different forms of persuasion and in many different ways.

This final section of the book shows some of the situations when persuasion happens and how trust, tension and closure appear within the more general patterns of 'pain and pleasure' and 'connect and change'.

25. Pain and Pleasure

Sigmund Freud is famed for his principles of Pain and Pleasure and their power as motivators, although Aristotle also noticed these a couple of millennia earlier.

'We may lay it down that Pleasure is a movement, a movement by which the soul as a whole is consciously brought into its normal state of being; and that Pain is the opposite.'

— Aristotle, *Rhetoric*, ~300 BC

Both pain and pleasure cause tension but lead to opposite reactions as we seek to avoid pain while being attracted to pleasure. These can also be found in the way people enact their preferences, with some people being more avoidant of pain while others play a more hedonistic game in seeking pleasure.

Pain and pleasure can happen together, resulting in a bizarre thrill that is at the root of such dysfunctions as masochism and shoplifting, where the pain of breaking rules is overwhelmed by the tense excitement of closing on 'something for nothing.'

We also think about pain and pleasure in the future and *anticipated* pain or pleasure can be as horrible or wonderful as the real thing. In fact sometimes our imagined exaggerations make the experience somewhat more intense than the real thing, which is perhaps why Robert Louis Stephenson said that 'It is better to travel hopefully than to arrive.'

Pain and pleasure are fundamental motivators and the avoidance and attraction they cause can be deliberate tools that are used in many different forms of persuasion.

Push and pull

The way we persuade others typically varies between 'push' approaches, where we coerce through the power of our position or other forms of threat, and 'pull' methods, where we seek to convince people to collaborate of their own free will ('pulling' from us rather than us pushing them).

Push methods have the advantage of creating immediate action, but they do not buy hearts and minds. They are most useful to kick-start a change, perhaps shocking people out of complacency, but are poor methods for creating sustained motivation. If you push a person, they are likely to push back or run away.

Pull methods of persuasion may require the time to build the trust, social capital and credibility of the persuader. Using pull is less predictable, as it allows target people to refuse or respond in ways that may cause us problems. It is fear of such problems that leads many to use coarser 'push' methods. On the other hand, when people do agree, it is likely that they are doing so for positive inner reasons and hence will remain committed for longer and through tougher circumstances.

Punishment and reward

In B. F. Skinner's Operant Conditioning (which he built on the back of Pavlov's Classical Conditioning) the simple fact was identified that you cannot get animals to do something by punishing them. Desired action comes only from reward, while punishment works best for prevention and extinguishing undesirable ways of behaving.

While people are more complex than animals, the same principle applies: to get them to do what you want, then reward and the pleasure it brings works best (although care is needed to ensure pleasure is linked to the desired actions and not just the reward).

Punishing people is not as straightforward as it is with animals, as people may react in unexpected and sometimes vengeful ways. When training children, for example, it is often recommended that undesirable ways of behaving are simply ignored. This can be because punishment can be seen as pleasurable in that it is giving desired attention, which is preferred to no attention. This can sadly lead to a spiral of abuse, where out-of-control parents simply increase punishment only to be frustrated by the child continuing to be naughty.

One-off vs. repeat selling

Coercive, pain-based methods that batter a customer into a purchase are typical of some traditional selling methods. A problem with this approach is where the customer later realizes they have been sold something that is of low quality or which they do not need (and which generates yet more pain).

This method of 'hard sell' works when customers have no form of redress and who are very unlikely to buy again from you, which means you have to have a steady stream of new customers. In most selling situations, customers are likely to return for repeat purchases and make recommendations about the seller to their friends, giving an amplifying effect of increasing or decreasing sales depending on their satisfaction.

As a result, much selling is a lot softer and ongoing customer satisfaction is of very real importance. This is one reason why sellers often focus on building relationships, understanding real needs and delivering good value for money, which of course all plays to the 'pleasure principle' and leads to repeat purchases and valuable positive references to other potential customers.

Competitive vs. collaborative negotiation

In a similar way to hard and soft selling, there are two ends of the spectrum in negotiation: one that is hard, pushy and pain-oriented and another that uses pull and promises more pleasure.

In competitive negotiation there is an assumption of a zero-sum, fixed-pie, win-lose situation. If you get more of the pie, then I get less. The game is hence seen as a straight fight in which each person tries to maximize what they get at the expense of the other. Deception is common and relative power is an important factor.

Against this, a collaborative approach assumes that the pie can be increased in size and that a smaller portion of a large pie is better than a larger portion of a small pie. Note that collaborative approaches are not weak or concessionary, and may well involve tough discussions and careful trading. But at least they are fair and deceptive tactics are minimized. This method was championed by Harvard's Roger Fisher and William Ury following their work in the nuclear weapons negotiations of the 1970s and 1980s.

Change and martial arts

Psychologist Kurt Lewin identified three phases of change: unfreezing, transition and re-freezing. Unfreezing, getting people to move even a little from their current position, is similar to martial arts where the notion of 'breaking root' is used to physically destabilize the other person. When they are unbalanced, it is then easy to move them where you will.

'Breaking root' in persuasion motivates a person to change. This often requires a brief period of pain, for example where they realize that their current position is no longer tenable. Pain as an ongoing motivator is not very effective and moving the person to the new destination is best done with pleasure, creating pull by selling the vision of a better future, involving them in the change and showing how they can make a real difference.

The list goes on

The dual hard-soft, pain-pleasure approaches appear in all kinds of other places beyond selling and negotiating. Table 25.1 shows some of the alternative approaches that can be found across a wide range of disciplines.

Table 25.1. Positive and negative methods

	Negative (pain)	Positive (pleasure)
Teaching	Strict discipline and 'injecting' knowledge with learning by rote	Lively discussion and instilling love of the subject
Romantic partners	Abusive demands and veiled threats	Loving concern and helpful suggestions
Managing	Coercive managers who tell you what to do	Inspirational leaders who sell the vision
Military strategy	Hand-to-hand large-scale fighting	Maneuvering and constrained action
Interrogation	Direct accusation that seeks confession	Get them talking with subtle questions
Begging	Nuisance wheedling and triggering guilt	Providing entertainment and giving thanks
Advertising	Hard-hitting descriptions of product benefits	Entertainment that builds positive associations

Hurt and Rescue

Pain and pleasure are both used in 'hurt and rescue', which is a fundamental pattern that appears across many methods of persuasion. The basic sequence is first to create tension by 'hurting' them in some way, then to 'rescue' them by throwing them a lifeline. By accepting the 'help', they achieve closure through the relief and satisfaction of removing the pain of the hurt. Note that 'hurting' includes creating positive tensions such as desire and exposing problems they will need to resolve.

Having accepted your help, you get the added bonus that they will feel obliged to repay your kindness, which you can use to lever further change.

Hurt and Rescue is little more than creating tension and then offering closure. It is a very common pattern that appears across many different contexts. Table 25.2 gives examples some of these.

Table 25.2. Hurt and Rescue

	Hurt (pain)	Rescue (pleasure)
Interrogation	Bad cop makes scary threats	Good cop offers way out
Selling	Show they have a problem	Offer product to solve their problem
Teaching	Give them work they cannot do	Show them how to do it
Leadership	Describe the current crisis	Show them the vision of a better future
Preaching	Talk about judgment, hellfire and damnation	Tell them how to live in order to get to heaven
Advertising	Tell them how bad breath loses friends	Explain that mouthwash freshens breath
Policing	Tell them what laws they have broken	Tell them you are letting them off this time
Parenting	Explain dangers of getting lost	Hug them then hold their hand
Romance	Talk about the pain of being apart	Propose marriage or living together
Coaching	Push person to painful exercise	Tell them how this will help them win

26. Connect and Change

The use of pain and pleasure is very common in persuasion and changing minds, as described in the previous chapter. Both are associated with tension that can be used to wind up the target person and move them towards closure, as epitomized by the pattern of hurt and rescue. There is, however, another approach that is more subtle in style and in the thinking behind it.

Pain and pleasure are sensations that the individual person experiences and which provide significant motivation, but what of the power of relationship? The bond between people is one of the most powerful forces on the planet. As a measure of the power of relationships, few would choose die for *things*, but many would die for the *people* they care for. If you connect well with others, then you can influence them in ways that many of the external and separate methods of pain and pleasure cannot touch.

The basic principle of this chapter is that if you truly bond with people, then when you move, you move together. In this way, you can connect and change, influencing them in very subtle ways.

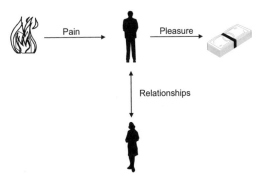

Fig. 26.1. Pain, Pleasure and Relationships

Integration and Isolation

When we are born, we exist in a strange but uniquely harmonious state where we do not think of ourselves as separate (or even think of our selves). We simply exist as a part of an undifferentiated universe. Psychoanalyst Jacques Lacan described this state as 'The Real', being as close to an external reality as we ever get.

As we grow and develop, we move away from this comfortable unity, distinguishing individual objects and the boundaries that define them. A classic shock point is when we look in a mirror or at another child and realize that we are individual beings, with a separate identity. This can cause a terrible sense of loneliness, yet we also revel in the power and control that individuality brings. From then on, we are torn between the two states: of integration and isolation, of oneness and separateness. Table 26.1 shows some of these.

Table 26.1. Integration and Isolation

	Integrated unity	Isolated identity
Society	Belonging to groups	Being an individual
Control	Giving control to a trusted person	Taking control and doing things by oneself
Sexual intercourse	Having sex, joining bodies	Separating, regaining identity
Relationship	Finding a partner, falling in love, sharing	Living one's own life, not having dependencies
In crowds	Losing oneself in the crowd, mob mentality	Watching the crowd, being sensibly separate

A further separation from that original sense of unity is created when we learn a language, with words that create a symbolic life where to describe something is to enable conversation and connection with others. Yet through that linguistic simplification we also separate ourselves further from the reality that the words symbolize.

Meditation, prayer, dance and many other rituals are methods we use as we seek to re-discover that original harmony. We seek one-ness with God, nirvana and obliteration of the self – and yet we cannot bear to give up our identities, for how else would we know what we had attained?

It is in this perpetual search for re-connection that our relationships go beyond functional convenience and reach out to connect our inner selves with those of others.

Connecting

A critical part of social life is in the sense of belonging we get when we join with others, and particularly so in the initial flush of togetherness when we connect with somebody new. In an echo of that early unity and connection with mother, we feel a warmth and happiness as we bond with the other person.

Shared identity

This state has several names: harmony, concord, rapport, friendship, kinship and so on. The joining together is not just two people feeling good about one another – it is also about two people *sharing* a sense of identity and, in some ways, becoming one extended person. In a well-formed state of harmony, there is a strong element of one-ness, of being with and a part of each other.

It also brings a shared fate and single purpose. What is good for one is good for the other, and vice versa. And therein lies the heart of what makes this a part of a powerful method of changing minds.

Of course a full joining of identities is an ultimate state and seldom happens in practice. Nevertheless, the principle still applies and even a relatively small connection with other people can be experienced as disproportionately pleasurable and fulfilling.

Social harmony

One of the basic principles of any group or society is to create a degree of harmony within its members. They share an identity that bonds them together. The group may well have a name which members proudly proclaim ('I'm British!') and have unique beliefs and rules, and where conformance is a critical part of the social harmony.

Trust and harmony

Trust is a core aspect of harmony. First, you need to gain trust in order to enable others to connect with you. When you have got through this barrier, then the connection gives automatic trust. If a person is a part of you, then you trust them virtually as you trust yourself. In the style of the Core Process for changing minds, creating harmony is an excellent way of achieving and sustaining trust (although breaking that trust creates a terrible dissonance).

Changing

Once you have achieved some degree of connected harmony, then you have the ability to change the other person's mind from the inside.

Disharmony

When the desirable state of connected unity is broken or disturbed, even a little bit, we feel the discomfort of tension as we perceive the gap between desirable total harmony and actual disharmony. One of life's forces is that we move towards harmony. Like water running downhill towards the sea, we seek to re-establish unity. Our immediate and primitive reaction to disharmony is to reach out and seek to restore the comfort of connection.

Disconnecting

The basic principle of changing a person with whom we have some harmony is therefore simply to start disconnecting slightly from the other person. As they feel their connection with you slipping away, they will feel a tension that seeks to reconnect more closely with you, maximizing the state of harmony.

Moving

In disconnecting from the other person, you should be moving in the direction that you want them to change. For example a sales person who wants to sell a particular car may start with the harmony of the customer's chosen car, then point out both small problems with this and then advantages that reconnect them with the target car.

The trick in disconnecting and moving is to find the degree of separation that leads to the maximum motivation for the other person to follow you without moving so far or fast that they let go to pursue more satisfying connections. A smaller gap will result in slower movement as they remain closer to their comfort zone. Too large a gap will create dysfunctional anxiety and potential feelings of betrayal (and subsequent reaction).

Change is often best achieved in a series of small steps of connection and separation, which create sensations of pleasure and pain. Importantly, the first step is the pleasure of connection and the feeling of trust, only after which the uncomfortable tension of separation can have a motivating effect.

Identity and control

Connecting and changing are linked with the basic needs for a sense of identity and a sense of control, which is perhaps why it is such as powerful method.

Connecting with other people increases our sense of identity, both because they are paying attention to us and also because we are gaining their identity and all of the associations that go with it, including their power and ability to control.

Change threatens and evokes the need for a sense of control, and when the other person moves away, the disconnection threatens the sense of identity.

Pacing and leading

'Pace and lead' is a widely used approach that is similar to connecting and changing, although it is typically framed in a simpler way and has a generally short-term focus.

Pacing

'Pacing' is typically achieved by echoing the other person's words and body language in some way, for example by using similar language. While this is a valid method of gaining short-term trust, it is not the only way of achieving this end.

Another form of pacing is to initially agree with the other person, giving approval for their ideas (and hence the person). When we align with others in any way, we form a connection with them. Even listening without comment or otherwise showing an interest is often enough.

Leading

'Leading' in this context is a way of creating change by demonstration, for example where you act in the desired way or otherwise work in an assumptive fashion.

Leading for change in operational contexts goes further than 'pace and lead' and requires significant work by the leader, as discussed on the next page. While people seek leaders they also suspect them and the leader must show *their* commitment before many will agree to follow them.

273

Leadership

Connecting and changing is a particularly effective method when you need to lead people, for example in the context of business change. As described in Chapter 18, leadership is different from management in that followership is voluntary and the leader needs to sell the vision rather than just tell people what to do. In essence, leaders do two things: knowing where to go and to persuading their followers to go with them.

Connecting

Leaders start with 'we', doing all they can to emotionally connect with their people. They do not sit in their ivory towers – they get out, walking and talking with their followers, building trust by showing competence in their work and demonstrating that they care.

If they are successful, then their followers will connect strongly with them and will be prepared to follow them through thick and thin, confident and comfortable in their shared identity.

Changing

Leaders typically promote change by expounding on a vision, creating a tension gap between a problematic now and a better future. They then take a step towards that future, encouraging their followers to join them on the journey.

A common way that leaders embody change is by behaving in a way as if the change had already happened. In this way they act as models, visibly showing the gap between how their followers behave and how they behave. Behaving is a strong part of identity and, in order to retain the connection, the followers must *change who they are*. This is not easy and perhaps highlights why it is so easy to fail in attempts to lead. If you do not make an effective connection or if you do not embody the change, then you may lose your followers (or never gain them in the first place).

Same and different

The leader's position is unusual in that they are both connected and disconnected at the same time. They maintain that important connection with their followers, yet they also stand apart. They are both one of us and someone different, someone to be admired and desired.

OODA

Colonel John Boyd was a remarkable pilot and strategist who identified a four-stage thinking model that is used by pilots and many others who must engage in rapid action in a responsive context.

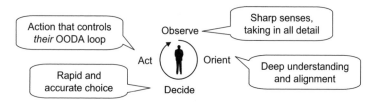

Fig. 26.2. OODA loop

Observation

Observation is the 'information' action, keeping senses wide open and taking in maximum detail from the surroundings. For a pilot, this includes instruments and other aircraft. In a social situation it includes monitoring the minute body language and inflections of other people.

Orientation

Orientation for a pilot is a rapid cognitive alignment to the situation, understanding what is going on and seeing what is real. In this way the pilot sensitively connects to the whole, complex context.

In a social situation a sensitive person orients themselves to the environment and to the cognitive and emotional states of other people, aligning with them and achieving remarkable rapport.

Decision

From the connected, sensitive stage, the pilot can decide what to do. In the heat of battle, the decision must be rapid and precise – one wrong choice can mean death. In a social situation, accurate observation and close orientation give effective choice that leads to the results you seek.

Action

After decision comes rapid action, which may be radical or just a slight course change. This results in others going through their own OODA loop. If your loop was effective, then you can intentionally *manage their loop*. In conflict and competition, the most effective OODA wins!

The romantic dance

Connecting and changing is a common pattern in boy-meets-girl scenarios. Author Eileen McCann describes beautifully the chase games that we play in our search for a romantic partner.

A typical flirting sequence happens when a boy looks at a girl, who holds his gaze for a second longer than might be expected (connecting), then looks down (a submissive action), then flashes a glance back to check that he is still hooked. He might then approach her (showing she caused a change in him), at which she acts coyly. This is then followed by a game of attraction and retreat, connection and change.

The reason for backing off after connecting with the other person is the same as in leadership: to get the person to change, in this case moving towards you. The principle of scarcity says that we desire more that that which we cannot get, and particularly that which is seems just out of reach. The gap between having and not having creates a motivating force that strengthens desire and, in the romantic setting, makes passion more ardent.

Domestic chase games

In the more mundane domestic setting, Eric Berne describes the 'Games People Play', including many dysfunctional and obsessive patterns that we compulsively repeat even when we know they are not good for us.

The domestic situation is potent perhaps because the connection is already there, and all it needs to change the other person is to threaten that connection. Domestic arguments, for example, often result in one person backing off, in effect inviting the other person to reconnect with them with an apology.

A similar pattern is where an addict forms a relationship with a doctor or carer of some kind. They connect, which feels good for the addict, as the doctor has a desirable identity and offers to connect this with the addict. But then, when the addict seems to have changed for the good, the doctor backs off, hoping that the addict is cured, but with the result that the addict has a complete relapse. What has happened here is that as the doctor backs away, this creates an uncomfortable change and the addict seeks to close this tension gap in the one way they know works: by going back to addiction square one.

Epilogue

Well, there you have it. Changing minds in more detail than you might find in many places. Reviewers of drafts of the book told me it was pretty dense but full of very practical stuff, which it is what it is all about, really. In a former existence I was an engineer, where two key questions were 'How does it work?' and 'How can I use it?' I guess some things don't change. And that's the critical metric: if in any way this book helps you change minds (or, for that matter, spot people trying to change *your* mind), then it will have succeeded.

I had planned to add further chapters with examples in assorted disciplines from argumentation to teaching, but I got to 250+ pages and concluded that enough was enough for now.

If this book sells well then I have a plan for a follow-up entitled 'Changing Minds: In Practice' that digs into how these methods and more are used in different disciplines and everyday situations. So if you like the book and want to see the sequel, do please recommend it to others!

Good luck and best wishes with changing minds,

Dave

References

This book is strongly targeted at practitioners rather than seeking to add to the academic canon, yet much of what is written here is based on a long reading, as well as a broad experience. The lack of references in the text is deliberate as, while this is important for academics, it can be very off-putting for the non-academic reader. In some compensation here are just a few of the places I looked along the way.

1. The SIFT-3M Model

(See chapters below for references)

2. Motivators

(See chapters below for references)

3. Needs

Alderfer, C. (1972). *Existence, Relatedness and Growth*. New York: Free Press.

Argyris, C. (1999). *On Organizational Learning (2nd edition)*, Oxford: Blackwell.

Bem, D. J. (1972). Self-perception theory. In L. Berkowitz (ed), *Advances in experimental social psychology*, (Vol. 6. pp. 1-62), New York: Academic Press.

Brehm, J. W. (1966). *A theory of psychological reactance*, New York: Academic Press.

Cooley, C. H. (1902). *Human nature and social order*, New York: Scribner's.

Darwin, C., (1859). *On the Origin of Species by means of natural selection*. John Murray, London.

Dawkins, R. (2006). *The Selfish Gene (3rd Edition)*, Oxford University Press, Oxford.

Deci, E. L. (1975). *Intrinsic motivation*. New York: Plenum..

Deci, E. and Ryan, R. (1991). A motivational approach to self: Integration in personality. In R. Dienstbier (Ed.), *Perspectives on motivation*. Nebraska Symposium on Motivation. Lincoln: University of Nebraska Press.

Freud, S. and Freud, A. (2005). *The Essentials of Psychoanalysis (new edtion)*, London: Vintage.

du Gay, P. Evans, J. and Redman, P. (2000). *Identity: A Reader*, London: Sage.

Gjesme, T. and Nygard, R. (eds). (1996). *Advances in Motivation*, Oxford: Scandinavian University Press.

Glasser, W (1984). *Control Theory -- A New Explanation of How We Control Our Lives*. New York: Harper and Row.

James, W. (1892). *Psychology: Briefer course*. New York: Collier.

Kruglanski, A. W. and Webster, D. M. (1996). Motivated closing of the mind: "Seizing" and "freezing." *Psychological Review, 103*, 2, 263-283.

Latané, B. (1981). The psychology of social impact, *American Psychologist, 36*, 343-356.

Maslow, A. (1943). A theory of human motivation, *Psychological Review, 50*, 370-96.

Maslow, A. (1998). *Toward a Psychology of Being* (3rd edition), New York: Wiley.

Morris, D. (2006). *The Naked Ape,* London: Vintage.

Mathes, E. (1981). Maslow's hierarchy of needs as a guide for living. *Journal of Humanistic Psychology, 21*, 69-72.

Tajfel, H. and Turner, J. C. (1986). The social identity theory of inter-group behavior. In S. Worchel and L. W. Austin (eds.), *Psychology of Intergroup Relations*. Chigago: Nelson-Hall.

4. Emotions

Arnold, M.B. (1968). *The nature of emotions*, London: Penguin.

Bowlby, J. (1969). *Attachment and loss* (3 volume set) New York: Basic Books.

Ekman, P. and Davidson, R.J. (eds) (1994). *The Nature Of Emotion: Fundamental Questions*, New York: Oxford University Press.

Frijda, N. H. (1986). *The emotions.* New York: Cambridge University Press.

Goleman, D. (1996). *Emotional Intelligence*, London: Bloomsbury.

Izard, C. E. (1977). *Human emotions*. New York: Plenum Press.

Pavlov, I.I. (1927). *Conditioned Reflexes*, Translated by G.V. Anrep, London: Oxford University Press.

Parrott, W. (2001), *Emotions in Social Psychology*, Philadelphia: Psychology Press.

Pert, C.B. (1997). *Molecules of Emotion*, New York: Scribner.

Skinner, B. F. (1938). *The behavior of organisms*, New York: Appleton-Century-Crofts.

Solomon, R. L. and Corbit, J. D. (1974). An opponent-process theory of motivation: I. Temporal dynamics of affect. *Psychological Review, 81*, 119-145.

Tomkins, S. S. (1984). Affect theory. In K. R. Scherer and P. Ekman (Eds.), *Approaches to emotion* (pp. 163-195). Hillsdale, NJ: Erlbaum.

Walton, S. (2004). *A Natural History of Human Emotions*, New York: Grove Press.

5. Beliefs

Csikszentmihalyi, M. (1993). Flow: *The Psychology of Optimal Experience*, New York: Harper Dilts, R., Hallbom, T and Smith, S. (1990). *Beliefs*, Portland, OR: Metamorphous Press.

Ellis, A. (1994). *Reason and Emotion in Psychotherapy*, NewYork : Birch Lane Press.

Fiske, S. T. and Taylor, S. E. (1991). *Social cognition* (2nd edn.). New York: McGraw Hill.

Higgins, E. T. (1989). Self-Discrepancy Theory: What Patterns of Self-Beliefs Cause People to Suffer?. *Advances in Experimental Social Psychology 22*, 93-136.

Jones, E. E. and Nisbett, R. E. (1972). The actor and the observer: Divergent perceptions of the causes of the behavior. In E. E. Jones, D. E. Kanouse, H. H. Kelley, R. E. Nisbett, S. Valins and B. Weiner (eds.), *Attribution: Perceiving the causees of behavior* (pp. 79-94). Morristown, NJ: General Learning Press.

Kahler, T. (1975). Drivers—The Key to the Process Script. *Transactional Analysis Journal, 5*, 3.

Popper, K. (1959). *The Logic of Scientific Discovery*, London: Springer.

Rockeach, M. (1960). *Open and Closed Minds*, New York: Basic Books.

Zajonc, R.B., Heingartner, A. and Herman, E.M. (1969) Social enhancement and impairment of performance in the cockroach, *Journal of Personality and Social Psychology, 13*, 83-92.

6. Models

Allport, G. (1954). *The nature of prejudice*, Reading, MA: Addison-Wesley.

Ashby R. (1956). *Introduction to Cybernetics*, London: Chapman & Hall.

Berne, E. (1964), *Games People Play: The Psychology of Human Relationships*, New York: Ballantine Books.

Cohen, C. E. (1981). Person categories and social perception: Testing some boundary conditions of the processing effects of prior knowledge. *Journal of Personality and Social Psychology*, 40, 441-452

Delia, J. G. and Crockett, W. H. (1973). Social schemas, cognitive complexity and the learning of social structures. *Journal of Personality*, *41*, 413-429.

Gilbert, D. (2007). *Stumbling On Happiness*, New York: Vintage .

Honey, P. and Mumford, A. (1992). *The Manual of Learning Styles*, Maidenhead, UK: Peter Honey Publications.

Kelly, G. A. (1955). *The psychology of personal constructs (vols. 1 and 2)*. N.Y.: Norton.

Kolb, D.A. (1984). *Experiential Learning*. Englewood Cliffs, NJ: Prentice-Hall.

Maslow, A. (2004). *The Psychology of Science*, Richmond, CA: Maurice Bassett .

McCann, E. and Shannon, D. (1985). *The Two Step*, New York: Grove Weidenfeld.

Senge, P. (1993). *The Fifth Discipline*, New York: Random House Business Books.

Tversky, A. and Kahneman, D. (1981). The framing of decisions and psychology of choice. *Science*, *211*, 453-458.

Weiner, B. (1986). *An attributional theory of emotion and motivation*, New York: Springer-Verlag.

Watzlawick, P., Weakland, J. and Fisch, R. (1971). *Change: Principles of problem formation and problem resolution*, New York: Norton.

7. Rules

Bachrach, B. and Klare, T. (1996). *Values-Based Selling: The Art of Building High-Trust Client Relationships*, Golden, CO: Aim High Publishing.

Deal, T.E. and Kennedy, A.A. (2000). *Corporate Cultures*, London: Perseus.

Deutch, M. and Gerard, H. B. (1955). A study of normative and informational social influence upon judgment. *Journal of Abnormal and Social Psychology, 51*, 629-636.

Klayman, J. and Ha, Y.W. (1987). Confirmation, Disconfirmation, and Information in Hypothesis Testing. Psychological Review, *94*, 211-228.

Hall, E.T. (1966). *The Hidden Dimension*, New York: Doubleday.

Hampden-Turner, C. and Trompenaars, F. (1997). *Riding the Waves of Culture: Understanding Diversity in Global Business*, New York: McGraw-Hill.

Hofstede, G, (1997).*Cultures and Organizations: Software of the Mind*, New York: McGraw-Hill.

Janis, I. (1972). *Victims of groupthink*, Boston: Houghton-Mifflin.

Kluckholn, C. and Strodtbeck, F. (1961). *Variations in value orientations*. Evanston, IL: Row, Peterson.

Simon, S.B. (1995). *Values Clarification*, Lebanon, IN: Grand Central Publishing.

Trompenaars, F. (2003). *Did the Pedestrian Die?*, London: Capstone.

8. Preferences

Conn, S. R., Rieke, M. L. (1994). *The 16PF Fifth Edition Technical Manual*. Champagne, Illinois: Institute for Personality and Ability Testing, Inc.

Cattell, R. B. (1957). *Personality and motivation: Structure and measurement*. New York: Harcourt, Brace & World.

Gilbert, D.T., and Malone, P.S. (1995). The Correspondence Bias. *Psychological Bulletin, 117,* 21-38.

Goldberg, L. R. (1990). An alternative "description of personality": The big-five factor structure. *Journal of Personality and Social Psychology, 59,* 1216-1229.

Johnson, J. T., Feigenbaum, R. and Weisbeg, M. (1964). Some determinants and consequences of the teacher's perception of causality. *Journal of Educational Psychology, 55,* 237-46.

Keirsey, G. (1998). *Please Understand Me II*, Del Mar, CA: Prometheus Nemesis.

Linville, P. W., Fischer, G. W. and Salovey, P. (1989). Perceived distributions of characteristics of in-group and out-group members: Empirical evidence and a computer simulation. *Journal of Personality and Social Psychology, 57,* 165-188.

Pronin, E., Lin, D. Y. and Ross, L. (2002). The bias blind spot: Perceptions of bias in self versus others. *Personality and Social Psychology Bulletin, 28*, 369-381.

Briggs Myers, I. and Myers, P.B. (1995). *Gifts Differing, Myers Briggs*, Mountain View, CA: Davies-Black Publishing.

9. Goals

Csikszentmihalyi, M. (1993). Flow: *The Psychology of Optimal Experience*, New York: Harper.

Fisher, R., Ury, W. and Patton, B. (2003). *Getting to Yes: Negotiating Agreement with out Giving In*, New York: Random House.

Tracy, B. (2003). *Goals! How to Get Everything You Want, Faster Than You Thought Possible*, San Francisco: Berrett-Koehler.

Lawler, E.E. (1974). *Motivation in Work Organizations*, London: Wadsworth.

Locke, E. A., and Latham, G. P. (1990). *A theory of goal setting and task performance*. Englewood Cliffs, NJ: Prentice Hall.

Munroe, M. (2003). *The Principles and Power of Vision*, New Kensington, PA: Whitaker House.

Niemiec, C. P., Ryan, R. M., and Deci, E. L. (2009). The path taken: Consequences of attaining intrinsic and extrinsic aspirations in post-college life. *Journal of Research in Personality, 43*, 291-306.

Pink, D. (2010). *Drive: The Surprising Truth About What Motivates Us*, Edinburgh: Canongate Books.

Straker, D. (1997). Rapid Problem Solving with Post-It Notes, Aldershot: Gower.

Watson, G. and Gallagher, K. (2005). *Managing for Results*, London: Chartered Institute of Personnel and Development.

10. Memory

Asch, S. E. (1946). Forming impressions of personality, *Journal of Abnormal and Social Psychology, 41*, 258-290.

Blaney, P. (1986). Affect and memory: A review. *Psychological Bulletin, 99*, 229-246.

Eysenck, M.W. and Keane, M.T. (2000). *Cognitive Psychology: A Student's Handbook*, New York: Philadelphia: Psychology Press.

Freud, S. and Freud, A. (2005). *The Essentials of Psychoanalysis (new edtion)*, London: Vintage.

Gilbert, D. (2007). *Stumbling on Happiness*, London: HarperPerennial.

Gardner, M. P. (1983). Advertising effects on attributes recalled and criteria used for brand evaluations. *Journal of Consumer Research, 10,* 310-318.

Goethals, G.R. and Reckman, R.F. (1973). The perception of consistency in attitudes. Journal of Experimental Social Psychology, *9,* 491-501.

Kilhstrom, J. F. (1996). the trauma-memory argument and recovered memory therapy. In K Pezdek and W. P. Banks (eds.) The recovered memory/false memory debate (pp. 297-311), San Diego: Academic Press.

Mather, M., Shafir, E. and Johnson, M. K. (2000). Misrememberance of options past: Source monitoring and choice. Psychological Science, *11,* 132-138.

Miller, N. and Campbell, D. T. (1959). Recency and primacy in persuasion as a function of the timing of speeches and measurements. *Journal of Abnormal and Social Psychology, 59,* 1-9.

Nelson. D. L. (1979). Remembering pictures and words: Appearance, significance and name. In L. S. Cermak and F. I. M. Craik (Eds.), *Levels of processing in human memory* (pp. 45-76). Hillside, NJ: Erlbau.

Rosnow, R. and Robinson, E. (1967). *Experiments in persuasion.* New York: Academic Press.

Tulving, E. and Craik, F.I.M. (2005). *The Oxford Handbook of Memory,* Oxford: Oxford University Press.

Von Restorff, H. (1933). Über die Wirkung von Bereichsbildungen im Spurenfeld (The effects of field formation in the trace field). *Psychologie Forschung, 18,* 299-34.

11. Musing

Argyris, C. (1999). *On Organizational Learning (2nd edition),* Oxford: Blackwell.

Claxton, G. (1997). *Hare Brain, Tortoise Mind,* London, Fourth Estate.

Frankl, V. (1946). Man's Search for Meaning, Uckfield, UK: Beacon Press.

Gilbert, D. (2007). *Stumbling on Happiness,* London: HarperPerennial.

Ogden, T. (1986). *The Matrix of Mind: Object Relations and the Psychoanalytic Dialogue.* London: Karnac Books.

Piattelli-Palmarini, M. (1994). Inevitable Illusions: How Mistakes of Reason Rule Our Minds, New York: Wiley.

Weick, K.E.. (1995). *Sensemaking in Organizations,* Thousand Oaks, CA: Sage

Wallas, G. (1926). *The Art of Thought*. London: Cape.

12. Sensing

Hall, E.T. (1966). *The Hidden Dimension*, New York: Doubleday.

James, T. and Woodsmall, W. (1989). *Time-line Therapy and the Basis of Personality*, Capitola, CA: Meta Publications.

Levine, M.W. and Shefner, J.M. (2000). *Fundamentals of Sensation and Perception*, Oxford: Oxford University Press.

Hall, E.T. (1959). *The Silent Language*, New York: Doubleday.

Petty, R. E. and Cacioppo, J. T. (1986). *Communication and persuasion: Central and peripheral routes to attitude change*, New York: Springer-Verlag.

Simons, D. J. and Chabris, C. F. (1999). Gorillas in our midst: Sustained inattentional blindness for dynamic events. *Perception, 28*, 1059-1074.

Styles, E.A. (2006). *The Psychology of Attention*, Philadelphia: Psychology Press.

13. Inferring meaning

Argyris, C. (1999). *On Organizational Learning (2nd edition)*, Oxford: Blackwell.

Austin, J. L. (1962), *How to do Things with Words*. Oxford: Clarendon.

Gilovich, T., Vallone, R. and Tversky, A. (1985). The hot hand in basketball: On the misperception of random sequences. *Cognitive Psychology 17*, 295-314.

Hastorf, A., and Cantril, H. (1954). They saw a game: A case study, *Journal of Abnormal and Social Psychology*, 49, 129-134.

Jones, E. E. and Nisbett, R. E. (1972). The actor and the observer: Divergent perceptions of the causes of the behavior. In E. E. Jones, D. E. Kanouse, H. H. Kelley, R. E. Nisbett, S. Valins and B. Weiner (eds.), *Attribution: Perceiving the causes of behavior* (pp. 79-94). Morristown, NJ: General Learning Press.

Kahneman, D. and Tversky, A. (1973). On the psychology of prediction, *Psychology Review, 80*, 237-251.

LaRossa, R. and Reitzes, D.C. (1993). Symbolic interactionism and family studies. In P. G. Boss, W. J. Doherty, R. LaRossa, W. R. Schumm and S. K. Steinmetz (Eds.), *Sourcebook of family theories and methods: A contextual approach* (pp. 135-163). New York: Plenum Press.

Pennington, N. and Hastie, R. (1986). Evidence evaluation in complex decision making. *Journal of Personality and Social Psychology, 51*, 242-258.

Pettigrew, T. F. (1979). the ultimate attribution error: Extending Allport's cognitive analysis of prejudice, *Personality and Social Psychology Bulletin*, 5, 461-476.

Watzlawick, P., Weakland, J. and Fisch, R. (1971). *Change: Principles of problem formation and problem resolution*, New York: Norton.

14. Formulating intent

Allport, G. (1954). *The nature of prejudice*, Reading, MA: Addison-Wesley.

Ajzen I. (1985). From intentions to actions: A theory of planned behavior, In J. Kuhl and J. Beckmann (eds), *Action-control: From cognition to behavior*, Heidelberg, Germany: Springer, 11-39.

Beach, L.R. (1994). *The Psychology of Decision Making*, Thousand Oaks, CA: Sage.

Chaiken, S. (1987). The heuristic model of persuasion. In M. P. Zanna, J. M. Olson and C. P. Herman (eds.), *Social influence: The Ontario Symposium* (Volume 5, pp. 3-39), Hillsdale, NJ: Erlbaum.

Chaiken, S., Liberman, A. and Eagly, A. H. (1989). Heuristic and systematic information processing within and beyond the persuasion context. In Uleman, J. S. and Bargh, J. A. (Eds.), *Unintended thought*, 212-252. New York: Guilford.

Claxton, G. (1997). *Hare Brain, Tortoise Mind*, London, Fourth Estate.

Klein, G. (1999). *Sources of Power: How People Make Decisions*, Cambridge, MA: The MIT Press.

Langer, E. (1983). *The Psychology of Control*. Beverly Hills, CA: Sage Publications.

Kahneman, D. Slovic, P. and Tversky, A. (1982). *Judgement Under Uncertainty: Heuristics and Biases*, Cambridge: Cambridge University Press.

March, J.G. (1994). A Primer on Decision Making: How Decisions Happen, New York: Free Press.

Nutt, P.C. (2002). *Why Decisions Fail*, San Francisco: Berrett Koehler.

Petty, R. E. and Cacioppo, J. T. (1986) *Communication and persuasion: Central and peripheral routes to attitude change*, New York: Springer-Verlag.

Plous, S. (1993). *The Psychology of Judgment and Decision Making*, New York: McGraw-Hill.

Pronin, E., Lin, D. Y. and Ross, L. (2002). The bias blind spot: Perceptions of bias in self versus others. *Personality and Social Psychology Bulletin, 28,* 369-381.

15. Translating into Action

Alm-Arvius, C. (2003). *Figures of Speech,* SwedenL Studentlitteratur AB.

Atkinson, M. (2004). Lend Me Your Ears: All You Need to Know About Making Speeches and Presentations, Vermillion.

Barthes, R. (1991). *S/Z: An Essay,* Hill and Wang.

Bly, R.W. (2007). *The Copywriter's Handbook (3rd edition),* Owl Books.

Goffman, E. (1959). *The Presentation of Self in Everyday Life,* New York: Anchor Books.

Hall, L.M. (2001). *Communication Magic: Exploring the Structure and Meaning of Language,* Carmarthen, UK: Crown House.

Hargie, O. and Dickson, D. (2003). *Skilled Interpersonal Communication,* London: Routledge.

Hughes, D. and Philips, B. (2004). *The Oxford Union Guide to Speaking in Public,* London: Virgin Books.

Maas, A. and Acuri, L. (1996). Language and stereotyping. In C. N. Macrae, C. Stangor and M. Hewstone (eds.), *Stereotypes and Stereotyping.* New York: Guilford.

Mather, M. and Johnson, M. K. (2000). Choice-supportive source monitoring: Do our decisions seem better to us as we age? *Psychology and Aging, 15,* 596-606.

Mehrabian, Albert, and Ferris, Susan R. (1967). "Inference of Attitudes from Nonverbal Communication in Two Channels," *Journal of Consulting Psychology, 31,* 3, 248-258.

Morris, D. (1978). *Manwatching,* St. Albans, UK: Triad/Panther.

Morris, D. (2002). *Peoplewatching,* London: Vintage.

Pease, A. and Pease, B. (2005). *The Definitive Book of Body Language: How to Read Others' Attitudes by Their Gestures,* London: Orion.

Searle, J. R. (1969). *Speech Acts: An Essay in the Philosophy of Language.* Cambridge: Cambridge University Press.

Trask, R.L. (2002). *Mind the Gaffe: The Penguin Guide to Common Errors in English,* London: Penguin.

16. State

Blaney, P. (1986). Affect and memory: A review. *Psychological Bulletin, 99*, 229-246.

Dweck, C. S. (2006). *Mindset: The New Psychology Of Success*. New York: Random House.

Eagly, A.H. and Chaiken, S. (1993). *The Psychology of Attitudes*, New York: Harcourt Brace.

Eich, E, Macauley, D and Ryan, L (1994). Mood dependent memory for events of the person al past, *Journal of Experimental Psychology: General, 123*, 201-215.

Forgas, J. P. (1995). Mood and judgment: The affect infusion model (AIM). *Psychological Bulletin, 117*, 39-66.

Hall, M. (1996). *Dragon Slaying*, Colorado: ET Publications.

Isen, A. M., Shalker, T. E., Clark, M., and Karp, L. (1978). Resources required in the construction and reconstruction of conversation, *Journal of Personality and Social Psychology, 36*, 1-12.

Mahoney, J. (2000). "Path Dependence in Historical Sociology," *Theory and Society* 29:4, pp. 507-548.

Sherif, C. W., Sherif, M. and Nebergall, R. E. (1965). *Attitude and attitude change: The social judgment-involvement approach*. Philadelphia: W. B. Saunders.

Martin, J. and McClure, C. (1985). *Diagramming Techniques for Analysts and Programmers*, Englewood Cliffs, NJ: Prentice Hall.

Thayer, R.E. (1996). *The Origin of Everyday Moods*, New York: Oxford University Press.

17. Relationships

Altman, I. and Taylor, D. A. (1973). *Social Penetration*, New York: Holst, Rinehart, Winston.

Cialdini, R. (1993). *Influence: Science and practice (3rd edition)*, New York: HarperCollins.

Berger, P.L. and Luckmann, T. (1991). *The Social Construction of Reality*, London: Penguin.

Berne, E. (1964). *Games People Play*, New York: Ballantine Books.

Byrne, D. (1971). The Attraction Paradigm, New York: Academic Press.

Cody, M. J. (1982). A typology of disengagement strategies and an examination of the role intimacy reactions to inequity and relational problems play in strategy selection, *Communication Monographs, 49*, 148-70.

Duck, S. W. (1982) *Personal Relationships 4: Dissolving Personal Relationships*, London and New York: Academic Press.

Feingold, A. (1988) Matching for attractiveness in romantic partners and same-sex friends: a meta-analysis and theoretical critique, *Psychological Bulletin, 104*, 226-35.

French, J. P. R. Jr., and Raven, B. (1960). The bases of social power. In D. Cartwright and A. Zander (eds.), *Group dynamics* (pp. 607-623). New York: Harper and Row.

Harris, T. (1996). *I'm OK-You're OK*, London: Avon Books.

Heider, F. (1958). *the psychology of interpersonal relations*, New York: Wiley.

Jones, E. E. and Davis, K. E. (1965). From acts to dispositions: the attribution process in social psychology, in L. Berkowitz (ed.), *Advances in experimental social psychology* (Volume 2, pp. 219-266), New York: Academic Press.

McClelland, D. C. (1975). *Power: The inner experience*. New York: Irvington .

McClelland, D. C. and Burnham, D. H. (1976). Power is the great motivator. *Harvard Business Review, 54(2)*, 100-110.

Miller, R. L. (1976). Mere exposure, psychological reactance and attitude change. *Journal of Abnormal and Social Psychology, 59*, 1-9.

Mintzberg, H. (1983). *Power in and Around Organizations*. Englwood Cliffs, NJ: Prentice Hall.

Murstein, B.I. (1970). Stimulus-value-role: A theory of marital choice, *Journal of Marriage and the Family 32*, 465-81.

Sternberg, R. J. and Barnes, M. L. (1988). The Psychology of Love, London: Yale University Press.

Zajonc, R. B. (1968). Attitudinal effects of mere exposure, *Journal of Personality and Social Psychology, 9*, Monongraph supplement No. 2, Part 2.

18. Groups

Asch, S. E. (1951). Effects of group pressure upon the modification and distortion of judgement. In H. Guetzkow (ed.) *Groups, leadership and men*. Pittsburgh, PA: Carnegie Press.

Brown, R. (2000). *Group Processes: Dynamics Within and Between Groups*, Oxford: Blackwell.

Corey, M.S. and Corey, G. (2001). *Groups: Process and Practice*, London: Wadsworth.

Festinger, L., Pepitone, A. and Newcomb T. (1952). Some consequences of deindividuation in a group. *Journal of Abnormal and Social Psychology*, 47, 382-389.

Granovetter, M. (1973). "The Strength of Weak Ties", American Journal of Sociology, *78*, 6, 1360-1380.

Gladwell, M. (2002). *The Tipping Point: How Little Things Can Make a Big Difference*, Lebanon, IN: Back Bay Books.

Hogg, M.A. and Tindale, S. (2002). *Blackwell Handbook of Social Psychology: Group Processes*, Oxford: Blackwell.

Janis, I. (1982) *Groupthink (2nd edn.)*, Boston: Houghton-Mifflin.

Jones, M.B., and Jones, D.R. (1995). Preferred pathways of behavioural contagion. *Journal of Psychiatric Research*, *29*, 193-209.

Lippmann, W. (1922). *Public Opinion*. New York: Harcourt-Brace.

Maass, A., Corvino, P. and Arcuri, L. (1994). Linguistic intergroup bias and the mass media. *Revue de Psychologie Sociale*, *1*, 31-43.

Stanley Milgram, S. (1967). "The Small World Problem", *Psychology Today*, 2, 60-6.

Moore, G. (2006). *Crossing the Chasm (revised edition)*, New York: Collins.

Morris, D. (1969). *The Human Zoo*, London: Johnathan Cape.

Moscovici, S. and Zavalloni, M. (1969). The group as a polarizer of attitudes. *Journal of Personality and Social Psychology*, *12*, 125-135.

Myers, D. G. and Arenson, S. J. (1972). Enhancement of dominant risk tendencies in group discussion. *Psychological Science*, *6*, 10-19.

Nohria, N. and Eccles, R.G.. (1993). *Networks and Organizations: Structure, Form and Action*, Boston, MA: Harvard Business School Press

Rogers, E. (2003). *Diffusion of Innovations (5th edition)*, New York: Free Press.

Sherif, M., Harvey, O. J., White, B. J., Hood, W. R., and Sherif, C. W. (1961). *Intergroup cooperation and competition: The Robbers Cave experiment*. Norman, OK: University Book Exchange.

Watts, D.J. (2003). Six Degrees: The Science of a Connected Age, London: Vintage.

Tajfel, H. (1982). *Social identity and intergroup relations*, Cambridge: Cambridge University Press.

LeBon, G. (1895) *The Crowd*, London: F. Unwin.

Yukl, G. (2005). *Leadership in Organizations (6th Edition)*, Englewood Cliffs, NJ: Prentice Hall.

19. The Core Process

See sections below for references.

20. Information Management

Barber, J. and Wilkins, R. (2005). *Good Question! The Art of Asking Questions To Bring About Positive Change*, Great Yarmouth, UK: Lean Marketing Press.

Bem, D. J. (1972). Self-perception theory. In L. Berkowitz (ed), *Advances in experimental social psychology*, (Vol. 6. pp. 1-62), New York: Academic Press.

BurleyAllen, M. (1995). *Listening: The Forgotten Skill*, New York: Wiley.

Cooley, C. H. (1902) *Human nature and social order*, New York: Scribner's.

Festinger, L. (1954). A theory of social comparison processes, *Human Relations*, 7, 117-40.

Freese, T. (2001). *Secrets of Question-based Selling: Sale Strategies for Spectacular Results*, Naperville, IL: Sourcebooks.

Frohart, P. (1998). *The Book of Fabulous Questions*, Minneapolis, MN: BRG Publishing.

James, A. and Kratz, J. (1995). *Effective Listening Skills*, New York: McGraw-Hill.

Nichols, M.P. (1996). *The Lost Art of Listening*, New York: Guilford

Poole, G. (2003). *The Complete Book of Questions*, Grand Rapids, MI: Zondervan.

Rogers, C. (1951). *Client Centred Therapy*, Boston: Houghton-Mifflin.

Straker, D. (1997). *Rapid Problem Solving with Post-It Notes*, Aldershot, UK: Gower.

21. Trust

Fisher, R., Ury, W. and Patton, B. (2003). *Getting to Yes: Negotiating Agreement with out Giving In*, New York: Random House.

Fukuyama, F. (1996). *Trust: The Social Virtues and the Creation of Prosperity*, London: Penguin Books.

Kramer, R.M. and Tyler, T.R. (eds.). (1996). *Trust in Organizations: Frontiers of Theory and Research*. Thousand Oaks, CA: Sage Publications.

Lane, C., and Bachmann, R. (eds). (1998). *Trust Within and Between Organizations*. Oxford: Oxford University Press.

O'Hara, K. (2004). *Trust: From Socrates to Spin*, Cambridge, UK: Icon Books.

Solomon, R.C. and Flores, F. (2003). *Building Trust: In Business, Politics, Relationships, and Life*, Oxford: Oxford University Press.

Ward, A. and Smith, J. (2003). *Trust and Mistrust: Radical Risk Strategies in Business Relationships*, New York: Wiley.

22. Tension

Cannon, Walter B. (1932). *The wisdom of the body*, 2nd Edition, 1939, New York: Norton.

Chaiken, S., Wood, W. and Eagly, A. H. (1996). Principles of persuasion. In E.T. Higgins and A. Kruglanski (Eds.), *Social psychology: Handbook of basic mechanisms and processes.* New York: Guilford.

Cialdini, R. (1993). *Influence: Science and practice* (3rd edition), New York: HarperCollins.

Cialdini, R., Vincent, J., Lewis, S., Catalan, J., Wheeler, D. and Darby, B. (1975). Reciprocal concessions procedure for inducing compliance: The door-in-the-face technique. Journal of *Personality and Social Psychology, 31,* 206-215.

Cialdini, R. B., Cacioppo, J. T., Bassett, R. and Miller, J. A. (1978). Low-ball procedure for producing compliance: Commitment then cost. *Journal of Personality and Social Psychology, 36,* 463-476.

Festinger, L. (1957). *A theory of cognitive dissonance*, Stanford, CA: Stanford University Press.

Freedman, J. and Fraser, S. (1966). Compliance without pressure: The foot-in-the-door technique. *Journal of Personality and Social Psychology, 4,* 195-202.

Joule, R. V., Gouilloux, F., and Weber, F. (1989). The lure: A new compliance procedure. *Journal of Social Psychology, 129,* 741-749.

Kallgren and Wood (1986). Access to attitude-relevant information in memory as a determinant of attitude-behavior consistency. *Journal of Experimental Social Psychology, 22,* 328-338.

Loewenstein, G. (1994). The Psychology of Curiosity: A Review and Reinterpretation, *Psychological Bulletin, 116,* 1, 75-98.

Matthews, G. (2000). *Human Performance: Cognition, Stress and Individual Differences*, Philadelphia: Psychology Press.

Milgram, S. (1983). *Obedience to Authority: An Experimental View*. New York: Harper/Collins.

Petty, R. E. and Cacioppo, J. T. (1986). *Communication and persuasion: Central and peripheral routes to attitude change*, New York: Springer-Verlag.

Rackham, N. (1995). *SPIN Selling*, Aldershot, UK: Gower.

Ury, W. (1992). *Getting Past No: Negotiating with Difficult People*, New York: Random House.

Watzlawick, P., Weakland, J. and Fisch, R. (1971). *Change: Principles of problem formation and problem resolution*, New York: Norton

Wilson, T.T. (2011). *Redirect: Changing the Stories we Live By*, London: Allen Lane

23. Closure

Burger, J. M. (1986). Increasing compliance by improving the deal: The that's not all technique. *Journal of Personality and Social Psychology, 51*, 277-283.

Donoho C.L. (2003). The "top-of-the-line" influence on the buyer-seller relationship. *Journal of Business Research, 56*, 4, 303-309.

Kruglanski, A.W., Webster, D.M. (1996). Motivated Closing of the Mind: "Seizing" and "Freezing". *Psychological Review, 103*, 2, 263-283.

Petty, R. E. and Cacioppo, J. T. (1986) *Communication and persuasion: Central and peripheral routes to attitude change*, New York: Springer-Verlag.

Hopkins, T. (1998). *Sales Closing for Dummies*, New York: For Dummies.

Richardson, R. (1997). *Stop Telling, Start Selling: How to Use Customer-Focused Dialogue to Close Sales*, New York: McGraw Hill.

Ziglar, Z. (1985). *Zig Ziglar's Secrets of Closing the Sale*, New York: Berkley Publishing.

Ingham, G. (2004). *Objections! Objections! Objections!*, Gavin Ingham.

24. Commitment

Becker, H. (1960). Notes on the concept of commitment, *American Journal of Sociology, 66*, 32-44.

Couch, D. (2007). *Chosen Soldier: The Making of a Special Forces Warrior*, New York: Crown Publishers.

Hassan, S. (1990). *Combating Cult Mind Control*, South Paris, ME: Park Street Press.

Karsten, P. (1999). *The Training and Socializing of Military Personnel*, New York: Garland Publishing.

Kohn, A. (1995). *Punished by Rewards: The Trouble with Gold Stars, Incentive Plans, A's, Praise, and Other Bribes*, Boston: Houghton-Mifflin.

Lifton, R.J. (1963). *Thought Reform and the Psychology of Totalism*, New York: Norton.

Lines, R. (2004). Influence of participation in strategic change: resistance, organizational commitment and change goal achievement *Journal of Change Management*, 4, 3, 193–215.

Reichheld, F.F. (1996). *The Loyalty Effect: The Hidden Force Behind Growth, Profits and Lasting Value*, Harvard Business School Press.

Schein, E.H., Schneier, I. and Barker, C.H. (1961). *Coercive Persuasion: A Socio-psychological Analysis of the "Brainwashing" of American Civilian Prisoners by the Chinese Communists*, New York: Norton.

25. Pain and Pleasure

Davis, B.P. and Knowles, E.S. (1999). A disrupt-then-reframe technique of social influence. *Journal of Personality and Social Psychology*, 76, 2, 192-199.

Dolinski D. and Nawrat R. (1998). Fear-then-relief procedure for producing compliance: Beware when the danger is over. *Journal of Experimental Social Psychology*, 34, 1, 27-50.

Fisher, R., Ury, W. and Patton, B. (2003). *Getting to Yes: Negotiating Agreement with out Giving In*, Random House.

Freud, S. (1975). *Beyond the Pleasure Principle*, London: Norton.

Jolles, R.L. (1998). *Customer Centered Selling*, New York: Free Press.

Rackham, N. (1995). *SPIN Selling*, Aldershot, UK: Gower.

Ralston, P. (1989). *Cheng Hsin: Principles of Effortless Power*, Berkeley, CA: North Atlantic Books.

Solomon, R.L. (1980). The Opponent-Process Theory of Acquired Motivation: The Costs of Pleasure and the Benefits of Pain, *American Psychologist*, 35, 691-712.

Ury, W. (1992). *Getting Past No: Negotiating with Difficult People*, New York: Random House.

26. Connection and Change

Berne, E. (1969). *Games People Play: The Psychology of Human Relationships*, London: Balantine Books.

Brown, D. (2007). *Tricks of the Mind*, London: 4 Books.

Coram, R. (2002). *Boyd: The Fighter Pilot Who Changed the Art of War*. New York: Little, Brown.

du Gay, P., Evans, J. and Redman, P. (eds) (2000). *Identity: a reader*, London: Sage.

Klein, M. (1984). The psycho-analysis of children (A. Strachey, Trans.). in R. Money-Kyrle (Ed.), *The writings of Melanie Klein* (Vol. 2). New York: Free Press.

Lacan, J. (1977). *Écrits: A Selection*. Trans. Alan Sheridan. New York: Norton.

McCann, E. with Shannon, D. (1985). *The Two Step*, New York: Grove Weidenfeld.

Index

Note: *italic* page numbers indicate specific methods, while **bold** page numbers indicate major sections on the subject.